MW00413787

OPEN WOUNDS

Hundreds of homicide cases go unsolved each year and with each one, the mutilated bodies of the victims cry out for justice. Will the parents of little Genette Tate ever learn what really happened to their daughter? After years of frustrating investigative work, can police ever hope to catch the brutal killers who raped and strangled pretty Krissie Povolish or cut the throat of Eve Stratford? New leads are rare in such cases and the trails are cold. But the files remain open until the search for truth is done.

Now, from the authentic files of *TRUE DETECTIVE* MAGAZINE, read about twenty-five cases of murder and mutilation that remain open and the killers still at large!

**PINNACLE BOOKS AND *TRUE DETECTIVE* MAGAZINE
TEAM UP TO BRING YOU THE
MOST HORRIFIC TRUE CRIME STORIES!**

BIZARRE MURDERERS	(486-9, $4.95/$5.95)
CELEBRITY MURDERS	(435-4, $4.95/$5.95)
COP KILLERS	(603-9, $4.99/$5.99)
THE CRIMES OF THE RICH AND FAMOUS	(630-6, $4.99/$5.99)
CULT KILLERS	(528-8, $4.95/$5.95)
MEDICAL MURDERERS	(582-2, $4.99/$5.99)
SERIAL MURDERERS	(432-X, $4.95/$5.95)
SPREE KILLERS	(461-3, $4.95/$5.95)
TORTURE KILLERS	(506-7, $4.95/$5.95)

Available wherever paperbacks are sold, or order direct from the Publisher. Send cover price plus 50¢ per copy for mailing and handling to Pinnacle Books, Dept. 654, 475 Park Avenue South, New York, N.Y. 10016. Residents of New York and Tennessee must include sales tax. DO NOT SEND CASH. For a free Zebra/ Pinnacle catalog please write to the above address.

FROM THE FILES OF <u>TRUE DETECTIVE</u> MAGAZINE

UNSOLVED MYSTERIES

Edited by
ROSE G.
MANDELSBERG

PINNACLE BOOKS
WINDSOR PUBLISHING CORP.

Acknowledgment

The editor wishes to express her sincerest thanks and appreciation to Sergeant Charles Stravalle who has vast experience in solving mysteries which he puts to practice every day.

For more true crime reading, pick up
TRUE DETECTIVE, OFFICIAL DETECTIVE,
MASTER DETECTIVE, FRONT PAGE DETECTIVE,
and INSIDE DETECTIVE magazines on sale
at newsstands every month.

PINNACLE BOOKS

are published by

Windsor Publishing Corp.
475 Park Avenue South
New York, NY 10016

Copyright © 1976, 1984, 1985, 1986, 1988, 1989, 1990, 1991, 1992 by RGH Publishing Corporation

For complete copyright information, see Appendix.

All rights reserved. No part of this book may be reproduced in any form or by any means without the prior written consent of the Publisher, excepting brief quotes used in reviews.

Pinnacle and the P logo are trademarks of Windsor Publishing Corp.

If you purchased this book without a cover you should be aware that this book is stolen property. It was reported as "unsold and destroyed" to the Publisher and neither the Author nor the Publisher has received any payment for this "stripped book."

First Pinnacle Books printing: November, 1992

Printed in the United States of America

TABLE OF CONTENTS

"WHO IS 'BABY HOPE?' AND WHO SMOTHERED HER?"

by Christofer Pierson

Much about her is mysterious. Even her real name is a mystery. All that is known about her is that she is between 3 and 6 years old, stretches a mere 3 feet 2 inches from head to foot, probably weighed no more than 30 pounds in her short life, and, most disturbing of all, had been sexually abused. No one knows where she came from or how she came to be where she was found—no one, that is, except for her killers.

"Baby Hope," as she is optimistically called by her present guardians—detectives seeking her identity and her murderer—is at the center of one of the most baffling and frustrating homicide cases in New York City's most murder-ridden police precinct: the 34th, which ranges on Manhattan's west side from 155th Street to the very northern tip of the borough.

The residents of the 34th are mostly Hispanic. Puerto Ricans and Dominicans make up the bulk of the precinct's Spanish-speaking population, just as they have for decades. But now the area's residents also include Mexicans, Guatemalans, Colombians, Peruvians, Ecuadorans, and other Latin American refugees. They have escaped harsh economic and po-

7

litical situations in their home countries to look for better opportunities — like millions of immigrants from every corner of the world before them — in this one corner of America. Descendants of older waves of immigration still holds to their shrinking Jewish, Irish, and African-American enclaves in the precinct, but the increasingly prominent flavor of the 34th is decidedly *latino*.

Unfortunately, while repression from juntas and guerrillas may no longer be a concern for the new immigrants, there are other concerns equally as dangerous and life-threatening. Drugs and the violence associated with them are only the most obvious of the new hardships awaiting the recent immigrant. More subtle and less expected, perhaps, is the sluggishness of the American economy in recent years, a sluggishness that has been felt especially hard in this already depressed section of the city.

The detectives who have "adopted" Baby Hope as their own think she probably came from their own troubled precinct. Although Baby Hope's ethnicity is unknown given the state of advanced decomposition that she was found in, most of the police artists and forensic anthropologists who have tried to reconstruct her features have agreed that Baby Hope looks Hispanic. Detectives believe the location of her body also suggests that whoever put her there had a familiarity with the area only a resident could have.

But clues in the Baby Hope case are depressingly hard to come by, and sleuths are groping in the dark for answers to even the most obvious of questions in the case. And the questions in this case, because of what was done to this particular victim at her vulnerable age and because of the amount of time that has passed since the questions were first formed, are ones that detectives desperately want answered.

On the Tuesday morning of July 23, 1991, members of a road crew were working on a section of the Henry Hudson Parkway, near the Dyckman Street exit just north of the George Washington Bridge in Manhattan. Over the last few days, the workers had become aware of a foul stench hanging heavy in the humid air. It seemed to be coming from below the section they were working on, from somewhere in a patch of woods on an embankment sloping down at a 45-degree angle from the highway to the Hudson River.

On this Tuesday morning, one member of the crew took it upon himself to investigate the odor. He climbed over the guard rail and followed a well-worn path ending at the foot of a tree about midway down the embankment. The limbs of the tree provided a natural umbrella over what appeared to be — judging from the amount of beer cans, cigarette butts, and other unsavory debris littering the area — some kind of partying spot.

The road worker discovered that someone who had used the spot had left a peculiar memento of their outing at the foot of the tree: a blue 30-quart Igloo ice cooler, about 13 inches wide, 13 inches deep, and 24 inches long. The cooler, in fact, seemed to be the source of the odor.

The workman alerted the others in the crew to his find. A contingent of the crew skidded down the hill and was soon standing at their co-worker's side, discussing the large blue container. The workmen decided to tip over the cooler and see what was inside. A rush of liquid spilled out, carrying with it several full cans of Coca Cola and an object wrapped in a black plastic garbage bag. The stench from the cooler's contents was horrific enough to send the entire crew gagging and scrambling up the hill.

In a matter of minutes, officers from the 34th Precinct were at the scene. They quickly confirmed the worst: the black garbage bag contained a human body wrapped in a light green linen-type cloth. Evidently, the cramped quarters of the 30-quart cooler had become a makeshift crypt for the tiny child in an advanced state of decomposition.

Detective Joe Neenan, whose gray hair seems to reflect more his 10 years as a cop than it does his age of 39 years, was one of the first detectives on the scene, arriving shortly before noon.

"My original thinking," Neenan would later explain, "when I looked down the hill and saw the cooler and the bag and the Coke cans scattered by the tree, was that this child was one who disappeared from a fair in New Jersey on Memorial Day. Not knowing the sex or description of the child, that was my first thought."

If there's one type of crime a detective finds hard to stomach, it's the murder of a child. It isn't only because many have children of their own that detectives respond to a child's murder this way, although basic human sympathy is undoubtedly a factor. It's also that homicide detectives see so much evil among the adults they deal with that the innocence of childhood stands out in stark relief. When a child is murdered, a detective feels an intense responsibility to avenge what is unquestionably a wrong.

Detective Neenan was hoping to solve two of these disturbing cases in one. In the New Jersey case, a mother took her child to the fair, took her eyes off

10

the child only long enough to get a soda, and when she returned, her child was gone. The child, a 7-year-old-blond boy, had been missing for almost two months by the time the blue cooler was found in Manhattan.

Neenan would be quickly disappointed. The crime scene technicians ripped open the black garbage bag and announced, "It's a female."

The tiny girl, wearing no clothes save for a linen-type cloth wrapped around her, was bound with a medium-weight ligature which was half rope and half venetian-blind cord. She was in a crouched position, her head resting on her knees. Her most distinguishing feature was her long, wavy black hair adorned with a yellow plastic ponytail holder that had come loose. Her front teeth, prominent in a mouth misshapen by death, must also have been prominent in life. Decomposition had already destroyed much of the victim's face and in fact had already made it impossible to determine the color of her eyes.

The victim bore no bruises or wounds to immediately indicate the cause of her death. It was clear, however, that the investigators were dealing with a homicide, if only because of the premeditated manner in which the body had been disposed of. Particularly suspicious was the presence of full cans of Coke in the cooler. The detectives theorized that the cans were meant to serve as a kind of decoy in case the perpetrators were stopped in the process of disposing of the body. Everything about the scene said that whoever put the body here was trying to hide a deep, dark, terrible secret.

The first plan of action when any unidentified body is found is to check it against a list of missing

11

persons. Detective Jerry Giorgio, a 32-year veteran who has spent 15 of those at the 34th, received a call from the scene requesting information on missing persons cases involving children.

"We were looking for a child anywhere from five years of age to nine years of age that was reported missing," Giorgio would later say. "We knew she was female, but we asked Missing Persons for any child missing. We got a list of children from all over the city who'd been reported missing in the last month. There were sixteen respondents, sixteen possibilities."

Ten on the list were boys and these were immediately eliminated. Two of the remaining six females were teenagers, and two were in their early teens, thus eliminating four more. The remaining two girls on the list were in the right age range, but they were black. None on the list fit the description of the body in the blue cooler.

The autopsy conducted the next morning sketched in a few more missing details while at the same time making it painfully clear that the case would be anything but open and shut. The victim had all of her original baby teeth, suggesting to the pathologists that the victim could have been no more than six years old. There was no evidence that she ever had dental work. This was an unfortunate break for the detectives; it eliminated the possibility that the girl could be identified by comparing her teeth with local dental records. Similarly, the pathologists determined that the girl had no history of broken bones, thus eliminating medical records as possible points of comparison for identification.

Although the body showed no bruises or other overt signs of physical abuse, the pathologists were able to determine that the girl had suffered severe

12

malnutrition. The doctors estimated that the body, which weighed a scant 20 pounds when it was found, had lost no more than 10 pounds of weight in fluids through decomposition. Even for a 3-year-old—the youngest the pathologists estimated the body to be—30 pounds is a dangerously low body weight.

But malnutrition was not the cause of death, the pathologists determined. Apparently, Baby Hope had been asphyxiated—smothered to death. The lack of broken bones suggested that she was freshly dead when her body was folded, tied with a cord, wrapped in the garbage bag, and then lain in the bottom of the ice cooler. The body might have been kept at the murder scene for a day or two before being disposed. The body's state of decomposition indicated that the victim had been left where she was ultimately found no more than three or four days, which would make July 18th the earliest date the murder could have taken place. But the pathologists did not rule out the possibility that the cooler may have been sealed well enough to retard decomposition for as long as seven days.

Tests on whether or not the girl had been sexually molested were inconclusive at that early stage of the forensic analysis. It was not until a month later, on August 28th, that tests for the presence of semen in the girl's body came back positive.

Until they heard this news from the pathologists, Detectives Neenan and Giorgio were skeptical about sexual abuse as a motive for the crime. They were busy tracking down dozens of other leads in the seamy areas of northern Manhattan and the South Bronx.

The detectives' boss, Lieutenant Joe Reznick, who had visited the crime scene and analyzed the evidence for himself, found the case to be so urgent that he took Giorgio and Neenan off every other investigation and allowed them to concentrate on what had quickly become known at the precinct as the Baby Hope case. The detectives hoped to inundate the news media with the victim's image in order to generate leads. They enlisted the precinct's resident artist, Sergeant Frank Domingo, to draft a speculative sketch.

The victim's lack of clear facial characteristics was only the first of many problems the sleuths encountered with their attempts to have her features represented on paper. The finished sketch presented another problem. As accurate as it appeared to be, it fooled the viewer into thinking the victim was much older than she really was. Many who viewed the poster told the detectives that the subject of the sketch, with her furrowed brow and her cheeks sunken by malnutrition, looked like a teenager or a woman in her early 20s. Nevertheless, Sergeant Domingo, a talented police artist, told the detectives that he found it difficult to render the victim as a young-looking girl. He was convinced that in life, Baby Hope did not look her age.

Unfortunately, the public does not respond as well to cases involving older victims as it does to ones involving young children. The last thing the detectives wanted was to have the public believe that Baby Hope was a teenage runaway. Detectives Giorgio and Neenan decided that Sergeant Domingo's sketch needed to be balanced by one that was more reflective of Baby Hope's actual age, not only for the sake of accuracy but also to help foster a sense of outrage in the public over the case.

Toward that end, the detectives turned to the National Center for Missing and Exploited Children in Arlington, Virginia, which has recently been equipped with the technology for computer-imaged composite sketches. When the investigators received back the fruits of the center's labors, they were stunned by what they saw. It looked not like a sketch at all, but like an actual posed photograph of a pretty, young, Hispanic-looking girl. The furrowed brow was smoothed out and the sunken cheeks were restored to a more youthful fullness. The victim still looked perhaps a few years older than she actually was, but it was as if the pain in the first sketch had been airbrushed away.

Neenan and Giorgio were impressed with the center's work, but once again, they were concerned about misleading the public into thinking that an imperfect sketch based on an educated guess was actually a photograph that perfectly reflected the girl's looks. So they asked Sergeant Domingo to make a charcoal sketch from the image. The finished product was finally released to the media on September 11th.

In the meantime, Detectives Giorgio and Neenan took the few solid clues they had and tracked them as far as they could go. Calling the Igloo Company of St. Louis, Missouri, with the serial number found on the cooler, the detectives traced it to a batch of 79 coolers of that size which had been shipped to the New York City area in the fall of 1990. The manufacturer was unable to pinpoint the exact store to which the cooler was sent, but the sleuths took some comfort in finding support for their theory that the killer was from the area.

Tracking the Coke cans found inside the cooler was a trickier proposition. The Coca Cola Company prints sale dates and distribution information in ink on the bottom of their cans. This information would have immediately established the earliest date the cans could have been purchased as well as the distribution area they came from. Unfortunately, the ink markings on the Coke cans that were found at the crime scene had been washed away by fluids— presumably body fluids and melted ice—that had accumulated inside the cooler. The fluids that damaged the markings on the Coke cans similarly erased any fingerprints the killer might have left on the cans or anywhere inside the cooler.

On Friday, July 26th, Detective Neenan enlisted the aid of Coca Cola's regional representative. Neenan learned that the bottler engraves a code into the aluminum on the cans that tells where and when they were bottled and to which distribution point they were sent. The representative deciphered the engraved code and revealed that all of the cans were bottled in Danbury, Connecticut, on June 18, 1991— five weeks before they turned up in the cooler off the Henry Hudson Parkway—and that they had all been sent to a distributor near the Hunt's Point Market in the Bronx.

The sleuths found out that the Hunt's Point distributor served only Manhattan and the Bronx. That added up to a daunting number of stores to check out. But once again, the detectives were encouraged to find support for their belief that the murderer lived not far from the crime scene. Somewhere close by the precinct headquarters on upper Broadway, someone must have seen the little girl, possibly with her killer.

At 4:00 a.m. on Monday, July 29th, Giorgio and Neenan met with the Hunt's Point distribution cen-

16

ter's drivers, handing out thousands of fliers printed with Sergeant Domingo's earliest sketch and a request for help from the public. The sleuths asked the drivers to give a poster to each of their vendors and have them display the sketch prominently in their storefront windows.

The posters began turning up in supermarkets and bodegas all over Manhattan. But, the detectives were saddened to find out, the stores closest to the killer's probable neighborhood were not cooperating. In a random sample that Giorgio and Neenan took in mid-August of stores in the immediate vicinity of the 34th Precinct Headquarters on 183rd Street and Broadway, not one single poster turned up.

Another source of frustration for the sleuths was the shaky quality of most of the leads they received. Many of the callers were armchair sleuths who, based on their limited knowledge of the case from newspaper or television stories, tried to second-guess the real detectives. Rather than helping, though, such calls usually accomplish little more than tying up the detectives' valuable time.

"The average layperson derives most of their ideas about police investigations from television," Giorgio said recently. "They want to be helpful, and we can't fault them for that. They're just trying to do their duty as citizens."

Detectives Giorgio and Neenan have also had to contend with spurious leads called in for less honorable reasons. A week after the news hit the papers, the detectives learned that someone was passing around posters in a Bronx neighborhood with a reproduction of the Baby Hope sketch and a photo of a man the poster alleged to be her murderer. Tracking the allegation to the source, the sleuths learned

17

that the man in the photo was actually being sought by the family who had made up the poster for the murder of a male family member.

"It was an affair of the heart," Detective Giorgio later explained. "The family claimed that this man [the man in the poster] killed their relative after the victim had stolen his girlfriend. They didn't report the crime to the police. They didn't want the man dead, they just wanted to flush him out. They figured that if this man thought the police were looking for him as the man who killed Baby Hope, they would get some attention.

"It certainly fit in with the information we have. Possibly the girl was kidnapped for ransom and the family didn't pay, so the kidnapper killed the child — and then *hid* the child, still in an attempt to get the ransom. I mean, it all fit. If you wanted to write a scenario for the thing, it comes out beautiful."

"A lot of different scenarios fit this kid," Detective Neenan added.

The scenario that the detectives find most convincing — the theory that would best explain the circumstances surrounding Baby Hope's death — is the one police most frequently encounter in child abuse cases. The most notorious example is the 1987 Lisa Steinberg case, in which New York lawyer Joel Steinberg beat his young stepdaughter to death.

"We're of the mind that this child was living in a home with her mother and dad, or mother and step-father, or father and stepmother — whatever combination you have — and was sexually abused," Detective Giorgio explained. "She either became a burden or rejected the person who was abusing her, causing that person to kill her. The abuse came from the male. The second party, which was more than

18

likely the mother, got caught up in this. We know from past experience. The classic is the Steinberg case, where the mother sat by and watched her child, not sexually abused, but physically abused, and did nothing about it."

Even when the detectives didn't know that Baby Hope had been sexually abused, they believed she had suffered some kind of abuse at the hands of the male head of her household while the female head, torn between her lover and her child, opted for the lover.

"It's pretty sick mentally to say, 'If I lose one child, I could always have another; but I'm not gonna give *him* up,'" Giorgio said. "But someone else — most likely the girl's mother — had to be a party to this."

Among the hundreds of calls that came into the precinct soon after the Baby Hope story hit the New York media was one that gave this theory strong support. The call from a reluctant witness has tantalized and haunted the detectives since Detective Giorgio took it on Friday, July 26th, three days after the investigation began.

The nervous-sounding caller, who accidentally let it out that she was from Westchester County just north of New York City, refused to identify herself except with the pseudonym "Judy Brown." She was calling from a pay phone. Giorgio guessed from the crowd sounds in the background that she was calling from a busy, commercial place, probably a shopping mall. She said she had seen something suspicious while on a family outing a couple of weeks before. Detective Giorgio asked for the woman's number and offered to call her back. The woman panicked. She said she didn't want to get too involved. Detective Giorgio calmed her down and asked her to be more specific with the details.

Judy Brown said that on the Sunday afternoon of July 14th, she was in a car traveling south into the city on the Henry Hudson Parkway. Just north of the Dyckman Street exit, the family came upon a traffic jam caused by the construction work being done in the area. As the car inched forward, Judy Brown watched a man and a woman heading north on foot by the side of the road. She told Detective Giorgio that the couple were both approximately 5-foot-6 and had a light brown complexion and dark hair. They were Mexican or South American, she guessed. The man, in his 40s, wore a light brown sports jacket. The woman, who had shoulder-length hair, was wearing a gray dress and high heels.

It wasn't a particularly extraordinary sight, but something peculiar about it stuck in Judy Brown's mind: In the steamy summer heat, along a stretch of road that had no rest stops, the well-dressed couple seemed to be en route to a picnic. They were carrying a large ice cooler.

The scene Judy Brown described set off alarms in Detective Giorgio's mind. It matched the location perfectly. It lent weight to the theory about the killers' relationship to each other and to the child. The time of day they were spotted supported the police theory that the killers had taken pains to make their unspeakable errand appear normal. Although the date did not exactly match the time frame the pathologists had set, being a full 10 days before the body was found, it was tantalizingly within sights of it.

Judy Brown, however, turned out to be a frustratingly reluctant witness. As soon as she finished laying out her details and before Detective Giorgio could persuade her to "do the right thing," Judy Brown hung up and vanished. Desperate to further jog his most intriguing witness' memory, Giorgio made a plea in Westchester newspapers for Judy Brown to come forward and call police. She did not, but a younger-sounding woman, who Detective Giorgio believes is Judy Brown's daughter, finally did call back—only to forcefully restate the witness' desire not to get any more involved.

Believing that their reluctant witness might make regular trips into the city on Sundays and not willing to give up on Judy Brown that easily, Detectives Giorgio and Neenan took a team of cops to the Henry Hudson Parkway on the Sunday afternoon of August 4th. Thousands of fliers were distributed to drivers as they crawled through the traffic due to construction work. The noble effort was, sadly, a futile one. None of the drivers or passengers admitted to being Judy Brown. None remembered seeing what Judy Brown said she saw on July 14th.

Now the sleuths were faced with three females in the case whose names they didn't know: The victim, the witness, and the woman they believed was an accomplice in her lover's murder of the child.

As the months passed, the case only took a turn for the darker. In October, a teenager walking along Route 46 in northern New Jersey, not far from the George Washington Bridge, found a discarded batch of Polaroid photographs. They showed a tiny, very young-looking, dark-haired girl being forced to perform oral sex on a man.

The New Jersey detectives who handled the photographs had also seen the Baby Hope sketches. They were immediately struck by the similarity between

21

the girl in the pornographic photos and the computer-imaged likeness of a girl found in the blue cooler. They sent the photos to the 34th Precinct while they began an investigation of their own to identify the subjects of the pornographic Polaroids. So far, they have been as thwarted in their quest as their colleagues in the city across the Hudson have been in the Baby Hope case.

Detectives Giorgio and Neenan agreed that the resemblance between the two young girls was astonishing. But they found some reason to doubt that the two girls were the same. The girl in the photos is clearly wearing small post earrings, while the pathologists who conducted the autopsy found no evidence that Baby Hope's ears were ever pierced. Nevertheless, it is possible that decomposition may have entirely closed up the holes in Baby Hope's ears. Forensic anthropologists are doing further tests to corroborate the original postmortem findings.

Even if it is determined that Baby Hope had pierced ears, the detectives are cautious about linking the girl in the photographs to Baby Hope. They are not, however, ready to rule out a connection.

The sleuths' open-mindedness toward any avenue that might lead to a solution has also led them to some unusual byways. A local psychic, who occasionally donates her services to the police for free, has offered her extrasensory readings on the case to the 34th squad.

"Green comes to her, the color or a name, an old-type station wagon and an underpass," a mildly skeptical Lieutenant Reznick told a *New York Times* reporter. "But God forbid she tells you something you ignore that turns out to be good."

As Lieutenant Reznick and Detectives Giorgio and

Neenan continue digging in the dark for clues to the girl's identity and that of her killers, they are still hoping to generate leads from media stories. While the evidence to the contrary is difficult to refute, the sleuths are willing to consider that Baby Hope is from somewhere outside of New York City and that she may be of some heritage other than Hispanic. On November 15th, they took their quest nationwide on the Fox television program *America's Most Wanted*. Now they hope *True Detective* readers can help. If any readers of *True Detective* have information relating to Baby Hope's identity or other aspects of the case, they are asked to contact Detectives Giorgio or Neenan at the 34th Precinct Homicide Squad at (212) 927-0825. All calls will be kept confidential.

"THE UNKNOWN HORROR BEHIND PRETTY PIXIE'S SLAYING!"

by Howard and Mary Stevens

Mary Beth Hale Grismore could do it all. She sang, acted, danced, played the piano, and organized and coached a barber shop quartet. She was a Sunday school teacher and often played the piano at church functions. She was a talented artist.

An Iowa beauty pageant finalist, 26-year-old Mary Beth was a cheerful, mischievous sprite who flirted and captivated all those around her. When Mary Beth was a child, her mother pinned the label "Pixie" on her, and the name stuck.

A striking blonde with specks of red in her hair, Pixie was the toast of Rockville, Indiana. Then, suddenly, she mysteriously disappeared.

One of her school chums, a girlfriend, was among the last to see Pixie alive. She described her last night with her friend to authorities. "Pixie had her night out on the town. We had dinner, went to a movie and then danced for a couple of hours at a night spot in Terre Haute. The movie was *Looking for Mr. Goodbar,* a story in which the female lead is murdered. The theme of the movie would come back to haunt us."

The young Parke County woman said the night

was to be a going-away outing before Pixie returned to Iowa and her new husband. The next morning, one of her night-on-the-town companions tried to call Pixie, to awaken her as she'd promised. There was no answer. She got into her car and drove to the old farmhouse near Marshall where Pixie was to have been.

"She was gone and so was her car. It was eerie. She had vanished," the friend told sheriff's deputies.

The date was February 22, 1978.

During preliminary interviews with Deputy Sheriff John Britton, Pixie's friend told of how she had helped her friend pack her car and van and how she was impressed by the fact that Pixie was taking turkey feed back to her husband for use on his turkey farm in Iowa. She reported that the pair also packed pieces of china and an old Regulator clock. "I expected her to walk up anytime," she concluded sadly.

For two months, March and April, volunteers combed the rugged Parke County hills searching for Pixie and the 1973 automobile she drove. Her parents offered a reward of $5,000 for information leading to her whereabouts.

At one point, in desperation, Pixie's parents hired a psychic to enter the case in an attempt to locate their missing daughter. The woman was flown in from Illinois and visited Pixie's home and the Turkey Run State Park where the missing woman had worked as a lifeguard.

While at the park, the clairvoyant told authorities that she could see Pixie walking from the pool area to the gatehouse. Later, she pictured her being attacked in the bedroom of the old house by a man hiding in a closet. He then forced her into Pixie's car and drove away.

The psychic told authorities that she felt a great pain in her head—a pain Pixie must have felt the night she was abducted from the rural farmhouse. She said she also experienced a sensation indicating that at least two shots were fired sometime during the ordeal.

During her stay in Parke County, lawmen drove the psychic along many country roads. They said that she kept her eyes closed much of the time, but that she was still able to tell the driver when to turn at country crossroads.

When local lawmen were unable to make any progress in turning up the missing woman, Indiana State Police were summoned and Detective Sergeant Loyd Heck was assigned to head the probe. Bloodhounds were called in to search for the beauty queen.

Heck learned that Pixie never locked her doors when she stayed at the farmhouse owned by her first husband. Her two children by her first marriage were cared for at her mother-in-law's residence.

"She wasn't afraid of anyone. She had a lot of spirit and spunk," Heck recalls.

Officers indicated that Pixie left behind some prescription medicine, her wallet containing $42, a package of cigarettes, and some clothing. The only unexplained material in the old farm dwelling were small particles of dust that had drifted onto a bedspread. Her coat and boots were nearby.

Investigators reported that there was no sign of forced entry or a scuffle. A black jump-suit she had worn at the party with friends was draped over the back of a chair.

Pixie's parents and friends were plainly worried and concerned about her safety. Each passing day

26

made them more fearful. A nationwide missing person report was circulated with a description of the missing woman, her photograph and instructions on how to alert authorities if spotted.

The family assured lawmen that Pixie was not the type of person to run away without telling someone. They said she was bold and brassy enough to tell friends her plans if she meant to disappear.

Detective Heck made no bones about the fact that he was extremely concerned about Pixie's disappearance. He noted that each day she remained gone, the possibility that she would return unharmed, shrank. A Valentine Day massacre of four youths in the area a year before did not relieve his or anyone's anxiety.

As the search continued, Heck shifted strategy. He ordered a helicopter search of the region's hills and deep ravines. He also contacted motels and airports in the area to see if someone had seen the missing woman.

A description of Pixie's missing car, a silver metallic automobile, was fed into police computers along with the Iowa license number, 93GYD485. Heck was now almost certain that the attractive beauty had met with foul play.

Missing-person posters reported that Pixie stood 5 feet 8 inches tall, weighed 129 pounds and had mid-length, curly hair. She was described as having brown eyes and a small, impish nose.

Ten agonizing weeks of frustration and speculation ended on May 3rd when Pixie Grismore's body was found in the trunk of her car parked in a motel parking lot in Whitehall, Ohio. Police in the suburb of Columbus were called to the scene by the motel manager who told authorities the car had been on the lot for nearly two months.

William Evans was one of the first officers to arrive at the scene. He noticed a distinct odor coming from the trunk, and was suspicious because the car carried no license plate.

Soon, officers converged on the parking lot and the vehicle was towed to the Whitehall police garage. A mechanic punched the trunk lock and inside, laid out full-length, was the badly decomposed body of a young woman.

Parke County authorities were notified and Detective Heck flew to Whitehall to view the body. He brought with him dental records which confirmed the victim's identity.

At the morgue, Heck noted that the upper part of the torso was wrapped in a waist-length yellow rain jacket with black snaps. Around the bottom half of the body was a pink blanket with satin trim.

Pixie Grismore's body was clothed, although she wore no shoes. Her flare-bottom blue jeans were unzipped. She was wearing a loose-knit, cream-colored sweater. The sweater was pulled up around her neck, exposing most of her chest except for her left breast.

An examination of the body revealed that all of the clothing appeared to belong to the victim.

A piece of clothesline was knotted tightly around her neck just below her adam's apple, with a large loop knotted to the left side of her face. A coroner's report ruled that Pixie had died of strangulation.

The tests conducted at the Whitehall morgue did not reveal whether the victim had been sexually attacked, but the position of the body and its placement in the car trunk indicated that she'd been assaulted.

Lending credence to this theory were the items found in the trunk with the body. The antiques she'd

28

packed were missing. A pair of battery jumper cables, a hand lantern and a white plastic tub with two bags of turkey grit were recovered. So were two empty bottles of beer.

Fingerprints were lifted from the beer bottles and from the rearview mirror. Police Chief Paul Jackson of Whitehall reported that the fingerprints were the only evidence authorities had to go on. The deterioration of the body, he noted, complicated the probe.

With evidence scarce and leads nonexistent, the FBI was called in to assist in the investigation. It was Heck's belief that the agency's vast resources would help generate life into a probe that had seemingly reached a standstill. He termed the FBI's involvement a "helpful development."

That the Feds were involved in the probe did not mean Detective Heck could pack up shop and return to Indiana. He remained in Whitehall and continued his probe from there.

For starters, he made a check of all motel guests during the period along with a list of airline passengers staying over in the Columbus area. The Columbus airport is within walking distance of the motel and many airline travelers register at the motel where Pixie's body was found.

Also of interest to the investigator was the fact that Pixie's car had traveled more than 667 miles since it was last serviced — a considerably longer distance than the actual mileage from Mrs. Grismore's home in Indiana to the spot where her body and car were found. Where had the missing woman traveled and who accompanied her on her journey?

With Ohio officers, Detective Heck attempted to determine when Pixie was murdered. Medical examiners at the scene said it would be difficult,

29

since several factors had to be considered.

For one thing, they explained, the body was in the car trunk during a long cold spell. For another, the car was parked in a shady area, probably prolonging the normal decomposure process. The coroner reported that the victim's body was partially mummified, and the head, arms and upper torso were blackened.

Photographs of the knotted rope were mailed to police and sheriff's departments throughout the country to determine if that method of strangulation had been used in other cases. It was indicated that the knot was one commonly used by cattlemen and was included in U.S. Navy training manuals.

"It was the same type knot you use to tie your shoes, only with one bow instead of two," the detective said.

Pixie's body had been found with earrings still attached, small hearts on the end of a gold chain, plus a necklace on a chain around her neck. The presence of jewelry on the body led probers to theorize that she had not gone to bed on the night she was abducted, as she'd been wearing the same jewelry the night before. Her clothes, however, were changed, indicating that she might have been rushed out of the house and did not have time to change her jewelry.

The Grismore case also had many similarities to three other unsolved murders reported within the same year in Indiana. The cases involved the strangling of an Indiana University student, a Purdue University coed, and a Mulberry, Indiana housewife.

In reviewing those cases, Heck said the housewife had been strangled and her body had been stuffed into a car trunk. Her body was also badly decomposed. The two students were also strangled and

30

both had been raped. Investigators agreed that if any of the cases were solved, the suspect would be regarded as a prime suspect in the Grismore murder, as well.

Memorial services for Pixie were held in the spring at the Marshall Federated Church. The minister read scripture from Isaiah. He also used passages from St. Paul. "We see through dark glasses now but soon it will be clear."

An uncle of the murder victim wrote a heartfelt tribute to the dead woman, which was read by the pastor: "She was witty, beautiful and a delight to know. She warmed both hands before the fire of life and loving nature."

A memorial service was also held in Pixie's hometown of Corydon, Iowa. The body was cremated.

As this was going on, ISP detectives were reporting several new, significant developments. In reviewing Pixie's last weeks alive, they discovered that she'd received several telephone calls. No one spoke to her during the telephone calls, but Mrs. Grismore told friends she was sure another person was on the telephone.

Heck said he didn't know what significance to attach to the telephone calls other than they were a nuisance and, for a while, alarming to Pixie, friends told the officer. Some of the calls continued after Pixie's violent death, Heck was told.

Finally, it seemed the probe was gaining momentum. New leads were being explored, new avenues of investigation were opening up. A break in the case seemed just around the corner. But 12 years after the brutal slaying, that corner is no closer in sight and Pixie Grismore still doesn't rest in peace.

Questions remain. Who killed Pixie? And why? A

frequent motive in many murders, insurance is not believed to be a factor in the Grismore slaying, since she had little coverage, Loyd Heck, who has since retired, reports.

If anyone is to crack the 11-year-old baffling Pixie slaying, the far-flung network of agents employed by the FBI is the hands-on favorite to prevail. Although the passing of time benefits the transgressor, the resources of the FBI is a force to be reckoned with, and they have not thrown in the towel and aren't likely to do so. Those close to the case say that the FBI office in Terre Haute made it known on the 10th anniversary of the unsolved mystery that the case remains a top priority.

A break in the case could come at anytime and the file in the Pixie probe remains open and viable, agents insist. A periodic review of the bizarre case is conducted by the FBI, Terre Haute director Martin Riggin notes.

Heck doesn't believe the Pixie murder was a random slaying. "Her slayer didn't walk in off the street. It was a well-planned and well-executed slaying. It was as neat as a hit-man."

Riggin reasons that she was not followed home by anyone from the nightclub where Pixie and her friends danced. "It would be difficult to find anyone on those country roads in the daytime, let alone at night. Whoever did Pixie in was at the house when she returned from her night out with friends," Riggin believes.

Both officers are at a loss to explain why the antiques in the dead woman's car never surfaced. Pixie's paintings (she was a talented artist) have not appeared, either. They were signed by the artist and many art dealers would have considered them extremely valuable. An old Regulator clock and chinaware is also missing.

Also missing is the Iowa license tag. The plate was removed from the vehicle, probably by Pixie's slayer.

At times, it seems that everything in the case has worked to the killer's benefit. Even the weather. Temperatures fluctuated like a yo-yo, causing moisture to build up in the car's trunk, obliterating fingerprints. Prints were lifted from the rearview mirror and the beer bottles, but how good they were was anyone's guess.

"There was some evidence collected," is all Riggin will say. How much evidence is another matter. There was the matter of the towels placed around Pixie's head. Were they used to sedate Pixie or to suffocate her?

Was she murdered in the motel, or was she killed elsewhere and transported in the trunk to the motel parking lot? Heck admits that there are more questions than answers in the case.

The autopsy conducted in Whitehall, Heck says, showed there was no food in the victim's stomach, although she had eaten in Terre Haute earlier. Medical experts say it takes three to four hours for food to clear the stomach. That would place the abduction at a later time than had originally been figured.

Whitehall investigators also say a motel key was recovered six feet from Pixie's car. However, they discount the key as a factor in the case since the room was thoroughly searched and no evidence was uncovered. Ohio investigators reason that the key could have been used several weeks before the murder and any evidence originating from the room would have vanished.

Authorities report that there were no tire tracks

visible in the yard of the old farmhouse. They were obliterated by a sudden freeze and thaw, and the tires of the moving van had taken care of those that remained.

There were reports in Rockville that a sports car with out-of-state license plates was observed near the town square by a man who waved at the occupant, a man, but got no response. The man who reported the incident said he looked in his rearview mirror and saw that the car was registered as an out-of-state vehicle. The car and driver continued on a route out of town and has not been seen since.

Investigators say that many informers who've come forward are convinced that at least two people were involved in Pixie's death. They are convinced that the planning and execution of the abduction and murder would've taken at least that many people. They reason that the spirit and energy of the victim would've been impossible for one man to crush.

At one point, Heck was convinced that the slaying would be solved. But, with the passing of time, he isn't so sure.

He says: "If this case is ever solved, I feel that it will have local roots or involve a hit-man who was paid well to do his dirty work. The person who committed this crime or paid to have it done must have a lot of bitterness in his soul. He cannot be proud of himself and he will take this dastardly deed to his grave.

"It was a cheap shot by someone who called the tune from a distance not too far removed from the victim and her family."

Director Riggin is more optimistic about an eventual solution to the baffling case. A photograph of the murdered woman in the FBI office serves as a daily reminder of the continuing task.

Readers of *True Detective* possessing information on the Pixie Grismore slaying are requested to communicate with their authorities. Your tips may bring her killer to justice.

...

"CATCH THE CRUISING CABBIE KILLER"

by Bud Ampolsk

Detectives of the Laconia and Wakefield Precincts in the East Bronx had no way of knowing on the early morning of Wednesday, March 7, 1990, that they were about to become the point men in one of the longest and most frustrating manhunts in Big Apple history.

The first inkling that they would came at 6:40 a.m., when a report of a "man down" at Wilder and Stouen Avenues in the Wakefield section crackled over the police radio network.

Minutes later, the first on-scene officers discovered 37-year-old Anton Jones, the driver of a radio-dispatched cab, slumped in the front seat of his vehicle. His bloody head rested against the cab's steering wheel. He was dead of a single bullet wound in his skull.

Detectives who were quickly summoned to the scene by uniformed personnel made their way through the gathering of early-morning gawkers who had been attracted to the murder scene by the profusion of police units jamming Wilder Avenue. From the blues present, detectives assembled bits and scraps of information into a somewhat cohesive account of the shooting.

It was learned that Jones' body had first been spotted by a second livery cab driver, who had become alarmed over the inert position of the victim and had then placed the emergency call.

An interview with the dispatcher on duty in the headquarters of the cab company that employed Jones was able to pinpoint the exact time of Jones' final communication. The ill-fated cabbie had radioed in that he had picked up a fare at 3000 Eastchester Road and was in the process of taking his passenger to 241st Street and White Plains Road in the Bronx. The fare for the trip would be six dollars. The dispatcher had received this information just minutes before the driver's corpse was found.

As reporters and police investigators talked to Jones' livery cab co-workers, they received a graphic picture of the terrors experienced by employees of operations that plied the streets where medallion cabs refused to go.

Said one 62-year-old veteran driver, "It's just miserable out there. How can you work when you think you're picking up the right man, and you might be picking up the guy who's going around killing people?" The man noted that he himself had been robbed twice.

Any hope that the Anton Jones slaying was an isolated event would be shattered within a week.

It was shortly before 5:00 a.m. on Wednesday, March 14th, that 43-year-old Elliot Whitaker, a husky former prison guard working as a cab driver while waiting to be hired by the New York City Department of Corrections, contacted his dispatcher. He announced that he had picked up a man in front of a produce store on Boston Road in the Bronx and was driving him to a train station on White Plains Road.

A few minutes later, the dispatcher received a telephone call from a woman. He would later tell police, "A woman called here and said, 'One of your cabs hit a parked car, and I think there is something wrong with your driver.'"

The report was instantly relayed to police, who sped to East 214th Street in the Williamsbridge section of the East Bronx. There they found the body of Whitaker. The father of three children had been shot numerous times in the back of the head.

On Monday, April 10th, the story was strikingly similar. This time the dead man was a 25-year-old student at Iona College who was working the late shift to help pay for his education.

Paul Burghard had picked up a passenger at Montefiore Hospital. He had been summoned to the medical facility by a caller who had used a direct telephone line to the dispatcher of the cab company to order a cab.

About 15 minutes later, according to the company manager, the dispatcher received a call from a driver for another company. The caller conveyed this ominous information: Burghard's cab was now at Wilson Avenue, off Gun Hill Road in the Williamsbridge section of the Bronx. Burghard was not moving.

For the third time in a little over a month, Bronx homicide detectives discovered the corpse of a hardworking cabbie who had been slaughtered wantonly. Burghard's cold-blooded killer had pumped two bullets into him: one into his cheek, the second into the back of his neck. After murdering his helpless victim, the killer had taken off with $60 Burghard had been carrying.

The police blotter showed that Burghard was reported slain at 2:40 a.m.

By now, the three murders of radio-dispatched cabbies who had earned their livings working the perilous early-morning hours had become almost an obsession with Bronx detectives. The slayings had also set off a growing sense of panic among other livery cabbies and the drivers' families.

The hub of the all-out police effort to apprehend the cabbie killer was the squad room of the 47th Precinct. Here, the 10 detectives regularly assigned to the precinct, plus scores of homicide bureau personnel, sifted through every aspect of the three cases hoping that some break would come soon.

According to their commanding officer, Lieutenant Anthony Vitaliano, shifts of officers were working around the clock on the cabbie killings.

Some investigators were canvassing areas where the killer might have placed calls to the cab company dispatchers. Other plainclothesmen were continually talking to residents of the East Bronx neighborhood in which the gunman had struck. They were seeking possible witnesses on the block where the drivers had pulled over to let their fare out moments before he had cut them down with the .22-caliber handgun he carried.

There was one optimistic note emerging from the series of talks with concerned and cooperating residents of the areas where the slayings had taken place, according to New York City Police Department Chief of Detectives Joseph Borelli. Borelli noted that detectives combing the teeming Bronx streets had come up with a witness who had been helpful in giving a detailed description of a possible perpetrator. The witness assisted police artists in making a composite sketch of the suspect.

Even as the chief of detectives revealed this information, it was said that copies of the sketch were appearing throughout the Bronx. They had been placed on store fronts and lampposts. One source described the handbills, grim as they were, as being like holiday banners amid their drab surroundings.

Detectives working the case agreed with their chief that the police sketch circulation represented the most positive development thus far.

Still, other officers remained at precinct telephones. They were fielding incoming calls from civilians who kept the police-installed hotline ablaze with over 100 calls.

Some of those responding to the police request for information on the killings were attracted by the $20,000 reward offered for contacts leading to the arrest and conviction of the perpetrator.

Just how valuable the telephone calls would prove remained very much in doubt. Some were coming from disgruntled wives seeking to tap their husbands for the triple murder. Many others merely whispered a street name before abruptly hanging up.

Nevertheless, the dedicated duty officers spared no effort as they took down copious notes relative to every incoming communication.

The officers followed up on every call. They developed identities from the proffered nicknames. They leafed through mugshots that might in some way be connected with these identities. They networked their lists of informants in hopes that one or more of them might know the assailant.

One thing the cops were not doing was going public with everything they had learned about the crime

40

wave against livery chauffeurs. For example, they hesitated to describe the killings to the press. Police feared that what was said to the reporters might reach the murderer. They pointed out that in all likelihood, the wanted man either read newspapers or watched television. If so, he might be alerted to the police activity and be able to change his M.O.

Said one investigator, "The search is like a street fight. Every bit of information they have, no matter how small, may be worked to advantage."

According to a second police source, there was another factor driving the cops to play it close to the vest. Veteran officers knew that in dealing with a serial killer, they were working against a depraved person with a supreme ego. They sought to avoid any press that would feed that ego and cause him to murder again.

Said one person who took part in the search, "We don't want to build up his credentials. Call this man a serial killer, and he will do it again."

Behind the scenes, however, the cops had enlisted the aid of an expert who was developing a psychological profile of the cabbie slayer.

Although at this stage of the manhunt no profile report had been filed, detectives felt that one vital aspect of his personality was clear. One officer put it this way: "The way he shot those drivers, he made sure they wouldn't walk away."

Although the assailant had operated within a single one-mile radius in the East Bronx, his activities had caused a sense of growing panic to race through the Big Apple's garages out of which over 20,000 livery cabs and 11,787 yellow medallion taxis operated.

The general feeling was expressed by the man who had employed Paul Burghard. The fleet manager

41

said, "Sure, everyone's uptight. Can you blame them? We're not just dealing with robberies here. We're talking about murder—and it looks premeditated. Obviously we're dealing with a guy who is getting into cabs and all he wants to do is shoot the driver."

Other livery company executives reported that they had been plagued by phone calls on the day of Burghard's murder. Their drivers were calling in to tell their employers they were not reporting for work. Some went so far as to say they didn't want to work at all.

Livery companies advised their drivers to exercise extreme caution in making their rounds. One fleet executive told drivers not to pick up fares at Montefiore Hospital unless given permission by the office.

Other dispatchers said they were attempting to confirm all telephone calls requesting cab service. They were also telling their personnel to avoid picking up any passengers who looked in any way suspicious to them.

One dispatcher reported that his company was instructing drivers to demand payment of fares at the beginning of a trip rather than at the destination. He added, "We're also saying, if you don't like the call, just pull away and roll."

One executive said his firm was not going to give up its usual routes. "We'll continue to drive in those neighborhoods, but if a call doesn't sound kosher, we won't go," he noted.

A dispatcher for the company that had employed Elliot Whitaker, the second livery chauffeur to be murdered by the serial killer, stated, "Robberies are much more common than killings.

"Robberies happen all the time. But we've only

had three or four killings here over the past three or four years."

However, there was little comfort to be gained by reviewing the past. Things were different now, and the potential was present for further bloodletting.

This was made painfully clear by the evaluation of NYPD Sergeant Frank Viggiano of the Laconia Avenue Stationhouse, who was spearheading his unit's search for the killer. He noted that the murderer had slain for relatively small sums of money. In each of the three cases the gunman had taken only $50 to $200 from his victims' pockets.

What worried Sergeant Viggiano was the fact that the wanted man had shot the cabbies to death although in no case was there any evidence that the victims had put up any kind of a struggle. In all three instances, the drivers had been shot from behind before they had a chance to defend themselves.

The fear that the robber might strike again in the East Bronx was a strong possibility. "We believe it's the same person," said Sergeant Viggiano. "And he knows the area well."

As the days passed without a major break in the case, police had another worry. When a serial killer is on the loose for any length of time, police worry that his literally getting away with murder may encourage other criminal types to try their hand at the same type of activity. This fear would prove warranted.

It was with a great deal of anguish in his voice that one detective said, "We have no suspects, nothing. We're begging the public for help."

The bad news came in the early-morning hours of Wednesday, April 11th. This time, the all-too-familiar crime scene was at East 169th Street and

43

Sheridan Avenue in the Bronx. The victim was 41-year-old Dennis Forbes. At first there had been some confusion in the identification, since Forbes' driver's license had been made out to another name. Forbes, a devoted husband and loving father of two young children, had been shot in the back of the head and was rushed to Lincoln Hospital, where doctors began a futile 24-hour battle to save him. The hardworking native Jamaican was beyond help.

Like just about every cabbie in the city, Forbes had been terrified by the three murders that had already rocked the Bronx.

A grieving relative reported, "He saw the news story about the killings on television and turned to me and said, 'I have to get out of this business.'"

The statement had been made shortly before Forbes had left his home, never to return. His last act there had been to set the family's VCR to pick up the 11:00 p.m. television newscast for later developments in the probe of Paul Burghard's death the day before.

As the police investigation into Forbes' shooting got under way, police noted the distinct possibility that the gunman had not been the same person who had slain Anton Jones, Elliot Whitaker, and Paul Burghard.

Investigators working the Forbes case noted that in the three prior slayings, the killer had called the cab companies to request a cab and had been given addresses on quiet streets in the Williamsbridge section of the Bronx before slaying his victims.

Commented Lieutenant Donald Stephenson, commanding officer of the 44th Precinct detective squad, "Not to say it couldn't be the same person or persons. But at this time, certain details are not the same. It is out of the area [of the earlier crimes], and it wasn't a radio call. At this point, the shooting doesn't seem to fit the pattern."

According to police sources, witnesses had seen two teenagers fleeing from Forbes' light blue cab following the shooting. But there was little more to go on. A .25-caliber handgun was discovered on the front seat of Forbes' vehicle as well.

Speaking for the distraught Forbes family, a close relative said, "There is a lot of anger right now. We can't understand why it had to be him." The relative told of Forbes' recent request that a bulletproof shield be placed in his cab. She said, "It's kind of like he had a feeling that something bad was going to happen to him."

That somebody else was ready to kill for the "innocent buck" Dennis Forbes had earned was obvious from the fact that the wallet he carried was completely empty.

It was late Saturday night, April 14th, when still another deserted Bronx street became the repository for the body of a cabbie who had been shot to death while working the night shift.

The driver, 38-year-old Rafael Montes de Oca, was found dead at the wheel of his car at East 188th Street and Webster Avenue in the Bronx at 11:55 p.m. The grisly discovery was made when the dispatcher for the company that employed Montes de Oca received a call from another cabbie reporting that the vehicle was parked at the curb and the driver was either unconscious or dead.

The dispatcher told police that Montes de Oca had gone to the 188th Street address to pick up a regular passenger who was identified only as "George." The man had called at 10:00 p.m. and had specifically re-

45

quested that particular car and driver.

Friends of the victim described Montes de Oca as a quiet, reserved man who worked 12-hour days and six days a week to support his wife and four children. His earnings ran from $50 to $150 a day.

On the day of his death, according to police, Montes de Oca had worked two shifts, pausing only to eat dinner.

When the 10:30 p.m. call came in for him, Montes de Oca had told the dispatcher it would take 10 minutes for him to arrive at the 188th Street site. He never radioed again to say whether or not he had picked up his passenger.

One co-worker and close friend of the dead man said of him, "He was such a nice guy. It's unbelievable. It's unreal."

The latest slaying of a Bronx cabbie caused police to review all of the open cabbie killings on their Bronx blotters. Sergeant Mary Wrensen, a police department spokeswoman, revealed that "their links are being investigated."

Later, police investigating Montes de Oca's murder shifted their probe into aspects of his personal life. One theory had it that there had been trouble between Montes de Oca and an acquaintance over a woman, which might have provided the motivation. At this time, the case is still considered open.

For their part, hundreds of drivers formed long motorcades in various boroughs throughout the city, protesting the violence now assailing the hack industry. Their anger and fear was heightened by the killing spree that continued to claim their co-workers.

Even as 300 cars returning from Montes de Oca's funeral drove across the Triborough Bridge during rush hour on Wednesday at 4:00 p.m., causing a mammoth tie-up because of their five-mile-an-hour crawl, the death of yet a sixth Bronx cabbie, Bakary Simpara, a native of the West African nation of Mali, was announced. Simpara had lingered between life and death for nearly a month after having been shot behind the ear at Underhill and Gildersleeve Avenues in the Clason's Point section of the Bronx on March 21, 1990. He had never regained consciousness.

The killer's motive remained a mystery, but Detective Irwin Silverman, who was investigating the case, said, "Robbery is a good bet."

Police did not think Simpara's death was the work of the serial killer.

However, Detective Silverman noted that many cabbies are robbed and fail to report the incidents. He held that if they did, their information might help catch the killers who prey on them.

And yet another victim, the seventh cabbie to be murdered within seven weeks in the Bronx, was to be added to the toll. This was 48-year-old Muhammad Salim, a Pakistani national. He was found slumped in his cab with a single bullet wound behind his left ear in the Tremont section of the West Bronx in the early-morning hours of Sunday, April 22nd.

Said one source close to the police investigation, "We believe it's part of the same pattern as the three consecutive murders that had claimed Anton Jones, Elliot Whitaker, and Paul Burghard."

The speculation among lawmen now was that the killer was targeting cabbies for some reason other than financial gain. Officers holding to this theory pointed out that most cabbies carry very little cash with them.

The latest driver to be found dead had been discovered with food still in his mouth and his wallet empty. His vehicle, with his body still in it, was taken to the 44th Precinct where forensic tests could be carried out with greater care. Meanwhile, New York City Mayor David Dinkins announced that he had instructed Police Commissioner Lee Brown to expand a task force of 30 officers. The augmented posse would include plainclothes cops who would pose as drivers of livery cabs in order to decoy perps bent on a fast hit.

In making the announcement, Dinkins said, "These killings represent more than a brutal attack on the drivers who have fallen victim. They have also become an assault on the vital link in our transportation system."

In all, the beefed-up task force now had 50 detectives, uniformed officers, and anti-crime and street crime cops. It had moved beyond the original Laconia Precinct area, although its prime objective remained the apprehension of the serial killer. Its new territory included the entire Bronx.

The move came as police reported that 16 cabbies had been killed in New York City in 1990 between January 1st and April 23rd.

Police spokesman Captain Robert Cividanes said a plainclothes task force would not pick up fares, but would cruise at night in livery-style vehicles or would tail cabs that already had passengers. A signaling system had been worked out for cabbies in distress.

The department also encouraged drivers to use well-traveled thoroughfares and avoid deserted streets.

Even with all the sustained efforts by lawmen, the actions of the serial killer and the others who might have been inspired by him continue to go un-

48

punished—despite the fact that the Bronx cabbie murders ran second only to the notorious work of the so-called Zodiac Slayer in the Big Apple's consciousness during 1990.

The search still goes on at this writing. Commenting on the situation at present, Sergeant Vitaliano, who remains the lead investigator heading the livery probe, reports that things have slowed down. A number of officers originally assigned to the task force set up by the police department and the Taxi and Limousine Commission have since been transferred to more current cases.

Public cooperation has also tailed off. Vitaliano notes that the outpouring of telephone calls from tipsters, which flooded police phones during March and April of last year, has now become a trickle. The lack of informant activity has been a severe setback to the probe.

All that can be said for certain is that a trigger-happy thug who might have inspired far more slayings than those three police hold him directly responsible for is still at large and still an ongoing threat to the community.

In all, the grim scorecard of cabbie homicides for 1990 stands at 35—16 in the Bronx, seven in Manhattan, nine in Brooklyn, and three in Queens.

Police made arrests in 10 of these cases, and further court action is pending against the suspected perps.

"TENNESSEE MYSTERY OF THE VANISHED NURSE!"

by Bruce Gibney

In November 1986, a pretty young woman named Teresa Ann Butler stepped out into a blinding rainstorm — and disappeared off the face of the earth. Since then, the search to find the pretty 26-year-old nurse has become almost an obsession for the men and women of the Shelby County Tennessee Sheriff's Office.

Eleven searches have been conducted, hundreds of leads followed up. Investigators have made trips to the morgue and to burial sites convinced that they have finally found the young woman, only to come away emptyhanded.

"We've have plenty of missing-persons cases before, but nothing like this," a weary detective said in 1987, after yet another fruitless search of the pine woods in eastern Shelby County.

And yet the case refuses to go away. "Will we ever solve it?" a detective responded to a reporter's question. "I don't know. But it seems like just when you are ready to give up, something else pops up."

Police have questioned several suspects. One of them, who confessed to raping and murdering the young nurse, led police on several searches.

Investigators don't know whether to believe him or not. What he says makes sense, and circumstantial evidence supports his claim. On the other hand, police have never found a body or any physical evidence connecting him to the crimes he confessed to—and later recanted.

"You aren't going to find a more complicated case than this one," drawled one investigator, who questioned several suspects and was involved in half a dozen searches. "I just don't know how this is going to end up. It's a real heartbreaker."

Heartbreak is the word for it.

With a population of 800,000, Shelby is the largest county in Tennessee. Most of the inhabitants live in Memphis, the state's largest city and former home and currently spiritual residence of Elvis Presley.

This story takes place outside the metropolitan hub, in the small towns that dot the state roads and highways of southwest Tennessee.

At nine o'clock on the evening of November 10, 1986, Teresa Butler finished her shift at the St. Francis Hospital and headed for her car parked in the faculty-employee lot.

A blinding, chilling rain had pounded southwest Tennessee for much of the day, and she likely hurried to the safety of her car without paying much attention to anyone around her. Normally, the pretty brunette was aware of her surroundings and people around the parking lot. Tonight, however, she was in a hurry and paid little attention.

Her husband, a night student at State Technical Institute at Memphis, was just getting out of classes, and she wanted to beat him home and have some hot food cooking when he got there.

Jamming her key into the front door of the Honda

Accord, she ducked in out of the rain. She pulled out of the parking lot and drove home.

Teresa's husband wasn't too far behind her. His last class finished at nine and he, too, was in a hurry to get home. He had gotten out of Memphis without too much hassle and was headed along Monterey Road when he saw a car parked along the road.

It took a second to register. Damn, it looked like Teresa's Honda! Quickly, he pulled off the road.

A glance at the license plate confirmed that it was her car. It was parked 20 feet off the road, with the engine running, the lights on and the radio playing.

Teresa, however, was nowhere to be found.

Her husband conducted his own search. Neighbors later joined him, but they did not find Teresa or learn what happened to her.

Finally, out of places to look, he called the Shelby County Sheriff's Office. Two deputies arrived. They searched in and around the car and questioned the husband and the neighbors before reporting back to headquarters.

More deputies arrived. By the next morning, two dozen had fanned out through the woods and dense brush looking for the missing nurse.

They were hampered by heavy rains which had washed away tire tracks and footprints that might have been present, and the thick brush which grew almost to the side of the road.

Investigators under the direction of Lieutenant Stanley White and Captain Jessie Gwin joined in the search. Old pros, they recognized that this was not your ordinary missing-person case.

Employees at St. Francis Hospital told lawmen that Teresa had been in good spirits and was in a hurry to get home to see her husband. Two said they

52

saw her pull on her coat and dash out the door to her car at nine o'clock. She was walking in the direction of the employee parking lot when she left.

Investigators searched the lot but found nothing significant. Hospital security had no recent reports of car thefts or assaults or of strangers loitering on the grounds.

Police estimated that it would have taken about 20 minutes for the comely nurse to drive from the hospital to Monterey Road where her car was found. That meant only minutes had elapsed before her husband, driving by, discovered the car.

The investigators were puzzled as to why the young nurse had pulled off the road. The car was in good working order and she had no reason to pull over, since she was in a hurry to get home.

They were also puzzled that she had left the vehicle with the lights on, the keys in the ignition and the radio playing. "No one is going to leave a car like that, unless they planned to stop just for a moment," one investigator commented.

Teresa's purse was also missing, indicating that she had taken it with her when she got out of the car.

Teresa's husband had found this strange, too. "She was very safety conscious," he told authorities. "If she had to leave the car for some reason, she would lock the car up and taken the keys with her. She isn't going to walk away from it, with the lights and radio on. It doesn't make sense."

The car was towed to headquarters. Lab technicians found fingerprints and bits of physical evidence but no bloodstains or signs of a struggle.

There was no sign of Teresa, either. Initially, police believed she had left the car and become lost in the woods. But after a thorough search that included

53

bloodhounds and trained trackers, they reasoned that she might have been abducted.

A possible scenario was that the pretty nurse had stopped to help a hitchhiker or someone who had flagged her down. Another possibility was she was forced off the road.

Police found no tire impressions or shoeprints indicating another person, but they reasoned that prints might have been washed away in the rain.

With each passing day, police had less hope of finding Teresa alive. News stories and a photograph of the woman were published in local papers. There were a few calls from witnesses who said they thought they had seen her or had something to report regarding her abduction.

On November 20th, the sheriff's office got a call from a farmer who said he had discovered a woman's body on his property. Detectives met with the man, who took them to a culvert off Interstate 20 and Norris Road and pointed into a culvert. At the bottom of the culvert lay the corpse of a young woman. She was half naked, though that was difficult to see at first because she was completely covered with a thick layer of mud.

The corpse was taken to the morgue where the mud was hosed off. The woman appeared to be in her early 20s; she was about 5 feet 5 inches tall and fit the physical appearance of the missing nurse.

She had been strangled to death and, judging from her ripped clothing and half-naked appearance, sexually assaulted. She appeared to have been dead for several days, perhaps as long as two weeks.

Teresa Butler's family was notified of the discovery and prepared for the worst. "At least we will know what happened to her," said one relative.

The young woman lying covered with mud in the bottom of the culvert wasn't Teresa Butler. Police didn't know who she was, except that she wasn't the missing nurse. Fingerprints proved that.

Family and friends of the missing nurse were relieved; however, they still didn't know what happened to their friend, who was not listed as missing for 10 days.

Investigators were puzzled, too. After the search failed to turn up anything, they reasoned that the girl had been kidnapped, possibly for sexual reasons, and that they would eventually find her corpse tossed in the woods or along a lonely stretch of road.

An APB was telexed to law enforcement agencies in the immediate area. Teresa was described as 26 years old, 5 feet 3 inches tall, 105 pounds, with blue eyes and light brown hair, and a chicken pox scar on her right cheek. She was last seen wearing a nurse's uniform and a light gray sweater.

When the telex failed to turn up any leads, her name was entered into the NCIC computer that links law enforcement agencies nationwide.

In December, Sheriff Jack Owens told a reporter that he expected to eventually find the woman. "It's a mighty strange case," he admitted. "We have some missing-persons cases on the books, but nothing really like this one. It looks like she simply disappeared into the thin air."

Several days after the announcement, the long search appeared as if it might come to an end. The break came after police spoke to a man who had been sitting in a bar and struck up a conversation with another man. Fueled on beer, their conversation gravitated around the subject of women.

"This guy told me he had had lots of women, but

the best piece he ever had was this woman he grabbed right out of her car," the witness told detectives. "Said she fought like the dickens, which made the sex even more fun." The man told him that he then killed the woman and buried her body in the woods.

"Let the smokies and the flatfoots look all they want," the man said, according to the witness. "They can search all they want, but they ain't ever gonna find that girlie. I got her hid too well."

The abduction, rape and murder reportedly took place off Monterey Road in the general vicinity of where Teresa Butler's car was discovered.

Lieutenant Stanley White instructed investigators to look into the lead. Undercover officers met with the idle boaster and pumped him for information about the woman he'd supposedly murdered.

Afterward, he was brought to the station, where he denied killing anyone or boasting that he had. He said he didn't recall talking to anyone in a bar about murdering a woman and if he had, he must have been pig-drunk.

"That ain't like me!" he insisted. "I got no reason to hurt women."

Investigators conducted a search of the man's house and three-acre spread. The search turned up nothing except discarded appliances and a few jugs of illegal moonshine.

Sheriff Jack Owens met with investigators. Convinced that they might be on to something more than idle talk made after too many beers, he ordered a massive grid search. Led by tracking dogs and deputies on all-terrain vehicles and in a helicopter, 150 deputies and volunteers returned to Monterey Road and conducted another search of the area where Teresa Butler's car was last spotted.

The search lasted three days. When it was over, investigators were not closer to learning the missing nurse's whereabouts.

In March 1987, CrimeStoppers offered $1,000 for information leading to the discovery of Teresa Butler. A videotaped reenactment of the abduction was shown on the local news, along with interviews of detectives and a snapshot of the victim.

The family offered a $10,000 reward. Anyone with information was asked to call CrimeStoppers, 528-CASH, or the Shelby County Sheriff's Department.

The search for Teresa Butler had been one of the longest, costliest and most publicized in recent years. But it was not the only one to catch the public's eye.

On April 16, 1987, 4-year-old Marlena Childress of Union City, Tennessee, disappeared while playing in her front yard, prompting a massive search. Police, state and federal agencies tracked suspects from Chicago to Memphis, where the little girl was reportedly seen in a local hair salon accompanied by two older women.

Volunteer organizations held rallies and bake sales to raise a $25,000 reward for information leading to the girl's return. A rally was held in which 10,000 helium balloons with the missing tot's smiling face printed on each one were let loose in hopes that someone might recognize the youngster.

Despite all the searchers and bake sales and dozens of leads, the little girl has never been found.

Authorities also conducted a publicized search for Martha Leanne Green of White Bluff, Tennessee, who vanished after she and her twin brother ran out of gas off Interstate 40, east of Memphis. Martha stayed in the car while her brother caught a lift to a gas station. When he returned, she was gone.

Despite an exhaustive investigation by the Tennessee Bureau of Investigation, and countless searches, she hasn't been seen since.

Shelby County detectives read through the reports and questioned investigators working those cases. Despite the fact that the 4-year-old and the teenager had disappeared under mysterious circumstances, the probers could find no connection between them and the Butler disappearance.

One case that was similar was the kidnapping and murder of a nurse from Beebee, Arkansas. On April 25th, Sandra Lynn Williams left a nursing home in Quitman. She never made it. Her car was found the next day parked off a road near Romance, Arkansas. Her body was discovered several days later in a ditch in Waite County. She had been raped and shot to death.

Shelby sleuths noted the similarities: both women were nurses, both were roughly the same age and physically similar, and both were abducted while driving home alone.

The Shelby investigators contacted Arkansas authorities and told them about their case. The Arkansas sleuths didn't have any suspects but agreed to keep in touch and share information.

Within days, however, Shelby sleuths were hot on another lead. On May 20th, they received a tip from a caller who said he had information about the Butler woman. He was switched to the detective detail and spoke with one of the investigators assigned to the Butler case.

The tipster said he had heard that the woman had been buried in a shallow grave in a 40-acre woods on the southeast corner of Raines Road and Hickory Hill.

The message was relayed to B.J. Patterson, emergency service director, who contacted Dr. Hugh Berryman, an anthropologist who taught in the pathology department at the University of Tennessee, Memphis.

Berryman is a legend in the Mid-South for his ability to excavate grave sites and reconstruct crimes from the tiniest of clues. He once gained fame by reconstructing the last hours of a woman's life after studying her skeleton and a tube of toothpaste found near her corpse.

Patterson told his old pal from the university about the tip. The two had been involved in nine previous searches for the missing woman, several conducted in the area where the tipster said the body was.

"What makes this one any different?" the anthropologist asked.

"Got me," Patterson said. "The detectives, however, questioned this guy pretty close and seemed convinced he's telling the truth."

"That's good enough for me," Berryman said. "Let's get going."

The two pored over topographical maps and planned the search. The next morning, wearing camouflage gear and gloves to protect their hands and prevent their contaminating the crime scene, they led deputies and volunteers to the intersection of Hickory Hill and Raines Road to begin the search.

Berryman instructed searchers to look for depressions, not raised mounds, explaining that soil settled when it was dug up.

He told them to be aware of subtle changes in

vegetation—a dead plant in a clump might indicate that somebody had dug it up to try to hide something. Another thing to look for was plants growing in the same area but of different heights. This might indicate that growth patterns had been interrupted.

He instructed the searchers to call him if they found a grave or depressed area and not to start digging on their own. His reason was that it took experience to do an excavation and an inexperienced digger might inadvertently destroy footprints or other physical evidence in his or her zeal to find the body.

"And one last thing," he said good-naturedly. "Be careful of snakes. It's damn hot out and we'll be up to our armpits in rattlers."

The search lasted all day. Armed with machetes, the searchers battled, in addition to the snakes, sweltering heat and swarms of bugs as they pushed and hacked through briars, brambles, poison ivy and great tangled beds of honey-suckle.

When it was over, they discovered the footprints of a raccoon, a dried-out crawdad hole and a .22-inch king snake that was big enough to make a good wallet.

What they didn't find was single earth depression or change in growth patterns or plant life indicating that a body had ever been buried there.

Sheriff Owens was informed of the findings. By now he was used to disappointment—it was the ninth search his men had conducted. Still, it hurt. He shook his head and wondered quietly if they would ever get to the bottom of this mystery.

His views were shared by detectives assigned to the case and by friends and family of the victim and just plain folk who had been touched by the tragedy.

The case was nine months old—yet, from the public response, it could have happened yesterday. Hardly a day went by when someone didn't call with a tip about "that Butler woman."

In August, police received a call from a self-described psychic who said she had a vision of the body of Teresa Butler. "I saw her plain as day," the woman told a detective. "You will find her buried in a triangular area near a stand of pine trees near Houston levee and Monterey roads."

The tip was passed back to Lieutenant White. "Got another one," he said. Investigators had a steady diet of calls from psychics reporting that they had seen the woman on her remains in various parts of the county.

This one was a little better than the others. "Well, let's check it out," the lieutenant said. "Who knows, it might lead to something."

Searchers returned to eastern Shelby County and began looking for the triangular spot where the body was supposedly buried. They didn't find it—but, by then, investigators were hot on another lead.

A few days earlier, investigators had received a call from the sheriff's office in neighboring Hardeman County. A 22-year-old mechanic and police reservist had been returned to the jail in Bolivar charged with impersonating an officer and abducting a nurse.

"He flat-out admitted it," the Hardeman detective said. "He said he did the same thing in your neck of the woods. Only, that time, he killed her."

The suspect was Ben Boyd, 22. Blond-haired and blue-eyed, Boyd had been arrested three times that summer, including once for rape in a Shelby County.

He was first arrested on June 1st by Germantown police after a woman told officers he was

61

following her after she left work.

When police stopped him, Boyd reportedly leaped from his car and flashed a Shelby County sheriff's badge, saying he was working undercover.

One of the officers taking down the report glanced in the backseat and noticed a shotgun. He ran a driver's-license check and saw that Boyd was not listed by the computer as a law enforcement officer.

When this was brought to Boyd's attention, he reportedly admitted he was only a reservist.

Further investigative work revealed that he was actually a former reservist who had entered a reserve class in November 1986, but was dismissed the following spring for poor attendance.

Boyd was arrested and charged with impersonating an officer. His badge was confiscated and he was booked into county jail, but was released the same day.

A week later he was back in jail on a charge of rape. A female employee at St. Francis Hospital said she woke up at 4:30 a.m. after falling asleep on her couch and saw a man standing in the bedroom. He showed her a gun, handcuffed her hands to the bed, then raped her.

In trying to talk the man out of the rape, the woman said, she learned he was acquainted with the neighborhood and even knew some of the people who lived there.

Boyd was picked up after police learned he had an old girlfriend who once lived in the neighborhood. He denied raping the girl but was arrested after the victim picked him out in a lineup. He was later released on $10,000 bond.

The next crime entry was July 22nd. A woman told police she was on her way home when she was stopped by a man in Shelby County sheriff's uniform.

The man told her she was under arrest for speeding. He told her to lock her car and go with him. She suspected something wasn't right because the man wasn't in uniform and reeked of alcohol, but she followed him anyway.

The man tried to put handcuffs on her. When she objected, according to the witness, he stuck a gun to the side of her head and said, "Do what I say, or I will blow you away."

The woman did not do what he wanted. Instead, she let out a bloodcurdling scream that made a passing motorist screech to a halt.

Meanwhile, the phony cop, jumped into his car and sped away.

The woman reported the incident to the sheriff's office. Later, she picked Boyd out of a lineup as the man who'd pulled her over and threatened her with a gun.

Police began receiving reports from other counties about a man posing as a police officer and pulling over female residents. In each incident, that man was out of uniform but wore a dark blue "huffy" police-style jacket and carried a badge. The women said that the man drove an unmarked vehicle, but they stopped because he had a blue flickering dash light, "like Kojak used on TV."

Investigators met with Lieutenant White. "That flickering blue light might explain why Mrs. Butler got out of her car," one investigator offered. "She probably thought she was talking to a real cop."

"It could have happened that way," Lieutenant White agreed. "She had no reason to think he was a bogus cop."

The sleuths also noted that the rape and two of the illegal stops had occurred near St. Francis Hospital, where Teresa Butler was last seen alive, and where Boyd's former girlfriend used to live. The crimes were also committed during the evening, about the time Teresa Butler left for home.

Investigators went to Shelby County Jail to question Boyd. Since his return from Hardeman County, however, the bogus reserve officer had hired an attorney and refused to discuss the Butler case or anything he had said regarding her disappearance.

Police still had his confession, though. In it, Boyd said he had kidnapped the young nurse, raped and murdered her, then disposed of her body in the woods. He didn't know exactly where in the woods, but he said that it was under a pile of leaves in a triangular area near a stand of birch trees.

Investigators then got a tip from a self-described psychic who said she had been following the story and had a vision of the body of Teresa Butler. "You will find her body near Houston levee and Monterey roads," she said with conviction.

Searchers went to the area and began looking for the triangular area near a stand of birch trees. The area had been covered in other searches and was as familiar to some of the detectives as their own backyards.

Still, they reasoned, one more search couldn't hurt.

As deputies and volunteers conducted their grid search of the thick and frequently hostile underbrush, detectives searched Boyd's home on Ayrshire Cove and a wooded area that adjoined it. They found nothing to link the suspect to the murder.

The search of Monterey road lasted five days.

Deputies found a rotting white blouse and an umbrella, neither of which belonged to the missing nurse, but no sign of a body or the triangular spot by the stand of trees.

"We found no tangible evidence to link our suspect to the case," Sheriff Owens told reporters. "That doesn't mean it doesn't exist, only that we couldn't find it."

Assistant District Attorney General John Pierotti said that without a body, it would be impossible to press additional criminal charges against Boyd. "It is possible to prosecute when the victim is never found," he admitted. "But not in this instance. We need a body and we don't have one."

On November 10, 1987, relatives acknowledged the anniversary of Teresa Butler's disappearance. "It is as painful now as it was a year ago," said one relative. "What can you do? We try to go on with our jobs and keep busy, but it always stays with us."

Another relative said she still got calls from people with information. "I had a call the other day from someone in Seattle who said, 'I think I've seen your daughter.' Things like that give you hope."

On December 10, 1987, Ben Boyd received a five-year sentence after pleading guilty to four charges arising from the attempted abduction of the St. Francis Hospital employee.

Since recanting his confession, he has said nothing about Teresa Butler, and no charges have been filed against him.

Meanwhile, the search goes on. Calls still trickle to the Shelby County Sheriff's Office. There is even talk about filming the story for the television program, "Unsolved Mysteries."

"It is just amazing how this case lives on," said

one detective. "Do we get discouraged? Sure, but we keep plugging away. You get a feeling for some cases and the feeling around here is that sooner or later, we are going to find that woman and learn what really happened."

EDITOR'S NOTE:
Ben Boyd is not the real name of the person so named in this story. A fictitious name had been used because there is no reasons for public interest in this person's identity.

"OREGON'S NO. 1 MURDER MYSTERY"

by Laura Grayson

The state of Oregon voices a philosophy about
tourists—only half in jest: "Visit us but don't move
here." Residents cling to the fond hope that they can
keep Oregon's natural glories free of the megalopolis
congestion that chokes the East and Midwest, the air
as crystalline pure as it was in the pioneer days when
weary travelers first glimpsed what must indeed be
the promised land. Oregon may very well be the
most ideal spot in America to raise a young family,
and the Medford area in the southern part of the
state is one of the choicest areas. There the orchards
grow fruit of a quality you rarely find anywhere
else—the kind that comes at Christmastime wrapped
in tissue paper and costs the sender a bundle.

The thick stands of towering fir alternate on the
horizon with dry chaparral, and gold and green rolling hills that disappear into infinity. Jobs are plenti-
ful for an able-bodied man willing to work. In the
orchards, the woods, and the many industries necessary to maintain the high standard of living local residents have come to expect and to cater to the
burgeoning tourist trade.

Twenty-eight-year-old Richard Cowden, who lived

in White City, was a logging truck driver, handling those behemoths of the blacktop with their loads of felled giants as easily as another man might pilot a VW. It was hard work, but the pay was excellent and he enjoyed the woods with the pungent smell of evergreens mixed with sawdust.

Cowden had a family to support and protect. There was Belinda June, 22, a beautiful dark-haired woman, five-year-old David James, and the new arrival, five-month-old Melissa Dawn. They lived in a three-bedroom, two-bathroom home, complete with mortgage, of course, but they were chipping away at that. They had two cars, one a 1956 Ford pick-up which they used for camping, and some new household furnishings. They were paying on the 1970 sedan and a vacuum cleaner. They still managed to maintain two savings accounts.

By Labor Day weekend, 1974, the freezer was filled for winter and Belinda's vegetable garden still thrived. Young David's room had just been redecorated and he was looking forward to starting kindergarten.

The Cowdens loved to camp out, but they hadn't planned to go camping on the Labor Day holiday. Cowden had arranged to borrow his boss' truck to haul a load of gravel for his driveway and spend the weekend getting that job finished.

The irony of fate, or chance, or whatever you choose to call it, intervened. The truck broke down. Not really a disappointment because it meant they could take a few days for fun instead of spending them shoveling gravel.

They packed supplies, fishing poles, disposable diapers for Melissa, and headed for Carberry Creek, 20 miles southwest of Medford. The camping area in the rugged Siskiyou Mountains is isolated. The town of Copper is nearby, but "town" means a crossroads and a country store, a few houses. There are a few farms downstream from the campsite they picked on Carberry Creek, but upstream the land becomes deep woods.

The drive to reach Carberry Creek was part of the fun of the outing. They passed through Jacksonville, once a booming goldrush town. Many of the fine old homes built by nouveau riche miners in the last century still stand in Jacksonville, with turrets, gables and intricate fretwork all advertising that they once belonged to men who had struck it rich. The old county courthouse is there, now a museum, filled with the rusting tools of the men who sought gold in the streams and earth of Jackson County. The Cowdens knew that even in the 70s, the challenge of a fortune in the ground drew miners, but they were only looking for a quiet spot to fish and picnic.

They reached their favorite site along Carberry Creek Road, and Cowden parked the pickup on the road above their campsite. There was a picnic table close to the creek, trees for shade. The creek itself was less than a foot deep this late in the summer, and as clear as glass.

They would camp until Sunday and then stop at Mrs. Cowden's mother's home for dinner on Sunday, September 1st, before returning home. The weather was so perfect and the scenery so beautifully peaceful they were glad that the truck had broken down. Melissa played happily on a blanket while young David and the Basset hound, Droopy, scampered around. Then David and his dad fished while Belinda prepared a picnic lunch on the campstove.

Even though the Cowdens knew the area well and

had been there many times before, there was always something new to discover. But the parents kept a close eye on David; there were still mine shafts around from the old days, wild animals, and deceptively deep spots in the tranquil creek.

Mrs. Cowden's mother lived only a mile from where they camped; her home was one of the few in Copper. If it grew cold during the night, or if the youngsters became ill, they could always pack up and be under a roof in no time.

The thought of danger was probably one of the farthest things from the Cowdens' minds as they enjoyed the lazy Labor Day camping trip. Beyond the normal caution that any young family takes while camping outdoors, they had nothing to fear — or thought they had not . . .

On Sunday morning, September 1st, Cowden and David hiked the mile into Copper and visited the general store. They bought a quart of milk and walked off. They appeared perfectly normal — happy, certainly not under any pressure, nor anxious about Belinda and Melissa left alone back at camp.

In Copper, on that day, Belinda Cowden's mother prepared a family dinner and waited for her daughter's family to arrive. The hot dishes grew cold and the cold ones warm as time passed. Too much time. It just wasn't like Belinda to be late for a dinner; she knew how much trouble it was for the cook when guests were late, and she was a most considerate woman. At length, she took off her apron and drove up to the campsite. She had no trouble finding it. The Cowdens' pickup truck was parked up on the Carberry Creek Road. She walked down to the creek, fully expecting to see the family.

They weren't there. Oh, they'd been there. There

was a plastic dishpan on the picnic table and the bottle of milk purchased that morning. The keys to the pickup were on the table. Fishing poles leaned against a nearby tree. Belinda Cowden's purse was there and Melissa's diaper bag. The camp stove was nearby, still assembled.

It looked as if the family had taken a walk into the woods, expecting to come back momentarily. The worried woman called their names, and her own voice seemed to hang in the air, startling in the silence that followed.

When does one begin to worry . . . to be afraid?

She walked closer to the creek itself. She was somewhat reassured to see how low it was, barely wading depth. And then her eye caught sight of something else. Richard Cowden's wallet lay on the ground. She picked it up and saw that there was $23 inside. Close by, she found his expensive wristwatch . . . and an opened package of cigarettes, her daughter's brand.

Even if the family had decided to go into the woods to explore or go berrypicking, she doubted that they would have left such valuable items as purse, wallet, watch and car keys behind.

She moved back to the truck. All the clothing that they had brought with them was there—with the exception of bathing suits. And bathing suits and blackberry thorns don't mix. If they'd meant to go hiking, they would certainly have changed into more suitable clothing.

Puzzled and more than a little frightened now, the Cowdens' relative sat down at the picnic table to wait. She tried to tell herself that they'd all be trooping into camp in a minute and she wouldn't have to admit how worried she'd been. She tried to be angry

71

because her supper was ruined, but her gnawing fear overcame the anger.

What could have happened? Was there a deep hole beneath the deceptively calm surface of the creek — or a whirlpool? Could David have fallen in and Richard and Belinda gone to his aid? Could they all have drowned? But what about Melissa? Left alone on the edge, she couldn't yet crawl, could barely turn over. And she was always kept in her plastic infant seat. Where was that?

Her mind raced, picking up and then dropping all manner of thoughts about tragedy and disaster. All right. Face it. If they all drowned, where was Droopy? A dog could survive where a human couldn't. And Droopy was gone, too.

She strained her ears for the familiar hoarse whooping sound of the basset hound's bark — but all she heard was the gentle sighing of wind in the fir trees and the lapping of water in the creek.

Although summer days are long in Oregon, Belinda's mother could see the sun sinking in the west and she knew she had to get help before it was full dark. With one last look around the deserted campsite, one last hard listen to the woods that might hold a terrible secret, she ran to her car. Moments later she called Jackson County Sheriff Duane Franklin's office.

The dispatcher listened to her story, tried to comfort her, but thought privately that the report didn't sound good. Sheriff's men and troopers from the District Three office of the Oregon State Police arrived at the Carberry Creek scene. It was just as Belinda's mother had described it. Certainly the young family had been there — and recently — but they were not there now. The men's voices echoed in the wind

72

as they called out the Cowdens' names and their shouts drew no more response than had hers.

An accident *could* have happened, of course — but to *an entire family?* They doubted that the creek was either deep or swift or wide enough to cause them all to drown. At any rate they agreed that the dog would have survived, but he was gone, too.

When it became too dark to effect a thorough search, the investigators departed for the night, with officers left behind to guard the spot. A full-scale search would begin again in the morning.

One member of the Cowden family did show up the next morning, but he couldn't talk. Early Monday morning, September 2nd, Droopy, the basset hound, scratched at the door of the general store in Copper. The only witness to the fate of the Cowden family had no way of telling the officers what he had seen. The dog was hungry and tired, but did not appear to have been injured in any way. Where had Droopy been all night?

There has probably never been a more massive search effort in the State of Oregon than the search for the Cowdens. Oregon State Police, Jackson County Sheriff's officers, the National Guard, Explorer Scouts, the U.S. Forest Service, volunteers.

Lieutenant Mark Kezar, assistant commander of the Oregon State Police District Three took over the overall coordination of the search and the subsequent investigation. Almost a year later, he was to remark wryly, "I felt like that campground was my second home."

The Forest Service checked every road and trail within a 25-mile radius of the campground. Planes and helicopters flew as low as they dared taking infra-red photographs. If the Cowdens had been

73

killed and buried, the freshly turned dirty and dying vegetation would appear bright red on the film, although this could not be seen with the naked eye.

Investigator at the camp looked in vain for footprints, tire tracks or for the sign of scuff marks in the dirt that might indicate a struggle had taken place. But there was nothing at all. It was almost as if some craft from outer space had hovered, landed, and carried off a typical American family to exhibit in some far-off planet.

More and more, it looked as if someone had kidnapped the Cowdens. But why? Robbery obviously had not been the motivation. Cowden's wallet, his watch, his truck — complete with keys — were there. A sexual attack was quite possible. Belinda Cowden was a lovely young woman; left alone at the campsite, clad in a bathing suit and with only a friendly basset hound for protection, she could have inspired lust in the minds of passersby.

But wouldn't that mean that only Belinda and Melissa should be missing? And, if Richard Cowden and David had walked back to find intruders in the campsite, and a fight had ensured, wouldn't there be evidence of a struggle? Why would the entire family be missing now?

Lieutenant Kezar and his fellow officers — Lieutenant George Winterfeld, Sergeant Ernie Walden, troopers Lee Erickson and Darin Parker — set up task force headquarters at the camp. They called for aid from State Police technical experts in Salem, the state capital. Sheriff Franklin made every man he could available to the search that was becoming more baffling every day.

Abandoned mine shafts were searched, as well as both sides of every creek, river, and gully for miles.

If, however, improbably, the Cowdens had drowned, their bodies would have surfaced and been caught in the rocks and debris downstream of the Carberry Creek.

But none of them did—nor was even a shred of cloth from a bathing suit found.

Bloodhounds were brought in, allowed to get the scent of the family from clothing left behind. The dogs stopped soon, ran in circles, and looked at their trainers as if to say, "What is it you want us to find?"

There were no footprints, no tire tracks to make moulages from. Some one—or some *thing*— had entered the Cowdens' camp and taken them away without a trace.

State police investigators talked cautiously to the press who soon sensed a story of highly unusual circumstances. Erickson commented, "That camp was spooky . . . even the milk was still on the table."

Sergeant Walden agreed, "It's getting to look really strange. It's not logical that a couple like that would take off with two young kids and leave all their belongings."

As the week-long intensive search continued, there wasn't a person in the whole Northwest who could read or watch television who hadn't heard about the missing Cowdens. But no one had seen them.

The closest thing to a clue was the report that hikers had seen a dog, a basset hound, on September 1st some four to six miles upstream from the campsite. But they hadn't seen anyone with him.

The Carberry Creek area is only a mile or so from the California border, criss-crossed with logging roads, honey-combed with abandoned gold mine shafts—some of them sunk as long as 100 years ago. Lieutenant Kezar and his men realized that the Cow-

75

dens might never be found if they had been killed and hidden in some mine whose existence had only been known to an old-timer long dead, the mine's entrance grown over with underbrush.

He did *not* believe that an *entire* family could have stumbled and fallen into such a mine.

One other possibility had to be considered. Could the Cowdens have chosen to vanish voluntarily? People do run away for private reasons — to avoid financial responsibility or some personal situation.

The Cowdens' background was scrutinized thoroughly. They had no more debts than any couple in their 20s, and they weren't behind on any payments. Moreover, Richard Cowden's paycheck was more than adequate to meet their monthly bills. Belinda was a good manager — as evidenced by the full freezer and the garden she kept up. Cowden was considered a valuable employee on the job, and he hadn't had any beefs with other loggers.

As far as the marriage went, it was described as very happy by friends and relatives. The handsome couple was devoted to each other, probably even more so since the birth of Melissa five months before. If there had been any breath of scandal about their marriage, it would have been well known in a town as small as White City — but there was none.

No, there was no reason in the world for the Cowdens to choose to disappear. Wherever they were, Lieutenant Kezar was convinced, they had been taken there against their will.

The searchers abandoned the organized efforts near the campsite in the Siskiyous a week after Labor Day. They had not found one scrap of physical evidence that might help find the Cowdens, much less the family themselves. They knew that the

76

couple and their two children could be thousands of miles away by this time.

The Oregon State Police and the Jackson County Sheriff's Office were flooded now with clues, suggestions, theories. Some were too ridiculous to consider, but others were checked out thoroughly. In the months to come, Kezar and his men would interview 150 people, compile a case file on the Cowden case that would fill an entire file drawer. They would come to know the Cowdens as well as if they'd known them personally for 50 years.

A $2,000 reward for information was set up. Just before hunting season began, more money was asked for. The grieving friends and relatives of the missing family felt that deer hunters might be in a position to unravel the puzzle that grew more inexplicable with each passing day.

On October 3rd, the missing man's sister wrote to the editor of the Medford Mail Tribune, appealing to hunters to be on the alert for "anything that could be connected to a man, a woman, a five-year-old child or a five-month-old baby. Even though we try not to let our hopes dwindle that they will be found alive, we ask that you will even check freshly turned piles of earth. We will truly appreciate any clue or help that some hunter may find."

It was a tragic request, proving once again that there is nothing worse than *not knowing*. Already, there were eight missing young women in the Northwest in 1974—women who had disappeared completely in Washington and Oregon, but the concept that *a whole family* could vanish was incomprehensible.

* * *

Two hundred concerned citizens wrote to Oregon Senator Mark Hatfield asking him to have the FBI actively enter the probe. But there was no evidence that the Cowdens had been kidnaped, taken across state lines. Hatfield and Kezar said that every law enforcement agency asked for assistance in the case had responded with full strength—but there was so little for any of them to go on.

The hunting season came and went, with no trace of the Cowdens. Christmas came. Snow covered the hills where they had picnicked, and then the torrent of spring rains washed the snow and topsoil away.

On Saturday, April 12, 1975 two men from Forest Grove, Oregon were taking advantage of the spring weather and had made a trip to the Carberry Creek area to do some prospecting for gold. They looked for the precious ore in the Upper Applegate region, which is six and a half miles upstream from the campsite where the Cowdens had disappeared seven and a half months earlier.

Forest Grove is a long way north of Medford, and the men were not nearly as aware of the disappearance of the Cowdens as were local residents. Their thoughts were only of gold as they approached a steep timbered, rocky hillside about 300 feet above the old Sturgis campground.

The found first one bone, and then another, looked with horror on what appeared to be the complete skeleton of a human being. Animals had scattered it over 100 feet in every direction.

The gold prospectors had no idea how long the remains had been there, but they noted bits of clothing, worn by weather, in the area too, and were pretty sure they were not looking at the unearthed skeleton of a long-dead gold miner. They ran back to their vehicle and called the Jackson County Sheriff's Office.

It was 3:30 p.m.

Sheriff Franklin dispatched deputies and notified Lieutenant Kezar and the Oregon State Police team. The officers were fairly certain that they knew what they had—at least one of the Cowden family. From the length of the femur bones and the configuration of the pelvis, the body would appear to be that of Richard Cowden.

Kezar knew that it would take extremely careful criminal investigation to preserve what evidence was left after almost eight months. He requested assistance at once from technical experts in Salem and from Dr. William Brady, Oregon State Medical Examiner.

The troopers and deputies searched the hillside for the rest of the afternoon but had to quit as shadows began to fall. They had waited out the winter and the spring; they didn't want to risk losing some vital clue because of darkness.

At dawn the next morning, they were back. At 9:30, they came upon a cave, a cave whose entrance had obviously been completely sealed up previously by rocks and dirt. But the fierce Oregon rains had pelted at the barricade and a small rockslide had resulted.

The officers looked into the opening. There were bones inside, obliquely reflecting the filtered light of the forest. Carefully, sifting the debris as they worked, they unearthed the body inside. It too was the skeleton of an adult, this skeleton smaller, though, with short, dark-brown hair.

They lifted the decomposed form out and shone their flashlights into the dim interior of the cave.

There were other bones. Small bones, those of a small child, and those of an infant.

The investigators were looking at last at what they were sure was the Cowden family, buried away from all the searchers until Nature herself revealed the secret.

Kezar, Franklin, and their men fanned out over the hillside. They went over every inch of ground, found more clothing, and a plastic baby carrier, its gay pastel coloring grimly incongruous to the grisly scene.

Everything found — no matter how small — was bagged and labeled; the Oregon State Police Crime Laboratory in Salem would analyze all of it.

The searchers looked, perhaps most of all, for a death weapon. If, for whatever unfathomable reason, Richard Cowden had killed his wife and children, and then killed himself, the weapon would be there. The investigators sought a gun — because the bodies of the woman and little boy in the cave had suffered bullet wounds.

There was no gun. There was no death weapon at all. If it was there, anywhere within the radius that a dying man could throw it, Kezar's men would have found it.

No, someone had taken the family far, far, upstream from their camp, probably at gunpoint . . . and, once there, killed them. The woman and children were stuffed into the cave then, and sealed up like victims in an Edgar Allan Poe horror tale. Cowden's body probably, was too large to fit into the cave and it had been hidden somewhere else, maybe even buried in a shallow grave, until the beasts of the forest scattered it.

Positive identification of the remains was made from dental records. Post mortems were begun by Dr. Brady in an attempt to determine specific cause of death.

Belinda and David had succumbed to .22 caliber bullet wounds, Brady found, and tiny Melissa from severe head wounds. But it was impossible to determine the cause of death for Richard Cowden. He *could* have been shot too with a bullet piercing vital soft tissue which had disintegrated with the passage of time, but Dr. Brady could not be sure. Such lethal methods of murder as strangulation and stabbing are often impossible to establish after so much time and when the body parts are scattered so widely.

Metal detectors were brought in and the entire area was scanned in an attempt to find the murder gun and/or bullet fragments—with no success. For days Kezar and his men literally *sifted* the earth of the cave and hillside, but the killer had been meticulous in leaving no sign of himself behind.

Lieutenant Kezar made a somewhat cryptic statement to the press that he felt the killer probably was a person who either lived in the area—or had once lived in the area—because the bodies had been hidden in such an obscure cave, a cave only a local person would be likely to know about.

The $2,000 reward for information leading to the finding of the Cowden family was paid to Proctor and West. Another reward, totaling $1,697, still stands for information leading to the arrest and conviction of the killer.

It seemed that Droopy, the family pet, might be the only living creature—beyond the killer himself—who knew what had happened. Campers had seen the basset six miles upstream of the creek—which was very close to where the bodies were eventually discovered, but, questioned again, they shook their heads helplessly. That's all they had seen . . . a dog.

One Copper resident recalled that he had talked to a young family on September 1st—not the Cowdens, but tourists who said they were from the Los Angeles area. "I remember they said, 'We're camping right across from you . . .' which would have meant the old campgrounds."

The witness said that the couple were in their late 20's or early 30's, and very friendly. The man had said he was in the computer field—possibly a programmer in Los Angeles. He'd had a beard.

The California couple had been traveling with three children—"with Biblical names—I can't tell you just what they were, but they were old-fashioned, from the Bible. One of the kids was just a baby in one of them backpack things."

The investigative team wanted mightily to talk to that family. It was possible they had seen someone in the area on the fatal September 1st, but their requests for contact published in Southern California papers drew no response. Lieutenant Kezar would still like to talk to them, and stresses that they are in no way suspect; he just hopes they may hold the key to the missing pieces in the case.

In the meantime, Lieutenant Kezar and Lieutenant Winterfeld, Sergeant Walden, Trooper Erickson, and Trooper Parker continue to wade through mountains of tips, clues, speculations. The Cowden case will never be closed for them until the killer or killers is caught, tried and sentenced. The crime is one of such consummate cruelty, so senseless, that every law enforcement officer who had anything to do with the investigation feels a personal sense of commitment to see it through to the end.

Lieutenant Kezar asks one specific piece of information from TD readers. He believes that somewhere — probably in Southern Oregon or Northern California — the components of a .22 still exist. Perhaps someone bought the gun, or found it. That .22 can make the case. If any reader has information on the .22 or its components, he is asked to contact Lieutenant V.L. "Mark" Kezar, Oregon State Police, P.O. Box 1488, Medford, Oregon 97501. All information will, of course, be held in strictest confidence.

The killer of Richard, Belinda, David, Melissa Cowden damaged forever a certain carefree style of life for everyone who lives in the peaceful Jackson County area. He should not go unpunished.

"FAMILY MASSACRE . . . BUT WHO DID IT?"

by David Pyle

The bizarre and brutal mystery began on Monday, November 16, 1987.

The previous day had been a normal day for the Dardeen family of the small southern Illinois community of Ina. They had spent most of that Sunday at a family get-together in Mt. Carmel, some 75 miles to the north. After a day of fun, the family of three decided it was time to return home.

The family consisted of 29-year-old Russell Keith Dardeen, his 30-year-old wife Ruby Elaine, who was seven months pregnant with their second child, and their three-year-old son Peter Sean. Mr. Dardeen was known by his middle name, Keith, and his wife by her middle name, Elaine. The Dardeens were at that moment a reasonably happy family.

After the long drive, the Dardeens arrived back at their mobile home in Ina. Their trailer was located just outside the small southern Illinois town, near the Jefferson and Franklin County line, and was visible from two state highways. Their closest neighbor was a quarter of a mile away. Twelve miles down the highway to the south was the community of Benton, Illinois.

After arriving at their home on Sunday, Elaine

called a relative to say they had arrived safely. As far as anyone knows, this was the last time anyone heard from the Dardeens. The events from the time of Elaine's last call to her family on Sunday until Wednesday evening still remain shrouded in mystery.

Keith worked the night shift at a local water plant. He was off Sunday and Monday during the day and due in at work at 11:00 on Monday night.

On Wednesday morning, November 18th, the plant supervisor was checking the schedule and noticed that Keith had failed to show up the previous day. He checked to see if Keith might have called in sick, but no such notice had been given.

Keith Dardeen had always been a good and reliable employee; it wasn't like him not to show up. The supervisor became concerned and phoned the trailer. The Dardeens' telephone rang, but no one answered. Maybe Elaine had gone into labor and Keith had forgotten to call in, the supervisor guessed.

Meanwhile, another friend of the Dardeen family was becoming worried about not hearing from them. She was Peter's babysitter, and Elaine was supposed to have left Peter with her that morning. After receiving no answer at the Dardeen home, the babysitter called the Dardeens' relatives, who had also not heard from Keith or Elaine since Monday.

The babysitter placed a call to the Dardeens' neighbor and asked her to check on the family. The neighbor drove to the Dardeen trailer. Peter's swing set was in the front yard, and everything on the outside looked as it should be. The neighbor observed only one thing missing: the Dardeens' late-model Dodge Colt. The family pickup truck was parked in the driveway. Everything seemed normal. The babysitter called the Dardeen relatives to give them the report.

85

Family members were becoming concerned. They placed a call to the Jefferson County Sheriff's Department in Mount Vernon, Illinois. Lawmen were asked to check on the family. One of those officers sent to the Dardeen trailer was Captain Mike Anthis.

"We were called to check on the well-being of the family," Anthis would recall. "We went to check on them that evening and made the discovery."

A squad car pulled into the Dardeens' driveway. Officers got out and knocked on the front door. It was locked.

"Keith? Elaine?" a deputy called out, receiving no answer.

"Let's go around to the back," another officer suggested.

"No big discoveries were made until we entered the residence," Anthis would later say.

Cautiously, the deputies entered the Dardeen trailer, again calling out for the family. Then one of the officers became pale as he looked in the bedroom. Part of a police officer's training is to try to be prepared for anything, but it was hard for anyone to be prepared for what was found — a sight that would have turned the stomachs of the most case-hardened sleuths in bigger cities. The officers managed to suppress becoming sick at the bloody sight.

Elaine and Peter Dardeen lay side by side in the bedroom, partially clothed. They had been beaten to death with a blunt instrument.

Immediately, the Illinois State Police were called to the scene and the area was sealed off. Detectives and the county coroner arrived and searched the place thoroughly. The murder weapon was not found. To make matters even worse, there were signs that during the attack, Elaine Dardeen had given birth prematurely to a baby girl. The Jefferson County coroner determined that the newborn had been murdered with the same blunt instrument that had been used to kill her mother and brother. The doctor could not determine if the birth had taken place before or during the attack.

After the initial shock of finding the bodies, lawmen realized that Keith Dardeen was still missing. A massive search for him began, since police had many questions to ask him. They soon learned that Dardeen had last reported to work on Saturday and had never picked up his paycheck on Monday. Authorities sent out his description: 5 feet 8 inches tall, 145 pounds, with brown hair and green eyes.

"He was the only suspect we had," commented State Police Lieutenant Richard Evans.

Meanwhile, in Benton, police discovered an abandoned car one block away from police headquarters. Not suspecting it might be connected to the Dardeen murders, lawmen nevertheless ran a check on it. They discovered that the Dodge Colt was registered to Russell Keith Dardeen. Bloodstains found inside the car were sent to the state police laboratory for analysis.

Ina is a small community of about 500 persons. Most of the residents thought nothing of leaving their doors unlocked at night. But the Dardeen murders changed that. Crimes like this were not supposed to happen in small towns like Ina—or so the citizens there had thought.

Though police continued to search for Keith Dardeen, his neighbors still hoped that he was incapable of committing such a crime. Family members told officers that Keith had never displayed any tendency toward violence. "Keith was a nice, polite guy, with many friends," one officer observed.

Lawmen had no idea where to look for the missing suspect. They could only hope he might contact a relative or co-worker, if he was able to. In the meantime, residents in the Benton-Ina area became frightened and started locking their doors. Home security took on a hard-edged reality in the friendly community.

Captain Anthis knew that Thursday, the 19th of November, would be a long day. So far, the only good fortune sleuths had was the discovery of the Dardeen family car in Benton. Captain Anthis then planned to question those family members who were not still in a state of shock.

Keith Dardeen's relatives were from Mt. Carmel, Illinois; Elaine's were from nearby Albion. Keith had been a member of the Pentecostal Assembly of God Church, while Elaine had grown up in the Olive Congregational Church. They were an average, if very religious, family, probers were told.

"The Dardeens were pillars of the community," a friend tearfully told police. "Elaine was like a china doll.

"She was an individual that when she walked into your presence, there was a radiance and happiness of life," said the family friend.

Officers talked to the victims' landlord and learned that in 1986, the Dardeens had leased the property on which their home was located. After leasing the property, Keith had moved the two-bedroom mobile home onto the lot. A relative told the detectives that Keith had mentioned plans to sell the trailer for $16,000, but had never discussed what he planned to do after that.

"With the three-year-old child and baby, it took something to kill them," commented a grim Lieutenant Evans. "I think it took a particularly angry person to kill the family."

Detectives did not know if they were dealing with a psychotic or a cold and cunning criminal.

Elsewhere in Franklin County, where Benton is located, two men were hunting in a wooded area adjacent to Rend Lake College. One of the hunters noticed something lying in tall weeds, just out of sight of a vacant baseball diamond. Out of curiosity, the two hunters approached.

"It's a body," one exclaimed. "Get the sheriff."

"Not another killing," remarked one lawman when the call came in. The Franklin County Sheriff's Department and coroner raced to another homicide scene. The area was cordoned off.

Officers recognized the dead man. Identification found in his wallet confirmed that it was the missing Russell Keith Dardeen.

Once again, surviving relatives were thrown into turmoil. An autopsy revealed that Keith had suffered bullet wounds to the head and had been badly beaten. Somebody had wanted to make sure he died. In addition to the wounds, Keith's pants and underwear had been pulled down to his knees and his body had been badly mutilated.

"While he was missing, some people assumed he did it," Lieutenant Evans told reporters. "We had been looking for him as a suspect."

With the body located in such a visible and busy area so near a junior college, Lieutenant Evans said he was surprised the corpse was not discovered sooner. Police believed the killer may have been trying to mislead them into suspecting Keith was the killer of his family. That way, all the police's efforts would be concentrated on looking for him.

"If the body had never been found, we would still be looking for Keith as a suspect," Evans added.

The coroner told police that Keith Dardeen had died around the same time as his family. Perhaps he had been killed at the trailer and hidden elsewhere, later to be disposed of in an area where he would not be immediately discovered.

"We can't develop a motive for the attack," Captain Mike Anthis observed. "We find what we think may be a good motive, then run out of information to support it, and we're back to square one."

"I think Keith was the object of the attack," Lieutenant Evans speculated.

A possible theory put forward by one investigator was that Keith might have been lured away by the killer. A phone call might have caused him to drive to Benton to meet someone, and he could have been beaten or possibly even shot at that point. The killer would have then taken Keith's body for disposal and continued on to the trailer to silence the remaining witnesses to his call.

Another possibility was that the killer was drunk, on drugs, or just crazed. The killer might have had a partner, not taking the chance that someone might phone or visit the mobile home before he could finish his grisly work.

The coroner placed the time of the wife and children's deaths between 7:00 and 10:00 p.m. Keith Dardeen could have been killed at the trailer, with his family tied up to prevent them from calling for help.

The tests revealed that the blood found in the family car was Keith Dardeen's. The question of exactly who had driven the car to Benton remained a mystery.

It would have been nighttime when the crimes occurred. The killer, lawmen reasoned, would have needed the cover of darkness since the victims' trailer was visible from two state roads.

The investigators remained undecided as to whether there was more than one perpetrator. An accomplice keeping watch on the helpless victims at the trailer might not have been aware of his partner's plans for Keith Dardeen and his family until it was too late to back out.

The coroner determined that Elaine and Peter Dardeen were tied up and terrorized with injuries and beatings for 15 minutes to two hours before they were murdered. There were no signs of sexual abuse to the mother or children, the coroner added.

At some point either during or before the attack, Elaine went into labor and delivered a baby girl. The killer may have panicked, or could have been too far gone to realize what he was doing. The baby was beaten and the family was murdered. Perhaps the killer considered killing the infant an act of mercy, since the child was orphaned and would probably die before being found.

"I have a hunch it was one person," Lieutenant Evans said. "I just don't think you could find two or more people sick enough to do this. Besides, the more persons involved in a crime, the greater the chance of someone making a mistake."

"A team of investigators came back with mixed opinions on how many were involved in the crime," Captain Anthis said. "I've not, and will not, narrow it down."

"I think it was break in, terrorize, terrorize, terrorize, terrorize, then bang-bang-you're dead," commented Jefferson County Coroner Richard Garretson.

Detectives attended the family's funeral in Mt. Carmel a few days later. Relatives had named the murdered newborn Casey Elaine and laid her to rest with her parents and brother. Hundreds of mourners filled the funeral home's chapel, as well as its parlor and hallways. After the services, the caskets were taken to the Albion cemetery for burial.

One young man collapsed at the chapel, presumably under the strain of grief, and had to be carried away. At the gravesite, a woman needed the arms of another mourner for support.

"The Dardeens were snatched from the community prematurely and tragically," one minister said during the services. "Those who knew the Dardeens can never be robbed of the beauty of their life."

Another minister said of the victims, "The family's growth in spiritual things was beyond measure."

The minister of the church the Dardeens had attended said Keith had recently voiced a desire to become more active in his church's Sunday School.

Captain Anthis had been working on the case since the first day. "I think it is solvable, and I think that at some point, it will be solved. The case is not closed yet," he said.

There were no signs indicating robbery or sexual abuse. Nor were there any signs of forced entry.

"I don't think they were picked out at random by passing psychotics," Lieutenant Evans said. "The killer may have planned the crime and been familiar with the area, even knowing beforehand where to dump Keith's body."

Some lawmen theorized the killer was someone whom the Dardeens knew and let into their home. They reasoned that perhaps the motive was some secret personal matter between the family and the killer.

Meanwhile, rumors began to spread throughout the Ina-Benton area that the Dardeens had been killed by devil worshippers. In a neighboring county cultist symbols had been found, as well as evidence of ritual animal sacrifice. An altar was discovered in another county, and animals had been sacrificed on this altar. People started to suggest that maybe the Dardeens were slaughtered in an unholy sacrifice.

But Jefferson County Sheriff Bob Pitchford discounted that theory. He said the slayings had been brutal, but they were not ritualistic. No cult symbols or markings had been found at the Dardeen trailer, and there was no evidence of sacrifice at the scene where Keith Dardeen's body was found.

Other lawmen agreed with Sheriff Pitchford in discounting the theories of cult involvement.

"We never had anything we felt was a cult type of crime," Lieutenant Evans said. "There were no signs or symbols left behind."

"There was nothing to support cult activity," Captain Anthis agreed.

Other rumors attributed the killings to professional hitmen. For that idea, police could find no justification whatsoever.

A task force was formed, made up of investigators from Franklin and Jefferson Counties and the state police. They considered the possibility that the killings might have been drug related, even in error, and they looked into that as a possible motive. The crime, however, just did not fit the pattern; the local lawmen knew that simple shootings characterized the few crimes of that sort in their area.

The drug motive fell close to the bottom of the long list of possibilities. Detectives realized that there need not be a logical motive for the crimes. The killer could be as insane as someone receiving messages from outer space that ordered him to kill—but still clever enough to avoid easy capture.

Rumors continued to spread throughout the little community. One person reported that a neighbor was so consumed with fear that she scared children with rumors and stories. Other tales had a gang of madmen who were loose terrorizing and killing.

Police did their best to reassure residents that there was no proof of a kill-crazy mob slaughtering at random, just a single, if terrible, incident. Eventually, things started to quiet down somewhat when no further killings were reported.

The investigative task force interviewed some 250 people and did clear up some troublesome loose ends. After 30 days, however, the task force was disbanded.

"The task force did what it set out to do in answering a few questions," Lieutenant Evans related. "Then there was nothing further to work with."

Some observers, noting similarities to other crimes, theorize the killer might have been taking a cue from a 1980 homicide case from across the state line in Evansville, Indiana. In that incident, the Patrick Gilligan family had returned home from a New Year's party and surprised a pair of intruders. In the attack, Patrick Gilligan, his wife and two children were murdered. Despite the similarities no connection was made between the two family murders, and being on death row at the time of the Dardeen massacre gave the convicted killer an airtight alibi.

Also compared to the Dardeen murders was the killing of another Indiana family in 1989. The Reverend Robert Pelley, his wife Dawn, and their daugh-

94

ters Janel, 8, and Jolene, 6, were discovered in their home in Lakeville, Indiana, hundreds of miles to the north. Like the Dardeens, the Pelley family was very religious. Unlike the Dardeens, the Pelleys were all killed by gunfire. Three other children not at home when the killings occurred survived the Pelley family slayings. Reverend Pelley had been pastor at the Olive Branch United Brethren Church.

"I'm not too sure there is any connection," Lieutenant Evans said, noting the way the families had been killed. The Pelleys had been shotgunned, while the Dardeen family had been beaten to death and terrorized. Like the killer of the Dardeens, the killer of the Pelley family has not yet been apprehended.

Lieutenant Evans used to drive by the Dardeens' trailer every day on his way to work. It has now been replaced. Occasionally, he pays a visit to their gravesite as he and other lawmen continue to keep trying to unravel the mystery.

"We need some information that will lead to some type of arrest and conviction," Captain Anthis says. "We are constantly in contact with the families involved as we investigate."

For the past three years, state and county police have been troubled by the haunting question: What kind of person could possess enough anger and hate to murder a family of four that included a newborn infant? So far, the only thing police can pray for is that the killer, or someone with knowledge about the crime, will develop a guilty conscience and come forward. Detectives continue to search for the answers and hope that somewhere there is someone who will provide a clue.

"CLEVELAND'S GRUESOME MYSTERY OF THE MAD BUTCHER'S DOZEN!"

by Christos Mirtsopoulos

No one has ever proved whether it should have been considered part of the official case, but the first dismembered corpse turned up about a year before the others, in the fall of 1934, not far from the city limits of Cleveland, Ohio. A man was walking on the beach along Lake Erie near the city's amusement park when he came across the strange object in the sand.

As he pushed away some of the sand to get a better look, what he saw sent a cold chill shooting down his spine. Before him was the lower torso and thighs of a woman.

Responding to the call, Cleveland police rushed to the scene and launched a homicide investigation. They searched up and down the beach until, some days later, they found the upper torso. They never did find the lower legs, the arms, or the head. It was impossible to identify the victim from what they had, so they closed the case, chalking it up as one for the unsolved files.

Although this case was never positively linked to the horrors to come, it was nevertheless a fitting prelude.

Officially, the Mad Butcher case began on the afternoon of September 23, 1935, in Kingsbury Run, a pass through which the Cleveland railroad tracks advanced out of the city's industrial valley on a southeasterly route. A desolate stretch, it was a choice scavenging area for children in quest of adventure and treasure.

That chilly autumn day, two young boys roving through the gorge found more adventure than they'd ever bargained for. Running and playing and scanning the ground for castoff prizes, they reached the far end of the Run. There, they discovered a small, weed-covered side-ravine that beckoned with the promise of secret hoards probably unseen by human eyes for years. One after the other, the lads worked their way through the weeds. Shortly, they came out into a small clearing.

The first youth stopped suddenly, his feet rooted to the spot, his jaw dropping open, his eyes widening in sheer terror. An instant later, he screamed. As his friend came up from behind, he, too, was terror-stricken.

On the ground in the clearing lay a pair of male corpses. They were naked—and headless.

Trembling, the two boys backed away slowly, whirled around and crashed through the weeds to the other side of the ravine. They tore out of there as if all the devils in hell were after them.

When Cleveland police reached the scene, they found the headless bodies arranged tidily side by side. The remains were completely drained of blood, yet no blood was visible anywhere on the ground. An added shock was the discovery that both victims' genitals were missing.

To the police investigators, the condition of the

97

bodies and the unmarred ground suggested that the two men had been murdered and mutilated elsewhere. The victims' blood must have been drained in another location, and the bodies must have been cleaned before being dumped in Kingsbury Run.

As they combed through the surroundings, the probers found three items — a flashlight, a kind of ladle, and a tin pail containing a weird, sticky substance. Later analysis established that the bucket contents was a mixture of oil, partly congealed human blood, and human hair.

Continuing their search, the officers soon made another disconcerting find. Not far from the pail lay the victims' cut-off genitals.

Then, about 50 feet away, the investigators unearthed a couple of human heads. Upon being brought to where the victims lay, they appeared to match with the bodies perfectly.

Later, at the city morgue, the autopsy revealed limited information about the victims. The coroner was able to determine that one man was about 28 years old, the other in his mid-40s. The younger victim had been dead for perhaps two or three days. The older one, in a more advanced state of decomposition, was believed to have been dead for more than a week.

The skill involved in the decapitations awed the medical examiner to some degree. Each head had been severed just above the collar, with the skin sliced in incredibly clean fashion. The retracted neck muscles of each victim led the coroner to conclude that each man's head must have been cut off either while he was still alive, or right after death when his reflexes were still functioning.

Apart from some rope burns on the younger man's

wrists, neither of the bodies bore any significant marks.

Because of its advanced decomposition, the older man's body proved to be impossible to identify. Not so with the younger victim, whose fingerprints were successfully taken. Through his prints, detectives were able to establish that in life he'd been Edward Andrassy, a local tough whose haunts had been in Cleveland's notorious Third Precinct.

In probing Andrassy's checkered past, homicide cops learned that he'd left behind an estranged wife and child. He'd had a job in a mental hospital, but mostly he'd made street crime his chief means of survival, employing toward that end the knife he carried.

Focusing on his sexual activities, investigators learned that although he'd gone the nightclub route with a number of women, he had also been seen picking up young boys.

The detectives checked his dwelling, questioned anyone who knew him even remotely, and sought links to the various items found near the bodies. They were able to learn nothing beyond Andrassy's wretched background.

In those Depression years, Cleveland was jampacked with immigrants from various parts of Europe. In the Third Precinct, which bordered Kingsbury Run, there was poverty, there were clashes between some members of striving ethnic groups, and there was crime. When passions ran high, vendettas flared up, often followed by brutal slayings. Thus, the authorities were inclined to view the murders of Andrassy and the unidentified man as just another local feud. Further investigation was dropped.

Within four months, however, horror once again reared its grisly head. More accurately, it was the lack of a head, and the Third Precinct had the dubious honor of providing the setting. It happened on January 26, 1936, when an area butcher found some burlap-covered bushel baskets containing a right arm, a pair of thighs and a lower torso.

According to the coroner, this victim was a short, heavyset woman of middle years. A very sharp knife had skillfully sliced through the skin and muscle, amputating the limbs at the joints. Of course, the head was nowhere to be found.

A dozen days later, more pieces of the body turned up behind an empty building. The head was never recovered. As was the case with the corpses of Andrassy and the unidentified man found earlier, the woman's neck muscles were retracted, suggesting that she'd been alive during the decapitation.

With the fingerprints from her right hand, investigators soon identified the dismembered victim as Florence Polillo, a 36-year-old streetwalker. Her life, they learned, had been as unsavory and wretched as Andrassy's. She was a boozer who drifted in and out of the local speakeasies and bordellos and had a record of two arrests for prostitution. A number of men had used her as a punching bag. Home for her was a room in a cheap boarding house where, in sharp contrast to her life and surroundings, she maintained a set of harmoniously arranged dolls.

Cleveland detectives wore out a lot of shoe leather in seeking out Polillo's acquaintances and trying to trace the burlap sacks and baskets. They reviewed whatever information they'd compiled in the Andrassy case. They even came up with the description of a mysterious individual who seemed to be linked to Andrassy. But after so many months of tracing objects, questioning associates of the victim, and going bleary-eyed from reading and rereading files, the sleuths realized that they were still up a blind alley.

Less than six months later, on the morning of June 6th, the fifth victim in the ghastly series announced himself in appropriately shocking fashion back on Kingsbury Run. A couple of hookey-playing juveniles were meandering along the railroad tracks toward Lake Erie when they discovered that there were worse things in the world than going to school. Under a tree along their path they saw what looked like a rolled-up pair of trousers. Yielding to their mischievous inclinations, they jabbed at the bundle with a long stick.

Suddenly, as the bundle came undone, out rolled a round object. As it stopped right at their feet and they got a good look at it, the errant schoolboys were overwhelmed by nausea and cold fear. The object was a human head.

Cleveland PD homicide cops observed that the victim was a good-looking young man. He had fine, sensitive features, but where was the rest of him?

The investigators found his shoes and socks carefully arranged not far from the pants. Not until the next day did they find the rest of his body. Dumped between two sets of tracks, the headless corpse was otherwise complete, unmarked, unbruised. As before, the neck had been sliced through with surgeon-like precision.

What offered some hope of coming up with an identification were the six tattoos on his body. Half of them contained names or initials.

After checking the tattoo joints around town and coming up dry, the cops distributed photographs of the victim in the Third Precinct. At the request of the authorities, about 2,000 persons came to the morgue to view the body. Another search was made of Kingsbury Run. Not a single lead turned up.

One other opportunity to try to get the victim identified arose with the Cleveland Exposition of 1936-1937. A plaster cast was made of the dead man's face and displayed at the fair. A grand effort by the investigators, it proved to be in vain.

Not long after the discovery of the fifth victim, another body turned up, this time on the West Side. It was apparent that this victim had been slain right where he lay. The condition of the dead man made fingerprinting impossible, and his clothes, which probers found nearby, held no clues whatsoever.

What the medical examiner did establish was that this victim had been killed before the tattooed man. He was never identified.

The West Side location gave rise to all sorts of speculation. Was the killer changing his hunting ground? Was the victim just a transient who'd had the bad luck to cross the killer's path? Many questions manifested themselves, but no answers were in sight.

On September 10, 1936, the seventh victim made his entrance in the usual, gruesome piecemeal fashion. A drifter waiting along the railroad tracks near the Cuyahoga River to hop the next freight train got the shock of his life when he glanced at a pool formed by the flow from several sewers just short of the stream. In that fetid pool floated two portions of a male torso.

In addition to the torso halves, police were able to recover a pair of thighs and lower legs. Neither the efforts of a diver nor the draining of the stagnant water yielded any more body parts. The investigators never did find the arms, the head, or the genitals.

By now, the authorities had no doubts that these mutilation murders were the abominable handiwork of one individual. They set in motion a citywide probe. Several aspects of the case confounded the probers, however. For one thing, why hadn't all the bodies been dismembered? Why had only three of the victims been castrated? There'd been no evidence of anger or frenzy—what motive could drive someone to commit such atrocities in so cool and deliberate a manner?

Meanwhile, horror gripped the city at all social and economic levels. Women stopped going shopping alone, if they went at all. Men who worked outdoors, such as railroad employees, looked over their shoulders while they performed their duties. The area hobo camps, prevalent during the Depression, shrank almost out of existence.

Now, every oddball character was quickly brought to the sleuths' attention by tips from the frightened citizenry. The detective force was beefed up and sent out to check into every weirdo who reared his freaky head. They rounded up dope addicts, reputed sadists, an occasional escapee from an insane asylum. They came up with nothing.

Within that same decade, 13 decapitated naked corpses had turned up in a swamp near New Castle, Pennsylvania, which was linked by rail to Cleveland. Cleveland sleuths paid a visit to New Castle looking for a connection. Although there seemed to be a similar M.O. involved, they could find nothing to relate the two series.

What did police believe about the Cleveland serial butcher up to this point? First, he had to know

103

something about anatomy or meat-cutting. Second, he had to live somewhere in the vicinity of Kingsbury Run. Third, it was likely that he met his victims before dispatching them. Fourth, he must have carried out his fiendish surgery in a room nearby. Fifth — and this was most crucial — he exhibited no signs of insanity in his everyday life.

On February 23, 1937, a female upper torso turned up on the very beach near the amusement area where the first corpse had been discovered before the official start of the Kingsbury Butcher case. The matching lower torso was found two months later, bobbing in the waters near the mouth of the Cuyahoga River.

Surgical precision was again the gruesome hallmark of the cut flesh. No arms, no legs, no head — these parts were never found. Because of dirt and plant matter in the skin, sleuths believed that the torso had been left lying on some section of earth before being dumped in the river.

About four months later, the Cuyahoga River gave up another cut-up torso. It was spotted at 5:30 a.m. on June 6th by the tender of the Third Street Bridge. The cadaver was the lower trunk of a man. The rest of the corpse floated by in the oily stream over the course of the next eight days. Not the head, however — that never showed up.

The coroner did find something unusual about this ninth victim. This time, the flesh was not so neatly sliced. The cuts were cruder, suggesting anger and violence.

The tenth victim was a woman. Her corpse made its spine-chilling debut in the river, too, nine months later.

On August 16, 1938, a lakeside dump yielded up

the eleventh and twelfth bodies. They'd been butchered like the others, and decomposition was quite advanced.

Public fear gave way to public rage. "The Butcher's Dozen" became the key phrase bandied about. The authorities were deluged by calls, letters, and telegrams demanding that something be done. Newspaper editorials echoed the call for action.

And action they got. The investigation was revived in massive terms. More investigators were assigned to review all the files and to follow the most trifling clue wherever it led.

The resurrected probe led nowhere. The score was Kingsbury Butcher — 12, Police — zero.

Whether the immense publicity and frenzied investigation had an effect is not known, but the killings did stop after the discovery of the last two corpses. Possibly the Mad Butcher had finally glutted his thirst for blood. Perhaps his psychotic urge burned itself out. Or perhaps he'd been hit by a car while crossing a street. Although the reason remained a mystery, the grisly murders stopped.

Cleveland police continued the investigation for a number of years, but eventually, it was deactivated, although the case wasn't officially declared closed for quite a long time to come.

Theories about the Mad Butcher multiplied and conflicted. According to the coroner, he had to be from an upper social level with above-average intellect. The sleuth who'd spearheaded the probe was inclined to believe that the killer was an uneducated sexual degenerate.

In fact, the head investigator kept digging into the case long after his retirement. He felt that the Mad Butcher never really called it quits, but just moved on to other hunting grounds. According to the detective, after the twelfth victim was found in Cleveland, another headless corpse turned up in New Castle, Pennsylvania, followed by three bodies in Pittsburgh in the spring. Another pair of decapitated corpses turned up in that city in 1942. Headless bodies sprang up all the way to the West Coast.

Like Jack the Ripper and a number of others of that ilk, the Mad Butcher of Kingsbury Run dissolved into infamous legend. It can only be hoped that he finally met justice at the hands of a higher power.

"GOLDEN GIRLS' HORRIBLE MUTILATIONS"

by Richard Walton

All eyes were on the beautiful blonde clutching the bouquet as she stood in the swaying London Metro train, and she knew it. Every jolt of the carriage as the engineer began to decelerate for the station just ahead made her arch her back instinctively to reach for the security of a hanging strap or a stanchion near the doors, outlining unconsciously as she did so the superb contours of her body.

All this appraising attention would normally have pleased her. The pert chin would have tilted up with no little pride — for Eve Stratford was "going places." Indeed, she could be said to have the whole world in the palm of one neatly-manicured hand.

Yet there was no trace of pride or satisfaction in her demeanor on that afternoon of March 18, 1975, for the clammy hand of fear had placed an icy grip on the 21-year-old blonde bunny-girl's heart. She had realized, with considerable trepidation, that she was being followed.

Perhaps one pair of eyes in the sea of faces staring at her in the crowded train was mentally stripping her voluptuous body . . .

There had already been sickie phone calls —

obscene, disgusting whisperings, particularly since her nude appearance in a famous "girlie" magazine as center-spread and cover-girl pinup of the month.

The price of such fame was beginning to have sinister connotations in her mind.

Perhaps lost in such troubled thoughts, she staggered and almost fell as the train rattled to a halt at Leytonstone Station. She recovered quickly from her morbid reverie and stepped lithely to the platform. After a quick glance over one shoulder, she joined the throng of travelers shuffling toward the exit.

The sky was leaden gray, cold and forbidding when she reached the street. A light snowfall was already flecking the sidewalk. Shivering with distaste, Eve Stratford looked about her. After a final backward glance at the station, she tucked the bouquet into the crook of one arm and set off hurriedly alone on the mile-long walk to her first-floor little apartment in Lyndhurst drive, Leyton. The time was 3:45 p.m.

She must have reached the apartment little more than 15 minutes later, for few people were lingering outside longer than necessary on that cold afternoon. But what happened after she arrived has been a puzzling mystery ever since.

What is definitely known is that by 5:30 that afternoon, "golden girl" Eve Stratford had become the mutilated victim of a sadistic and lustful killer.

Who was this beautiful girl who died, bound like a sacrificial lamb for the slaughter, with her throat cut?

There were, it seemed, two faces of Eve. One looked out on the harsh world of fact; the other dwelt in fantasy. The former was the home-loving, highly-intelligent girl adored by her parents; the lat-

108

ter, the nightclub bunny-girl and girlie magazine model who called herself Eva Von Bock and was quoted in one issue as saying that she got a kick out of turning men on.

She was born in Dortmund, West Germany, in December of 1953, when her father was serving in the British Army of Occupation on the Rhine.

The child became a brilliant pupil at school with both Advanced and Ordinary levels in German, art and business studies.

So Eve was far from being the classic dumb blonde and her good looks and figure flowered early enough for her to win three beauty contests in Germany before the family went back to England in 1969, eventually taking up residence in Warrington, Lancashire, not far from the former giant USAF base at Burtonwood.

But the North of England was not for Eve. She had already decided that London would be her springboard to stardom.

That leap to success took time, however. She worked first as a secretary, then in public relations. A short spell followed in a trendy boutique, before she joined the German Tourist Office in Mayfair, where her ability as a linguist made her an ideal eye-stopping receptionist. And the area, with her future in mind, was ideal, too.

Contacts were soon made in and around the niteries of that district, and she became a trainee cocktail "bunny" at the Park Lane Playboy Club on November 19, 1973, earning about three dollars an hour for a 35-hour week, plus generous tips from the clientele.

The Playboy organization's "Playmate of the Month" pictorial feature in its popular magazine was

109

sought after by many of these lovely girls; Eve was considered for this plum spot during the summer of 1974.

But the American photographer who flew over to London to take the pictures told her she would be successful only if she lost a little weight. She was ideal in the upper regions, but a little heavy at the hips.

Was he being unkind? Well, Eve, with her height of 5 feet 5 inches and 34-24-35 figure, clearly thought so. In fact, she was bitterly disappointed.

Had she not already been picked because of her sparkling personality and intelligence for several Playboy Club publicity promotions, and been photographed with famous figures from the show-business world?

Her sights now became firmly fixed on a modeling career, with its outlets into TV and the film world. When the chance came in December of that year to pose for a set of pictures for one of Playboy's rival girlie magazines, she eagerly accepted.

In an issue of that rival publication for March, 1975 — it was on the streets a few days before her death — she was featured as a long-haired lorelei, living alone with a cat called Eric, a vast collection of records, a wardrobe of clothes and a jewel box glittering with gold ornaments. (As police observed later, there seemed to be no residential cat, plenty of people — three members of a pop group shared the house with her — and the gold was mostly imitation.)

The 19 color pictures of her in the magazine included a semi-nude front cover and a full-frontal nude centerfold. They were accompanied by a highly-imaginative interview which detailed Eve's preferences in men, sex and jewelry. The latter, she

110

admitted, involved expensive tastes.

The accompanying feature went on to describe how Eve got a kick out of turning men on, totally in contrast to the reserved and a bit shy impression she gave journalists, including the author, who met her from time to time at show-business cocktail parties around Mayfair.

It pulled out all the stops: "I try to wear very sexy clothes, like tight sweaters and see-through shirts. With my height and figure, it seems quite easy to turn men on."

The interview concluded: "If a man is truly a man and not effeminate in any way, he'll know how to handle me. I like to be dominated. Not whipped and tied up, or things like that. But just kept in my place."

To some people, looking for kicks, those imaginative words could be provocative.

A month before her death, Eve had asked the Playboy Club for a few weeks' leave of absence to try to further her ambitions in the modeling world. It was not an unusual request for a bunny to make. Being generous employers, the club management granted it.

On that fateful March 18th, Eve visited London's West End to see her agent about arranging a series of pictures for promotional purposes. It was a modeling date she was never to keep, for she left the West End carrying her bouquet of flowers and dried grasses and took that Metro train to Leytonstone.

Was she followed on that walk home from the station by someone who pushed his way through the door with her at knifepoint? Did she actually walk at least the last few yards with someone she knew and trusted? Or did someone knock on her door soon after her arrival and did she permit her visitor to enter?

Significantly, the bouquet of flowers was found discarded in the hallway of the apartment ground-floor entrance and not up in her first-floor rooms. This suggests that she was confronted by her killer almost immediately.

There was no sign of forced entry. So, unless the killer had found a key somewhere, how else could he have entered?

Neighbors remembered hearing voices in the apartment that afternoon, but no screams or cries of protest to alarm them. They had heard a heavy thud, then silence. Some recalled hearing footsteps descending the stairs toward the street door. And then the telephone rang—and rang on unanswered.

Eve was found at about 5:30 p.m. by her boyfriend, one of the pop group sharing the house with her, when he returned home from work. She lay in the corner of her bedroom, hands tied behind her back, dressed only in filmy pink bra and panties and a flimsy blue nylon negligee open at the front.

Her head was lopsided, almost severed, the throat deeply slashed several times, with extensive mutilation to neck and face.

There was no sign of a violent struggle in the room, or of apparent sexual assault, but medical examination soon revealed from seminal stains and minute traces of a different hair that she'd had sexual intercourse some time shortly before death.

Had it been voluntary, or had she been forced to submit to her killer, his hand clamped over her mouth or with a knife to her throat, before he terminated her?

There was one thing alien to that room, however.

A peculiar cloying scent, not from any of the perfume bottles in Eve's own bathroom, and not emanating from her body.

Police inquiries began swiftly and have continued to this day, for in baffling cases like this, Scotland Yard keeps its murder files open.

Nearby gardens, dust bins from surrounding houses and a local garbage dump were all searched for the murder weapon, which has never been found, either.

Even street drains were siphoned dry in the hope that the telltale glint of metal might reveal the killer's knife or axe, for the weapon could have been either.

A badly-torn copy of the magazine which had featured Eve was found in one of the garbage bins, but so were other such girlie magazines.

News vendors in the locality who sold such magazines were questioned, and so were the regular customers in nearby Mayfair.

A side-street shop specializing in soft-porno magazines and treatises on bondage and flagellatory fetishism was also in the dragnet. That didn't particularly help the inquiry.

"Photofit" pictures (similar to "Identikit" in the U.S.) were released to the press of two men seen in the vicinity of the murder locale that day—men police wished to question. One was a man of medium height, in his late 30s or early 40s, with a peculiar limping gait and a ruddy complexion. The other was about the same age, but taller and with thick, black wavy hair. Yet nothing came of these appeals for assistance.

Names and addresses in a diary found in Eve's flat included those of men she had known in her short

113

life. Many were questioned by the police and were eliminated from the case. A few of these men were never traced, either being no longer in Britain or because the names were false.

The Playboy Club offered a reward for information that would lead to the arrest and conviction of her killer. That move, too, met with no success. Club members and staff were also interviewed, to see whether anyone had shown more than usual interest of late in the beautiful "golden girl."

One of the club officials recalled Eve as a very wonderful girl — a "natural" beauty with tremendous personality. A neighbor in Lyndhurst drive, Leyton, echoed this statement, saying that Eve was "really glamorous — the sort of girl to make any man's head turn."

The inquiry widened to include people she had met in the North of England when she'd first arrived in Britain, and the people she had known at the tourist office in Mayfair. Naturally, the inquiry ran back to Germany, too, and her beauty contest days there.

A squad of nearly 50 detectives were working tirelessly on the case, around the clock, interviewing between 800 and 1,000 people who had known her. They fingerprinted 250 of them.

As with the address book, it was not easy to trace many of the people she had known in the course of modeling and working as a bunny.

She had been particularly friendly with Arab clients of the club, rich men, some of whom delighted in taking three or four girls out at a time to night spots of the city.

Many bunnies dreamed of fame and stardom and ended up as ordinary housewives and mothers in the

114

end, but Eve was determined to climb the ladder to fame.

Every time there was a promotion where bunnies were needed, she volunteered for the job. And when she was rejected for the Playboy modeling assignment, she immediately took on the one for a rival magazine.

Normally she would have been dismissed for that breach of house rules at Playboy, but she was so well-liked that they kept her on, after a stern warning and temporary suspension.

A sickie turned on by the feature could not have traced her address that way. The magazine doesn't give out that sort of information. The killer had to be someone she knew, to either enter the house with her or be let in soon after her arrival. Otherwise, her instant scream of alarm would have alerted the neighbors.

Her boyfriend told the inquest officials on September 28th that a few days before her death, she had been receiving strange phone calls; the caller either hung up before speaking or whispered obscenities over the line.

She had also complained of a man seen lurking near the house, but she never gave her beau a detailed description, beyond saying that the stranger seemed to have a peculiarly strained and stiff walk.

She had also told friends of a sleek Chinese businessman she'd met at the club who had pestered her to take the offer of a hostess job in Hong Kong. She'd fobbed him off, believing it to be a crude vice trap.

At that same inquest, Professor Keith Simpson, the pathologist who examined the body three hours after she was found, described the mutilation marks

115

on the face, in particular the throat. Death had been more from downright shock than multiple hemorrhage, he said. To describe her panties as being on was perhaps incorrect. They had been pulled down, twisted around one naked foot.

Her throat had been slashed from ear to ear, left to right from behind, by a right-handed man, one enormous straight cut with a razor-sharp blade at least eight inches long.

She had certainly had sex shortly before death. Swab stains of semen were taken from her vagina, but although genetic matching would have been possible today, at that time there was not enough technology to establish the blood group of the man.

Consequently, a verdict of murder by person or persons unknown was recorded by the coroner. Later, detectives mingled with mourners at the funeral in Warrington, where the officiating cleric commented that God's love and forgiveness would flow out to the killer — a statement that clearly upset many of the mourners.

The boyfriend felt upset, too. He and the other members of the pop group had all been suspects at one time, as residents of the apartment, but all had cast-iron alibis for the time of the murder. So had the neighbors.

Was Eve, then, perhaps a high-priced hooker? The suggestion was made, but colleagues at the Playboy Club derided it. She might have been ambitious, a little ruthless where using men for her own ends was concerned, and an obvious flirt, but there was nothing to indicate that she was hooking for money or needed vice earnings to buy drugs.

One thing was eminently clear to anyone who had seen Eve's mutilated body and the unspeakable look of disbelief and horror frozen on her face. Whoever killed her in that ritualistic way must have hated her, for it was not the work of an emotionless, fastidious hitman.

This killer was a sicko who got Eve into that ultimate pose by fear or deception for straight sex or sodomy—and then topped his own climax in the act by almost cutting her head off.

And so, as the inquiry rolled on, fear swept through the ranks of London bunnies, wondering who might be next. Some had already received weird phone calls, particularly if they had modeled in girlie magazines.

And it didn't help one bit when, in January 1979, only five miles from where Eve died, another bunny was found slain in a similar throat-slashing ritual. She was 31-year-old Lynda Farrow, found in a pool of blood by her young daughters. Like Eve, she would never willingly let some stranger into the house.

So, with no sign of this similar crime being connected, time passed, until in 1981, back came that call-girl theory with an assertion that Eve might have been a hooker, after all.

Allegations of a vice racket at the Playboy Club came up during an official inquiry in London, during which the club lost its valuable casino gaming license.

Police were anxious to trace and interview a wealthy Arab known as "Doctor Sex" who was allegedly running the racket using bunnies with the help of club staff.

Clients were mainly fellow Arabs, including the sons of well-known princes lusting for the soft white flesh of European bunnies.

Eve had her throat slashed from ear to ear, a way Arabs kill prostitutes in Damascus and Cairo if they give a client VD, and a way desert Arabs kill women who defy their wishes. And Eve had certainly defied "Doctor Sex."

Just before her death, she'd had a violent quarrel with the suave Islamic flesh-peddler who had taken offense at her intimate quotes in the girlie magazine, and the photographs therein. One showed her kneeling submissively, a favored posture for the doctor's clientele, and another in similar pose, with a hand between her thighs as if fondling herself intimately.

He was violently angry when he saw this and, according to another bunny, told Eve: "You're crazy advertising yourself like that. The next thing you know, the vice squad will be around at the club asking questions. You're ruining my business, you stupid white cow!"

And it was apparently very good business indeed for the white slaver, who happened to constantly chew those little violet-scented cachous, so popular among Levantines to sweeten the breath after eating spiced food.

Remember Peter Lorre's superb portrayal of the homosexual pervert Joel Cairo in *The Maltese Falcon?* And remember that strange unidentifiable scent in Eve's room?

"Doctor Sex" was clipping his Arab friends $500 a throw to spend the night with one of his bunnies. The girls got a kickback from that fee and rich presents like Cartier watches and diamond bracelets from the bug-eyed clients.

After all, there was nothing quite like the bunnies — with or without the bobbing whitetails — in back of the goatskin tents of the desert.

118

The girls, of course, were breaking every rule in their club contract. They were not even supposed to have dinner or a date on their own time with clients of the club and casino.

Soon after the quarrel, a dark stranger had tried to run Eve down with his car as she'd left the club one night in Park Lane to walk past the Hilton Hotel. Someone had obviously marked the 21-year-old blonde for death.

When it came, one significant thing seems to have been overlooked at the time. That gimpy stranger had been near the house, described as walking a little like a penguin, as if he had pain in the groin—the sort of pain you get with a sudden dose of VD—and witnesses said he could conceivably have been an Arab.

There is, of course, quite clearly no evidence that Eve had any disease, but another bunny could have given it to him. To a sicko, the carrier would be immaterial. The burning pain would be associated with the desire to simply kill a bunny.

One of the men in Eve Stratford's diary was a well-known 35-year-old Lebanese gambler at the Playboy Club, although often banned there.

His name came up at the inquiry, too, as did the allegations of his cheating. He says he was introduced to the club by a gambling film superstar, has increasingly denied press reports that he, too, was procuring bunnies for wealthy friends.

A millionaire, he is said to have started on his road to success as a barefoot doorman in a shady Beirut clip-joint, where a donkey was included in the cabaret.

He has admitted dating bunnies in the past and going to orgies. There was no need to run a vice racket, he says. The bunnies willingly threw themselves at men.

He knows, too, the notorious Indian woman running a house of vice in London, who also provided bunnies for rich Arabs, but denied having had a business connection with her. As for being in Eve's diary, the diminutive dark-skinned Levantine had the right answer: so were a lot of other men.

Now, he says, he is happily married and a deeply religious man in the Moslem faith.

So there it all rests, unsolved and uncomfortably so.

"It's unsolved," Detective Chief Superintendent Don Gibson, head of the precinct police, recently stated in an interview. "An inquiry is on hand—quite an important one—but I can't tell you anything that's being done, and I can't even tell you if later we may have some answers to all of the questions."

Not the most cooperative of responses. Perhaps, like all intriguing murder mysteries, one cannot see the forest for the trees. Think, for example, about the case of Jack the Ripper. One or two researchers suggested that he might have been a policeman, the one person whose presence late at night on the streets of London would have never been questioned.

In the case of Eve Stratford, everything points to someone at the Playboy Club, possibly an Arab, but certainly the same person she never would have suspected until too late.

And if that's so, then why are not other bunnies talking, because they must know him—or are they too scared of the sicko to come forward?

"STRANGLED BIBLE LADY CLUTCHED A BIZARRE CLUE!"

by Gary C. King

The case which follows is a classic whodunit from anyone's point of view, from the avid mystery reader to the frustrated investigators who have spent more than a year working, day and night, trying to unravel the mysterious clues that might point them towards a potential suspect in a most unusual, seemingly senseless, killing. This case is by far the most baffling one this writer has encountered in the many years spent investigating such matters.

Eunice Karr, 74, was a religious, God-fearing woman who went to church every Sunday and read from the Bible daily. Some would say she was fanatical; others, those who knew her well, simply said that she had strong, deep-seated religious convictions. At least one person, her killer, felt she made intrusions into and moral judgments about areas she knew nothing of, namely sexual preference, all in the name of God and religion. It should be noted that only her killer knows the precise reason Eunice Karr was killed, and that the theory outlined in this article was arrived at from the careful study of evidence left at the crime scene, some of which the killer or killers went to great lengths to provide for the investigators. Here's what happened.

On Saturday, July 28, 1984, Eunice Karr arose at her usual time, after which she took care of the routine chores in and around her single-level home, located in the 4700 block of Northeast 100th Avenue in Portland, Oregon, a quiet, well-kept neighborhood. The house Karr occupied was a rental, dark gray with white trim, but she nonetheless took pride in it and kept it up as if she had owned it. To help her with the household chores, Eunice Karr occasionally paid two neighborhood boys to do yard work and minor repairs.

That night, at approximately 7:00 p.m., the two boys who occasionally did chores stopped by Eunice Karr's house to say hello and to ask if there was anything they could do. When they walked up the front walk to the door, they hesitated when they noticed through the outer screen that the front door was ajar. Since it was still daylight and the middle of summer, the boys reasoned that it really wasn't all that unusual for someone to leave their door ajar, particularly since the evening sun tended to make staying indoors nearly unbearable.

They knocked, but received no answer. They knocked again, louder, and called out the woman's name. Still receiving no reply, the two youths entered Eunice's home, and slowly made their way from room to room. When they reached the bedroom they found Eunice Karr, but not in the condition they'd expected or hoped to find her in. She was grotesquely sprawled on her bed, quite dead. One look was all it took for the youths to realize that she had been murdered, a fact which prompted them to turn on their heels and run quickly out of the house.

When they reached their home, the boys told their parents of their macabre find; and the parents, in turn, notified the Multnomah County Sheriff's Department.

When a team of sheriff's department homicide detectives arrived at Karr's home a short time later, they were met by the two shaken teenager boys who found the woman's body. The youths, accompanied by their parents, told the investigators how they'd come across the body, and assured the detectives that they had left everything, including the corpse, undisturbed.

The detectives discovered Eunice Karr's body, just as they had been told they would, sprawled on the bed in her bedroom. The body was bloody, as if it had sustained a violent beating, and bore many of the tell-tale signs of death by strangulation, such as a grotesquely protruding and discolored tongue, froth mixed with blood around the mouth and markings about the neck area. The woman's body had been bound, but detectives would not reveal what parts of the body (hands, feet or both) had been bound, nor would they reveal what type of material was used to tie her up. It was important, they explained, that certain details remain known only to the police and the killer(s), as that information could prove valuable during the interrogation of a potential suspect — provided, of course, that a suspect was apprehended. Several other details, however, some of which proved quite bizarre, were released.

Among those bizarre details was the fact that detectives, when they closely examined the crime scene, discovered a small scrap of paper next to Karr's body. It read Romans I and II, the significance of which was not immediately known to the investiga-

123

tors. However, also lying on the bed near the woman's body, was a stack of books, one of which was a Bible. Instead of looking up the passages right away with the Bible at hand, the detectives instead made a note to do it later. It was possible, they reasoned, that the Bible on the bed, as well as the other books, bore the perpetrator's fingerprints, evidence which they certainly didn't want to jeopardize through hasty reactions and curiosity.

When the deputy medical examiner arrived at the scene, he briefly examined Karr's body and determined that she had been killed earlier that day, at least several hours prior to the body's discovery. He also concurred with the detectives' observation that she had been strangled. He said that additional details may be learned from the autopsy.

As the victim's body was being placed on a gurney, preparatory to being transported to the county morgue, the investigators discovered a small white paper cross that had been placed upside down in the palm of Eunice Karr's left hand, a startling discovery that raised several questions. Was the cross placed in the victim's hand by the victim herself? Or had it been placed there by her killer? What significance did it have, if any? And why was it upside down? Did the latter fact indicate something satanic, perhaps a ritual? The detectives pondered over their many questions, but did not quickly arrive at any sound and satisfying answers.

An inventory of the victim's property and possessions indicated that several credit cards may have been missing, but detectives could not quickly substantiate that suspicion. Other than that possibility, everything else seemed in order, making robbery seem a slim possibility for motive.

As the investigation continued, detectives interviewed numerous people, including Eunice Karr's relatives, friends, acquaintances and neighbors, all of whom provided them with many interesting details and aspects of the woman's life and habits. Among the things they learned and were able to release to the public was the fact that Karr liked to make daily trips to downtown Portland via the bus, where she often ate lunch at a moderately priced restaurant. She was known to stay out for hours at a time, walking the streets of downtown Portland, often stopping at a park on West Burnside Street where she engaged in people-watching. The area she was known to frequent is largely inhabited by transient types, many of whom are homeless, and detectives eventually ascertained that Karr often talked with many of the people she encountered. But she always made it home safely, usually at or near the same time, without encountering any trouble from the strangers she met.

Did Eunice Karr know the person who killed her? The detectives pondered the question. Was it possible that she met her killer during one of these downtown excursions? It seemed possible, and was at least worth checking out. But what would have been the killer's motive? Anger? Revenge? Or had Eunice simply met up with a psychopath bent on murder? Of course, the detectives had to address the possibility that perhaps Eunice Karr's killer was a complete stranger who had targeted the elderly woman for death for whatever reasons. Possibly, it was someone who had perhaps burglarized her home and had not expected her to be there at the time, in which case she would have had to have left her house unlocked, as there were no signs of forced entry. Suffice it to say, there were many viable possibilities that had to be considered, enough to keep the detectives busy for months.

The results of the autopsy, performed by the Oregon State Medical Examiner's Office in Portland the next day, revealed that Karr had sustained injuries to the head and had sustained three broken ribs, both indicative that she had been severely beaten. It was also revealed that postmortem lividity, which are dull, blue discolorations that appear on the undermost parts of the body shortly after death due to the gravitation of blood, was present in more than one anatomical location of her body, a strong indication that the victim's body had been moved long after death. Additional pathological tests confirmed that Eunice Karr's body had been moved at least eight hours after she had been killed. It was a fact that was not only shocking, but one that raised many new questions as well.

Had the body been moved by her killer? If so, why would anyone, the detectives wondered, return to the scene of a crime and risk being discovered? Furthermore, the detectives wondered, had the white paper cross been placed upside down in the victim's hand at the time the body was moved? Or had it been placed in her hand right after she had been killed? These were, of course, questions which have answers. Unfortunately, however, the investigators were unable to uncover the truth while the trail was still hot and could only theorize as to the answers.

Among those theories during the initial stages of the investigation was the possibility that the killer had left some article or item inside Karr's home, perhaps something that could lead investigators to his or her identity, and the killer had returned to retrieve

126

the item and to leave behind additional evidence to serve to confuse the investigators, such as the white paper cross. But why, they wondered, had the killer found it necessary to move the body, if it was in fact the killer who did so? Needless to say, it was not an often-encountered occurrence in police work, and at this point the stymied investigators were understandably reluctant to speculate as to why the corpse had been moved, much less by whom, until additional facts were known.

In the meantime, sleuths learned that the message found next to Karr's body on the bed, which came from Romans I and II, had been written by the victim's own hand! When the investigators looked up the passage in a Bible, they learned that portions of it condemned lesbianism and homosexuality and made references regarding those who pass judgment on others. Portions of the passages which proved important to the investigation are as follows, taken from the *GOOD NEWS BIBLE:*

. . . And so God has given those people over to do the filthy things their hearts desire, and they do shameful things with each other.

Romans I-24

Because they do this, God has given them over to shameful passions. Even the women pervert the natural use of their sex by unnatural acts. In the same way the men give up natural sexual relations with women and burn with passion for each other. Men do shameful things with each other, and as a result they bring upon themselves the punishment they deserve for their wrongdoing . . . They know that God's law says that people who live in this way deserve death . . .

Romans I; 24-32

127

Do you, my friend, pass judgment on others? You have no excuse at all, whoever you are. For when you judge others and then do the same things which they do, you condemn yourself.

Romans III-1

Needless to say, the biblical passages raised some new questions about the case, which had been confusing enough without them. However, the detectives quickly learned that Eunice Karr had not been a lesbian. Her friends and relatives attested to that fact, as did her strong religious convictions. But was it possible, the detectives wondered, that she had known a lesbian or perhaps a male homosexual? Someone she had perhaps met during one of her trips downtown and had befriended, possibly had even preached to against homosexual activities? Sleuths agreed that anything was possible, but what they really needed were answers instead of more questions. With that in mind, they hit the streets, not only in Karr's own neighborhood but downtown as well.

At this point in the investigation, residents in Karr's neighborhood were becoming accustomed to detectives and sheriff's deputies knocking on their doors in search of additional information. That's not to say, of course, that people had gotten over the murder; quite the contrary. Most residents were upset, visibly shaken that such a brutal murder, or any murder for that matter, could have occurred in their quiet neighborhood. Nonetheless, the residents were more than cooperative with the sheriff's department officials, as they were just as anxious as the detectives to have the killer or killers apprehended and brought to justice.

During the early phase of the investigation, detectives learned from subsequent interviews with Karr's neighbors that Karr had been seen in the company of a young female several days prior to her death. It was not known if Karr had taken the young woman in to live with her or whether the young woman was merely a frequent visitor during Karr's final days. It was said, however, that Karr had not previously had overnight visitors or boarders. No one could say for certain whether the young woman had actually stayed overnight with Karr but, following the interviews, sheriff's detectives had a good description of the young female.

The woman was described as 18 or 19 years old, 5 feet 4 to 5 feet 5 inches tall with a medium build, approximately 120 to 130 pounds, on the "husky" side, a full face with smooth clear complexion, straight sandy-brown shoulder-length hair, small eyes with no make-up, a "button" nose, and small, thin lips. She was last seen carrying a small gray backpack.

"The woman we are looking for was seen at Karr's home several days (prior to Karr's death)," said Deputy John T. Drum, spokesman for the sheriff's department. "She was known to have gone to the bank with (the victim). We don't know who the woman is. She is not necessarily a suspect, but we would like to talk with her." Drum added that detectives learned Karr had been trying to sell her automobile prior to her death, and detectives hoped that maybe the young woman they were seeking had seen or heard something important that might aid them. Drum did not say whether or not Karr had been successful in her attempts to sell her automobile.

In the days that followed, sheriff's department detectives ran down one fruitless lead after another, each time with their backs against a brick wall. As they pored over the police reports and took new ones over the phone regarding the case, they reflected that there had been 130 homicides in Oregon in 1984 including Karr's death, most of which had been solved. But as one day turned into another with no suspect identified nor in custody, the investigators began to feel as if this case might go unsolved if they didn't receive a lucky break soon. However, much to their dismay, leads slowed to a trickle and finally stopped.

Then, nearly a month after Karr's death, detectives received an anonymous letter from two Portland women who claimed to be lesbians, and the Karr case was off and running again. In the letter, the women stated that they had rented a room to another lesbian named Abby Anderson, after which they had discovered some interesting things about the Eunice Karr homicide. One evening, after Anderson had gone out, the women said they made a decision to search her room, during which they uncovered some evidence, or so they thought.

During the search, they found a shoe box among Anderson's belongings. When they opened the box, the women said they found several newspaper clippings of articles regarding Karr's murder on which "Ha Ha" was written across the top of one of the articles. The women, in subsequent anonymous telephone calls to the sheriff's detectives, also said they found a cheap bracelet inside the box which they said they thought had been taken from Eunice Karr. At the urging of the detectives, the women mailed the items to the sheriff's department. The items were subsequently analyzed for clues, but no findings, if

130

any, were made public.

A few days later, an ad appeared in the classified section of *The Oregonian* which caught the attention of the investigators. The ad read: "Silver bracelet, coins, news clippings taken from my shoebox, return for Muff. Abby." Needless to say, sheriff's detectives considered the ad an interesting new twist to the unusually bizarre case, and they wasted no time in checking out the new lead. At this point, it was vitally important that they learn the identity of the two anonymous lesbians who had been tipping them off and as much about Abby Anderson as possible — provided, of course, that she indeed existed.

After checking with *The Oregonian,* the detectives learned that someone named Mike Moore, or at least someone using that name, had placed the ad in the newspaper. The billing files at the newspaper office listed his address as 4709 N.E. 100th Avenue, directly across the street from Eunice Karr's home! Checking further, the detectives learned that the address did not actually exist. The only building across from Eunice Karr's house was a garage and a corner house whose address faced the cross street.

So who was Mike Moore? the detectives wondered. And who were the so-called lesbians who had placed the anonymous telephone calls, wrote the letter and sent the items taken from Abby Anderson's shoebox? Detectives relentlessly tried to uncover the identities of the two women, all to no avail. And who was Abby Anderson? Did she really exist?

It occurred to the detectives that Mike Moore and Abby Anderson were possibly fictitious names, and that the sleuths had been made the butt-end of a sick joke perpetrated by the two lesbians for reasons known only to them. But they had to take it all seriously, at least until they could prove otherwise, as they were dealing with a brutal, unnerving murder of an innocent old lady and they desperately wanted to bring her killer or killers to justice.

At another point in the investigation, the detectives received another telephone call from the two lesbians. The probers made additional inquiries into the ad placed in *The Oregonian*, and they asked the two women what Muff referred to. Muff, they explained, was the name of their dog, who had mysteriously disappeared shortly after the women sent sheriff's detectives the contents of Abby Anderson's shoebox. Although an attempt was made to trace the telephone call, the callers hung up before the trace could be completed, ultimately leaving the identity of the two women a mystery. It was the last telephone call the detectives ever received from the two women, and clues stopped coming in altogether.

Days quickly turned into weeks and weeks into months as the homicide probers worked on this difficult case, achieving, much to their dismay, no significant results. They had been unable to determine whether or not Abby Anderson and Mike Moore were fictitious or real persons, or, if real, whether they were two individuals or one and the same persons. They had also failed in their attempts to learn the identities of the two lesbians who had been so busy making telephone calls and writing letters. In short, all indications were that the case would go unsolved. And because of a burgeoning work load and manpower shortages, the case, although it remained officially open, had to be temporarily shelved until additional clues and evidence was uncovered or surfaced.

The case remained more or less dormant until the

spring of 1985 when Detective Sgt. Rod Englert asked to take a crack at it. Englert, an authority on unsolved murders, is in charge of the sheriff's department's Scientific Investigations Unit and had, over the past 10 years, solved six "unsolvable" murders with the help of his partners.

Englert considers the Karr homicide a "classic" case which depicts the many-faceted problems such a case produces. The trim, salt-and-pepper-bearded detective who, at age 43, has had 22 years experience in law enforcement, settled into the chair behind his desk in Room 207 at the sheriff's department headquarters and began a methodical study of the Karr case. He requested as his partner, this time out, Deputy Chris Peterson, 41. Although an experienced undercover cop who has posed as a heroin dealer and played a major role in breaking up a crime ring operating in the Northeast, Englert chose Peterson as his partner not because of his experience in dealing with homicides — which had been very little — but because he is "extremely street-wise," an attribute Englert felt would be of particular help because of its connections to the homosexual community.

Together, the two men spent days going over the Karr file, formulating theories and trying to make some sense out of a seemingly senseless killing. They made lists of people they would interview, which grew to an enormous 400 or more names, and studied the evidence uncovered at the crime scene as well as that which was sent to the sheriff's department via the mail. They paid particular attention to the fact that Karr was extremely religious while at the same time, as described by the woman's relatives, somewhat senile, and they concentrated on Karr's frequent trips to the downtown area.

133

During the course of their investigation, Englert and Peterson hit the streets of Portland and became familiar with the homosexual community, particularly the lesbian community. The tips they received also brought them into close contact with burglars, drug dealers and male and female prostitutes, some of whom Karr may or may not have inadvertently came into contact with while in the downtown area. The two detectives finally concluded that Eunice Karr met her killer either in the restaurant she frequented or in the park where she regularly talked with strangers.

"No one goes in and kills an old lady for no reason," said Englert. "There was no dope involved, no money and nothing was taken . . . (on the other hand it's) a phenomenon we are seeing more of. People can drive from one state to another in a matter of hours, and it's easy to carry out fantasies. Some people's fantasy is to kill someone, just killing for killing's sake . . .

"I think she met some street girl who talked her way into Karr's home," Englert continued. "(The girl's) a lesbian, so Karr starts preaching about how evil it is. The kid figures she's had enough and wants to shut her up. It gets out of hand and Karr's killed. I think there was more than one person involved because Karr was a strong woman and it would have taken two people to kill her," he theorized. "The autopsy showed she had three broken ribs and had been hit around the head pretty good." On the other hand, if Karr's murder was merely a random killing, Englert said that it would be among the most difficult type of cases to solve, if it could be solved at all.

"I think my most important asset is my intuitiveness with people," said Englert, when commenting about the more than 400 people he and Peterson interviewed. "Our break on this case, or on any similar case, will come from people. The break can drop out of the sky, and the skill is in recognizing it."

As the investigation continued, Detectives Englert and Peterson went over the files again and again and reviewed the numerous photographs of the death scene. They tried relentlessly to determine whether or not they missed a clue, a vital piece of evidence or a potential suspect, but they continued to come up with zero.

One thing that particularly bothered them was the bizarre fact that Eunice Karr's body had been moved long after she had been killed. Another thing was the small white paper cross found in her hand, and the mysterious telephone calls and letters, all of which they just couldn't understand.

"I don't think there's enough there to make it a satanic ritual," said Englert, "although it's damn strange. If it was just an everyday burglary that went bad, why the anonymous calls and letters? It doesn't make sense, but you can't think logically when it comes to crooks."

Reacting to a tip, Englert and Peterson hit the streets again, this time in Southeast Portland, looking for a business owned by two lesbians. The detectives declined to name the business or the two lesbians, but confirmed that the trip had been worthwhile. As it turned out, the detectives showed the two women the composite drawing of the young woman who had been seen in the company of Eunice Karr shortly before her death, and hoped the lesbians could help identify her.

The two women looked carefully at the drawing and, after several minutes, one of them told the sleuths that the girl looked like someone she had gone to high school with in the 1970s. "But she was thinner then," said the woman.

Admittedly, it wasn't much of a clue, the detectives agreed, because the woman in question would be by now in her late 20s or early 30s. The woman seen with Karr had been described by earlier witnesses as approximately 18 to 19 years old but, they reasoned, it was possible that the witnesses had been mistaken about her age or perhaps the mystery woman looked much younger than she actually was. At any rate, they had to check out the lead, and the two probers went to the Portland School District headquarters to review old files.

As they went through the countless files, more than 10 years' worth, Englert and Peterson paid particular attention to females with the last name of Anderson and/or the first name of Abby. However, after a considerable time spent searching, each sleuth realized their efforts had again proved fruitless and they gave up that avenue of pursuit.

"Well, another crash and burn," said Peterson after their efforts failed to yield results. "But you never know what a shred of evidence will lead to. We'll exhaust every lead and start over again. We do it day in and day out. One day we'll hit the right button." Englert agreed with his partner.

"You only get one chance on a case like this . . . ," Peterson added. ". . . There's disappointment each time you turn the corner. The rewards are few and far between . . . On a burglary, you know you're going to get a chance at (the perpetrator) again in six months. On this kind of case, you mess up and they're gone . . .

"We found one lady we were sure was Abby Anderson, and we circled her like a shark," continued Peterson. "But after a 45-minute interview we knew she wasn't the person we were looking for. For all we know Abby Anderson could be dead, out of state or not even exist." The same holds true for Mike Moore.

Did the gay or lesbian connection cause any undue difficulties with the case? Englert and Peterson don't think so now, although at the outset, they admitted they feared it might. However, they found the gay community very cooperative and willing to help.

"Working on this case blew away a lot of my stereotypes about the gay community," said Peterson. "They're not anti-social, and they went out of their way to help us on this case. I guess a homicide cuts across all walks of life."

Another lead took Englert and Peterson to a Northeast Portland home of a woman and her mother. The detectives had been told by a source that the woman might know something about Karr's murder. However, when they arrived they were met at the door by the woman's mother and were informed that the person they sought to interview was not at home.

At Englert's urging, the woman retreated into the house to obtain the phone number where her daughter could be reached. While waiting for the mother to return, Englert eyed a small dog inside the house. Getting an idea, he called the dog through the screen door.

"Here, Muff," called Englert. "Come on, Muff." However, the dog didn't move, and that proved to be yet another disappointment for the detectives. "It was worth a try," Englert said, shrugging his shoulders. "You just never know." The woman returned and handed the telephone number to the two detectives on the porch. They thanked her and left, and never revealed whether their conversation with the woman yielded any significant clues.

Following up on still yet another lead, Englert and Peterson went to the home of a 17-year-old girl and, with her mother's permission, picked the girl up and took her out to lunch at a nearby restaurant. The girl, whom they initially believed may have been involved in Karr's death, was understandably nervous, even after they were seated at a table inside the restaurant.

"So why did you kill Eunice Karr?" Englert asked the girl, never taking his eyes off hers. There was no reply. "That's what we're going to talk about today."

The girl denied any involvement in Karr's death, and even volunteered to take a polygraph test. The detectives soon realized she had nothing to do with the murder after all, but they learned the girl was a lesbian and a former drug addict who was trying to straighten out her life.

"So what's the talk on the street about some old lady being snuffed last summer?" Peterson asked the girl. She responded by saying that she'd heard other street kids talking about an old lady being robbed, but had not heard anything on the streets about a murder. She provided the detectives with the names of the kids she heard talking about the robbery.

"I think you can help us," said Englert. "Did anyone ever spank your butt and tell you to knock off the drugs?"

"Yeah, my lover did," the girl replied. "She said it broke her heart."

"Eat and get your health back," Englert told the girl. "Change your life and stay off the street . . .

138

Start getting good food in your body. And if you think of anything, call us. What you think may be unimportant may break the case. Take the time. Call." When they finished their meal, Englert and Peterson drove the girl home, again empty-handed and no closer to discovering or apprehending Eunice Karr's killer or killers.

"I'll personally never quit," said Englert. "I may not be out there knocking on doors as hard as I did, but I'll keep working it. But realistically and economically, it just isn't possible to work it full-time forever."

As of this writing, case number 84-14836, the homicide of Eunice Karr, has not been solved. Detectives still have not located Abby Anderson or Mike Moore, nor have they ascertained whether they even exist.

"WHO BLASTED THE BELOVED TEACHER IN THE GOLD CAR?"

by Bud Ampolsk

"We have a problem in our society," says the director of the New York City Board of Education's office of school safety. "And when you have a problem in society, it will make its way to the schoolhouse."

The problem the Board of Education official refers to is violence. And violence in all its terrifying forms appears to be escalating in New York's places of learning.

Bitter memories of recent violent outbursts in schoolhouses and on the streets immediately surrounding them have alarmed educators fearing for their very lives. The panic stems from no melodramatic overappraisal of the situation. It comes instead from the actual day-to-day experience of many members of school staffs.

Says a young English teacher assigned to an intermediate school in Brooklyn's Bushwick section, "In the two years I have been teaching in Bushwick, I have been threatened, shoved around, and cursed at. I have had eggs, rocks and bottles thrown through my classroom windows. I have been karate-kicked, half-strangled with my own tie, and hit in the side of the face.

140

"And never once did any of the perpetrators of these acts fear the consequences of inflicting corporal punishment on me."

The teacher tells of a particularly harrowing incident. While sitting in his parked car immediately outside the school, he was surrounded by a group of neighborhood toughs. One of the educator's tormentors hurled a brick through the rear window of his Chevy hatchback. The missile completely shattered the glass and narrowly missed the victim's head.

Luckily for the trapped teacher, at that moment, a police car on routine patrol pulled into the street. The teacher was able to attract the attention of the officers. Apprised of what had been going on, the cops took off in close pursuit of the perps and managed to round them up. Arrests were made. The police officers did everything they could under the circumstances. However, because the brick hurler was 14 years old, he had to be treated as a juvenile. Within days, the assailant was attending classes at the school once more, all too ready to strike again whenever the savage mood struck him.

Recalling what happened to him, the teacher cited 10 chronic offenders who were members of his embattled school's student body. He said of them, "In ten years' time, I'm sure they'll all be dead, or on Rikers Island, where they will join the ranks of other notorious graduates from my school who now are serving hard time: one for strangling an eighty-year-old man; another for setting fire to a vagrant as he slept on a subway; still another for killing a cop."

A teacher at a Manhattan high school, who is also the faculty's representative to the United Federation of Teachers (UFT), talks of the presence of gun-toting students in her school's corridors. She says,

141

"It scares the teachers to death. Even one gun in the school is too much. When you have one gun, the potential is there for more."

The teacher/union executive's fears are borne out by the grim statistics. During the last school year for which figures are available, there was an average of 20 serious incidents a day reported in city schools. They included seven assaults, one robbery, and 10 weapons seizures. These figures do not include the confiscation of weapons through routine surveillance with metal detectors. It is said there were 800 such incidents reported in only five of the city's high schools during that period.

For its part, the UFT reports there are an average of four assaults a day carried out against teachers, either on school property or on the streets immediately surrounding schools.

This is how the statistics are being written in blood:

—On the first day of the 1989-1990 school year, Duane Lewis, an 18-year-old student at Prospect Heights High School in Brooklyn, was shot to death by an unknown assailant right outside the school building.

—On the second day of the term, police entered De Witt Clinton High School in the Bronx to confiscate a loaded handgun from a student.

—Later in the year, at Herbert Lehman High School in the Bronx, a student was arrested for menacing a classmate, as well as two faculty members, with a loaded .357 magnum revolver.

—At Brooklyn's Paul Robeson High School, a 15-year-old student was sitting with friends on the school steps. She was suddenly and viciously attacked by a group of youths who wielded sticks and

142

golf clubs, and at least one gun. The girl was shot in the neck, as well as beaten.

—A dispute that had begun in the cafeteria at Manhattan's Julia Richman High School spilled out into the Lexington Avenue subway. It reached its hideous conclusion when one student was shot to death at 2:30 p.m., in full view of fellow passengers.

—Seventeen-year-old Alexander Stephens Jr. became the first Big Apple high school student in a decade to actually be killed violently inside a school building. He was cut down by another student, according to police, as the boys were "horsing around" with a handgun belonging to Stephens. The other youth has been charged with second-degree manslaughter in Stephens' death. Further court action is pending against the boy.

Not only are teachers overwhelmed by the carnage surrounding them, but concerned students express exactly the same fears. A poll taken recently in five typical New York City schools found that one third of those queried named the top problems they faced as drugs, crime, gangs, violence, weapons, fighting, stealing, and security.

In all five reporting schools, teenagers of all races and ethnic groups concurred that these were their greatest preoccupations.

What does this mean in the life of individual kids? It is perhaps best expressed by a 19-year-old student who travels daily from Brooklyn to her classes at Louis Brandeis High School on Manhattan's West Side. Says the Haitian-born student, "I don't feel safe here. They [the students] carry knives in class. Some people have drugs and beepers. If you're different, and they don't like you—then they want to fight."

143

Of all the terrifying memories of what went on in and around schools during the 1989-1990 school year, none has had a more chilling impact on teachers and students alike than the brutal slaying of 33-year-old Maureen Smith, a former nun who immigrated from Guyana.

To all who knew her, Smith was the embodiment of all the best qualities one could look for in a teacher. A brilliant and dedicated person, she had brought a special flair to her work. It had earned her an outstanding reputation among supervisors, colleagues, and students alike. The 60 special-education students who reported to her classes daily at Franklin Delano Roosevelt High School in the Bensonhurst section of Brooklyn benefited markedly from Smith's innovative methods, which she developed to combat their learning disabilities.

The slightly built young teacher spared no effort to give the youngsters in her biology program the absolute optimum in teaching aids. Smith had undertaken the exhaustive and exhausting project of tape-recording their daily lessons. Because of her efforts, Smith's students, who ranged in age from 14 to 21 years old, could work at their own pace, whether they had been absent from classes or had needed more time to cope with their course work.

In the early days of September 1989, Maureen Smith had been busy at work, preparing herself for the term that lay ahead.

On Tuesday, September 6th, Smith traveled to Staten Island with a group of fellow teachers to attend an intensive educational meeting there. She was happily aware that in a matter of days, the yongsters who were so dependent on her sense of responsibility and energy would be returning to her classroom.

In the early afternoon, the biology teacher, accompanied by others who had been at the Staten Island session, drove back to Brooklyn. Her colleagues bade her a fond farewell in front of FDR High School. They watched as she walked to her gold Hyundai two-door sedan, which she had left parked in front of the Brooklyn school. Feeling that once Smith was behind the wheel of her own vehicle, she would be safe, the other teachers then drove off.

They would never see Maureen Smith alive again.

At 5:30 p.m. on September 6th, one of Smith's neighbors, a civil engineer employed by the Board of Education, returned to the house in the Crown Heights section of Brooklyn where the teacher had lived.

The man noticed that Smith's mail was still stuffed in a slot in her door. At 8:00 p.m. on the same evening, the engineer passed Smith's door once more as he left the building to keep an appointment. Her mail remained where he had spotted it before.

Thinking this was unusual because of his neighbor's inherent neatness and orderliness, the Board of Education employee asked his son to remind Smith of her apparent neglect in not having made the pickup.

Still concerned over the unusual lapse, the man decided to check once more. At 2:00 a.m. on Wednesday, September 7th, when he returned from an appointment, the neighbor called at Smith's apartment. Receiving no answer to his knock at her door, the man contacted Smith's relatives.

He reasoned that there must be some logical explanation for the young biology teacher's continuing absence. If there were, the closeness between Smith and her family members would probably have led her

145

to contact them. The civil engineer had every reason to hope that everything was all right with Maureen Smith.

But that hope was to prove vain. A relative of Maureen Smith, who lived in the same Crown Heights building, reported that she had received no calls or messages of any kind from Maureen.

Thus began a period of 11 days of mounting agony for all those who had known and loved Maureen Smith. As the minutes, hours, and days passed, the telephone of Maureen's relatives remained ominously silent. However, there could be no comforting sense that no news would prove to be good news.

Said one of Maureen's understandably distraught relatives, "If she could call somebody, I know she would."

Added another relative, "It's getting pretty bad. The longer it gets, the worse the situation could be."

Word of the beloved educator's disappearance began to spread like wildfire among concerned neighbors, friends, and colleagues. Civilian car searches were organized by people in the area. Fliers were posted throughout the streets. They provided a physical description of the missing woman and what little was known about her disappearance.

By now, police at the 71st Precinct had been informed of the baffling situation. Detective Jim McCabe of the 71st, who had been assigned to the missing-person case, commented, "This is quite unusual. There are people who wander away, and people who don't. This woman just doesn't wander off."

At that point, the police had little to go on. They knew Maureen Smith had migrated from her native Guyana in 1985. They knew there was nothing in her private life to account for her disappearance.

They knew she had been seen by close colleagues getting into her Hyundai with New York license plates LMZ-204 at 3:15 p.m. on Tuesday, September 6th.

Earlier on that day, she had mentioned to both colleagues and a relative that she had planned to stop off at an automatic teller machine at a branch of the Crossland Savings Bank at East 42nd Street and Avenue D in the Flatbush section of Brooklyn.

A police check of bank records showed that Maureen Smith had indeed made the stop. She had deposited her paycheck and had withdrawn $40 at the same time. The transaction was encoded on ATM tapes as having taken place at 4:20 p.m.

Obviously, the question now became whether Smith had been alone at the time she entered Crossland. One theory had it that somebody lurking near FDR High School might have accosted her and forced her to accompany the perp to the bank.

Another possibility was that whoever was responsible for the teacher's disappearance had tailed her from her school parking spot, spied on her as she took care of her banking chores, and then kidnapped her.

A third and just as plausible scenario had a perp watching the comings and goings of bank customers from a vantage point near Crossland and selecting Smith as a likely target. It was noted that because of Maureen's slight build and the fact that she wore eyeglasses, it would not be difficult to overpower her.

Adding to the confusion was that the Crossland branch was not located close by the high school where Smith taught. This made it virtually impossible to determine where and when she had been intercepted, if indeed she had been kidnapped.

The continued absence of the popular educator sent shock waves through FDR High School. A typical comment was that of the school's vice principal. "She's [Smith's] a person who would give of her own time, do anything to help her students. Her students are quiet, withdrawn. They can't believe it happened to her," she said.

Nor could anybody else who had known Maureen Smith over the years. They talked of her deep religious convictions that had caused her to enter a convent in her native Guyana.

Smith had then opted to migrate to the United States. Detectives learned that in 1985, Smith had begun her American studies in Texas. After a short time in the Lone Star State, the aspiring young educator had moved to New York City, where she took courses in education at Medgar Evers and Brooklyn Colleges. By February 1989, she had earned her master's degree in biology from Brooklyn College.

Commented the dean of academic affairs at Medgar Evers, "She was an A student . . . quiet, unassuming, ladylike, very well poised. Just a very fine person."

In the police bulletins and privately sponsored fliers put out about Maureen Smith's disappearance, she was described as being 4-foot-10 and having brown eyes and medium-length black hair. She usually wore eyeglasses. On September 6th, when she vanished, she had been wearing a dark blue skirt, a cream-colored blouse, and a white jacket with a black pattern.

Police set up a hotline at (212) 374-6913 in hopes that anybody with information about the missing Maureen Smith would contact detectives. Complete confidentiality was promised. However, there were no incoming calls to give tangible promise that the mystery would soon be solved.

While the missing-person case was the subject of tremendous agitation and concern throughout Brooklyn, it had created scarcely a ripple in the bedroom communities surrounding the Big Apple's five boroughs.

Across the Nassau County border in Uniondale, Long Island, for example, residents of quiet, residential Webster Avenue and Bedford Street paid scant attention to the small gold-colored vehicle parked at the curb. A number of days were to pass before the car attracted anybody's curiosity.

.Gradually, it dawned on passersby that the two-door sedan was not one normally seen in the neighborhood. Obviously it did not belong to local residents. More confusing was the fact that the car had been left in one spot over the course of a week and a half. Normally one might expect that in such a period of time, the car's owner would have at least moved it from one spot to another.

Thus, those who lived along Webster Avenue and Bedford Street were faced with a knotty puzzle. Why was a relatively new and well-kept vehicle remaining where it stood? Perhaps it had been abandoned. But there were no signs that it had been vandalized in the way derelict automobiles are generally disposed of.

At some point, somebody thought the continuing presence of the small Hyundai warranted police attention. At 2:00 p.m. on Saturday, September 16th, an RMP (Radio Motor Patrol vehicle) with Nassau County Police Department insignia emblazoned on its sides pulled alongside the mysterious foreign-made car. Officers checked the interior of the mysterious gold Hyundai sedan.

149

The search for 33-year-old biology teacher Maureen Smith came to a sudden and nerve-jarring climax.

Scrunched down on the right-hand passenger seat was Smith's frail body, already in an advanced state of decomposition. It lay partially hidden by a green plastic bag that covered the head and by several car mats camouflaging the arms, legs, and torso. A preliminary crime scene examination revealed that Maureen Smith had been shot twice in the head. However, actual determination of cause of death would have to await a more complete autopsy, which was scheduled for Sunday, September 17th.

Because Maureen Smith had to all intents and purposes been murdered, and because her body had been recovered across the city line, investigation of her slaying now became the province of the Nassau County Homicide Squad.

Detective Sergeant William Cocks of that unit told a hastily convened news conference that the $40 Smith had withdrawn from Crossland Bank on September 6th was missing. So were the teacher's pocketbook and a ring she was wearing when last seen alive.

Commented Cocks, "We're not ruling out robbery, or any other motive. It could be many things."

What Cocks did not reveal at the time was the fact that the victim was *not* last seen at the Crossland Bank, but had left there to do some grocery shopping.

Sergeant Cocks assigned 26-year-veteran Detective Vincent Donnelly to the case. Donnelly, a redheaded, no-nonsense sleuth with "cop" written all over his face, returned to the area of Brooklyn where the victim was last seen. He questioned several

150

people, showing them the victim's photo and asking them whether they had seen Maureen Smith.

Donnelly's next step was to go over the victim's Hyundai thoroughly. It was here that Donnelly found out something interesting. Apparently, the victim's last stop had not been at the automatic teller machine, but rather at a Pathmark supermarket not far from the bank. In the trunk of the victim's car, Detective Donnelly found three bags of groceries that contained women's personal items, apparently purchased right before the victim was killed. Maureen's killer(s) did not attempt to steal them and left no prints on the bags. Donnelly would later learn that the victim bought these items with the intention of sending a care package to relatives back in Guyana.

Detective Donnelly also found something that helped narrow down the time frame of the victim's death — he discovered the register receipts from the purchased items. These receipts had the date September 6th and the times noted were 5:07 and 5:08 p.m. Apparently, Maureen Smith had made two separate purchases, hence the two receipts.

Donnelly questioned clerks who remembered Maureen Smith as having used coupons to make the two separate transactions. This revealed to the sleuth that the victim was seen more than a half-hour after she left the bank machine.

Could Maureen Smith have been accosted in the supermarket parking lot? This was a definite possibility that Detective Donnelly knew had to be explored. Donnelly theorized that there was more than one attacker because of the angle of the shot. It suggested that one assailant was in the backseat and one beside Maureen.

Regarding the motive behind the murder, Donnelly believed it might have been robbery as well as sex. The victim's torn pantyhose indicated that an attempt at sex was made, but it was not completed.

There was no indication that the slaying was related to any personal or romantic problems the victim was having.

Declared Sergeant Cocks, "There is nothing to suggest that she had a strong relationship with someone in her life. There's nothing in her background to indicate that she would meet her death in this manner."

One mystery complicating the baffling circumstances of Smith's slaying was where, in fact, she had actually been killed. No slugs or casings were discovered by police in the Hyundai's interior. This led probers to wonder whether Smith had been shot someplace else.

The victim's family members were unable to shed any new light on who might have taken the life of their beloved and deeply mourned relative.

Stated one relative, "She had no enemies; nobody who knew her could have done this.

"She came to this country to study and to fall in love with it. We are all shocked and saddened."

Other relatives told of the terrible ordeal of Sunday, September 17th, when they had to travel to the Nassau County Medical Center to make a positive identification of the remains.

Said one of her relatives, "We looked at her tiny hands and we knew it was Maureen."

However, the finality of the occasion did have some therapeutic quality for the family's pain. A relative said there was a certain relief that Maureen's death was no longer a mystery. The relative had flown to the United States from her own home in England.

Declared the woman, "You always imagine. Imagination is worse than reality. . . . We went through all the possibilities. You hoped she would come back, but then, after all this time, you wonder. Whatever pain or trauma she was in, she's in peace now."

Also easing the family's burden somewhat were the joyous memories of those who had known Maureen Smith.

The assistant superintendent for special education at FDR High School recalled, "Many special-education students have trouble writing, taking notes. Maureen was doing the whole year's work for biology, little by little. She was just starting it this year. And she was doing it all on her own time."

The admiring faculty supervisor told of how Smith's deep early religious fervor, which had once caused her to become a novitiate to an Ursuline order, had had a profound bearing on her caring relationship with her students. Among other things, Smith had collected clothing her own younger relatives had outgrown and given the items to less fortunate youths.

Stated the assistant superintendent, "We have some students who are very, very poor. But they don't want to be embarrassed in front of their peers, carrying the clothes from school. So she would put the clothes in her car and take it to their homes and drop it off."

As a teacher, Maureen Smith was both inventive and disciplined, according to the assistant superintendent. "She gave the students as much hands-on as possible, because students don't learn from what we

153

call 'chalk and talk.' Every day she had something new that was being done."

Nor was Smith somebody who could be pushed around. The assistant superintendent noted, "She may have been only four-foot-ten, but she could handle those kids. If she said this is the way it had to be done, that was the way it had to be."

In addition to her regular teaching duties, Smith had often taught catechism classes at St. Ignatius Roman Catholic Church in the Crown Heights section of Brooklyn.

Of her work there, a reverend stated, "She was a teacher, and quite a good one."

That, in death, Maureen Smith would remain an ongoing inspiration to the young was the force behind efforts to establish a memorial fund in her name. The fund would give an award to a special-education student who showed particular merit.

On this point the assistant superintendent reported, "I think I know who I'm going to give it to next year, when he's a senior. There are two students Maureen had really worked with. Back in June she'd bring in a sandwich and really work with them, because she knew if she worked with them a little bit longer, they would make it. This student, he wants desperately to pass, but he didn't pass the test, by only two points.

"I'm going to make sure he passes it this year, for Maureen."

On Monday, September 18th, faculty and students of FDR High School paused to observe a moment of silence for the well-loved and highly respected teacher. Outside the building, the flag was flown at half-mast.

Said the FDR principal, "We hear about violence

154

in our society and it usually rolls off our backs until it hits someone we knew well. We're hurting, there's no doubt about it."

Students who had studied under Smith joined in the eulogies.

Remembered one 17-year-old boy, "She was really a sweet person. Really quiet, a polite lady."

The boy told of how there had been occasions when Smith had asked him to leave because he was disrupting the class.

"But she'd come down and talk to me. She'd say, 'You're only hurting yourself,' " he recalled.

A 16-year-old told of how the biology teacher had met with him every Thursday afternoon to help him prepare for his exam.

On Wednesday, September 20th, a crowd of 500 jammed into St. Ignatius Catholic Church to pay their last tributes to Maureen Smith. They heard the reverend ask, "Why are we deprived of her company so soon?"

The reverend answered his own question, "The Lord does not tell us why some people are called home so early."

A relative of the slain teacher offered these words of comfort to the grieving. At the end of a poem she had written for the funeral came this two-sentence message: "I am somewhere just around the corner. All is well."

But there was no stifling the underlying sense of outrage that gripped the congregation. It was articulated by a dean of Medgar Evars College who said, "It makes me angry. It's senseless . . . a senseless waste of a good life."

The dean said she was concerned that the killer or killers were still at large. She added, "That's a question I think we should pursue, to find out how she was murdered."

A teacher at an elementary school agreed with the college head. She stated, "The whole thing made me mad. That a good teacher is no longer here to help New York."

For their part, police assigned to the case felt the same need to solve the brutal slaying.

On September 18, 1989, Sergeant Cocks reported that sleuths had recovered a gun and two slugs thought to have been used in the murder. However, progress since that announcement has been slow. The case remains very much in the active file. Over a year later, no arrests have been made.

And still, the violence that claimed Maureen Smith remains a part of the everyday experience of all those who teach and of the army of law-abiding students who learn from them.

The views of the United Federation of Teachers' director of school safety are widely held. Of violence in the schools, the UFT official says, "It's pretty bad. I don't think there's such a thing as a teacher's standpoint on this issue. There's only a human standpoint. We must make the schools safe for teachers — and everybody else."

"TWO INFERNOS — THREE CORPSES — NO SUSPECTS!"

by Howard and Mary Stevens

Nashville, Indiana, is a charming little town. Sassafras, sorghum and squash are offered to visitors at colorful roadside stands. Sidewalks can barely accommodate all the kids, dogs and skittish skateboarders. And the local theater puts on exceptional performances in the summertime.

Yes, Nashville, Indiana, is most charming indeed. But it's not all peaches and cream. It has been nearly two decades since the charred, limbless body of a man was discovered in the smouldering ruins of a weatherbeaten barn on the hilltop homestead of Clarence Roberts.

The mystery began on November 18, 1970. The first authorities summoned to the Roberts' property assumed that the victim had been accidentally caught in the inferno. Closer inspection revealed that the fierce blaze had burned away the ends of the man's arms and legs. Volunteer firemen called to the rural scene commented openly about the fire's destructive force and its reduction of the barn to fiery embers which glowed a golden color in the brisk November air.

The Roberts family members were fixtures on the

Nashville scene. A former sheriff, Roberts was a respected businessman, and his demise, if indeed the body was his, represented a complicated and confusing turn of events.

Many of the onlookers, who were attracted to the black smoke that billowed up, blotting out the sun, and to the wail of volunteer fire sirens, had heard stories that Roberts had fallen on hard financial times. Others suggested that the one-time lawman had been drinking heavily to drown out dark thoughts of his mounting money problems. For such a proud man, suicide might be a way out of his crumbling lifestyle, they agreed.

But the actual fire scene presented complications to his theory. Roberts' handsome Masonic ring was discovered near the body, unmelted and undamaged. His wedding ring, however, was missing. He always wore the gold band wherever he went, one of those present volunteered.

Investigators from the Indiana State Police district post at Bloomington were called in to conduct a probe. One of their first revelations proved to be a bombshell. Roberts, they learned, had taken out a $1.2 million life insurance policy with four different firms weeks before the blaze. The beneficiary, lawmen learned, was Geneva Roberts, the frail, diabetic wife-widow.

Troopers assigned to the chilling case could not agree on how the victim died. A shotgun, the barrel twisted and charred from the intense heat of the fire, straddled the middle of the torso. The man's skull was so badly burned that authorities couldn't tell whether the charge from the weapon had killed him or the man had died from overpowering flames from the inferno.

One authority, Brown County Coroner Earl Bond, refused to certify the cause of death. He flatly refused because, as he explained, "It is impossible to determine the cause of death due to the intensity of the fire and the disarray of evidence at the scene."

Bond made it clear that firemen at the scene had not secured the area and that, later, investigators allowed passersby to trample through the region, making it extremely difficult to reconstruct the events leading up to the fire and, more important, to identify the fire-singed body.

Despite inconclusive evidence, members of the Roberts family buried the corpse as one of their own. Bond labeled the torso as a "John Doe."

One month later, the body was exhumed for another look. Experts, including Dr. John Pless, a highly respected forensic pathologist, concluded that the body was not Roberts.

"When it came down to the nitty-gritty, most of those involved in the case, didn't think it was Roberts," Pless recalls. "The family counsel came to me since they were about to sue for the life insurance and I simply told them that Roberts, in my opinion, did not die in the fire. It was as simple as that."

Pless was bombarded from all sides. He stuck to his guns. He continued to insist that the body in the fire was not Roberts.

More than two years after the fire, an eerie feeling permeated Nashville. Reported sightings of a man closely resembling Roberts filtered into town. The "ghost" of Roberts marched on and before long, Roberts look-alikes were reported in a number of communities surrounding Nashville.

One man, a respected businessman who had dealt with Roberts on a number of occasions, reported that he had seen a man resembling the former sheriff in animated conversation with a vagrant. Others related that they had seen Roberts as far south as Mexico. One told authorities he saw the missing man closer to home. He swore he saw a man answering Roberts' description slipping into his widow's cabin on the edge of town.

A ghost in Nashville? Not on your life, several businessmen complained. The story of a man flitting around town would not be good for business, especially one who many thought perished in a fire in the hilltop.

In 1975, community leaders had had enough of the Roberts' legend. A county grand jury indicted Roberts for murder and arson. Finding the missing man and bringing him to trial would be another matter. But that was not what hounded townspeople most. Who was the man who perished in the fire on the hilltop that bleak November day?

Amateur sleuths in Nashville — and there were many — wondered how Roberts could have carried out the startling slaying. Had the vagrant he befriended, as some reasoned, been led cunningly to his death in the barn? A bold plan, but it could have worked, some natives reasoned.

Several grand jurors were convinced that it would have been possible to rig the hilltop scenario. They noted that Roberts was a well-regarded, well-liked businessman, an influential citizen who might have been down on his luck but able to bounce back.

Another grand juror explained he assessed the case as involving the "good old boy outlook." He posed

160

his theory with a question. "Who is going to question the ethics of a former sheriff, a brother who was a lawman and a bunch of state policemen who regularly had coffee and doughnuts and perhaps breakfast at the Brown County Jail? We have all seen those marked cars parked outside the jail. Tell me, please, who is going to throw a monkey wrench in that system?"

One juror said he was also familiar with the buddy system as it pertained to county government. He suggested that Roberts had a lot of clout in the hill country, that he was one man people who wanted favors made a point to see.

Nearly 10 years after the blaze, in 1979, Geneva Roberts went to court to get her mate declared legally dead in order to collect the insurance money. But Monroe Circuit Court Judge James Dixon ruled in favor of the insurance companies, noting that the evidence introduced in the hearings didn't prove conclusively that Roberts died in the fire. Dental and medical records, the magistrate insisted, were sketchy and unreliable.

Geneva Roberts' lawyers appealed the ruling against them, but in the fall of 1980 the court upheld the ruling. The town of Nashville returned to near normalcy. But not for long.

A month later, fire again figured in the saga, destroying Geneva Roberts' cabin. In the ruins, firemen found the charred bodies of a man and a woman and this time, authorities were in agreement. The man was Clarence Roberts and the woman, his wife, Geneva.

Roberts' heirs refused to claim the body following the second fire. They informed burial representatives that they had buried their loved one a decade ago. They insisted that the remains not be disturbed.

One man who lived with the bewildering Roberts case for most of his long career in law enforcement was Dave Anderson, an Indiana State Police detective assigned to the Bloomington post. Anderson spent a good portion of his time trying to keep track of the Roberts' movements. His assignment was not easy.

"Only a handful of people could get past a guard dog kept tied to the back door of Geneva Roberts' cabin. The dog was part German Shepherd and an excellent watchdog. Someone who could get into the house and past the dog surely set the fire that consumed the pair," Anderson is convinced.

The veteran investigator concedes that while he can't prove it, he believes a third person slipped into the cabin, set the fire, and escaped before the inferno destroyed the structure and the two occupants. Anderson says he personally saw a number of persons enter the property but was unable to get close enough to positively identify who they were. "The cabin's windows were boarded up, so it was impossible to see anything at night," the officer explained.

If anything, the mystery surrounding the Roberts case has added another dimension to Nashville's popularity among tourists. The mystique of a full-blown whodunit draws many to the old brick courthouse and into the jail courtyard beyond. A few hardy souls also visit the neatly manicured cemetery where the Roberts' family plot commands a prominent position on a rolling hill near the cemetery entrance.

Horse-drawn carriages have been added to the luster of the quaint Indiana village and the sharp crackle of the leather harness admittedly creates a homey touch to the rustic countryside. Students from nearby Indiana University mingle with the crowds and attend performances of the summer theater in the heart of the community.

In 1983, a Brown County grand jury issued a report on evidence collected in a fall session of the group, suggesting that Clarence Roberts attempted to kill his wife by setting fire to the cabin in which Geneva lay unconscious. It was believed that he, too, was overcome by flames after passing out in an alcoholic daze. A diabetic, Geneva Roberts, the report sets out, might have succumbed to a diabetic coma following the night of drinking with her husband.

Lawmen also learned while collecting information for the presiding grand jury that a large quantity of turpentine had been poured in a circular stream from the rear door of the cabin to and around a cot Geneva Roberts rested on. Others, beside Anderson, speculated that a third person might easily have set the fire before disappearing into the heavily wooded area surrounding the cabin.

During the grand jury probe, jurors took officers to task, charging that evidence had been lost, misplaced or tampered with at the crime scene. The jury's report further alleged that the investigation of the case was hindered to a great degree by disputes between state and local authorities over who should investigate and how.

Anderson has not tried to dodge the grand jury's findings of official foulups. "It is a blemish we will have to live with. It is a performance we cannot be proud of to any degree," he acknowledges.

163

While probers finally concluded that the man in the second fire was Roberts, the man in the first fire was never identified. At least one person has come forward and said he saw the man now believed to be the fire victim and Roberts together in a small town near Nashville. The man appeared to be of the same stature as Roberts, the man volunteered.

Testimony was also presented to the grand jury alleging that Roberts had befriended a vagrant shortly before the fire. It is not clear if both reports involved the same man. The secrecy of grand jury deliberations have frequently led to confusion and conflicting opinions. Arson investigations are particularly difficult and divisive, Anderson admits.

"Concealing a crime by arson is one of the leading motives in use by criminals in this decade because it is so difficult to prove. Evidence is often tampered with before fires and after firemen work over the scene with powerful water streams, valuable clues are simply washed over or blown away. An eyewitness to someone setting a fire is a rare happening."

If friends and relatives breathed a sigh of relief when it was announced that Clarence and Geneva Roberts died in the second fire, officials of four insurance companies who held death-benefit policies on the pair were elated. They all agreed that they were happy the decade-long ordeal was over and they were off the hook.

One insurance official indicated that throughout the affair, he was convinced Clarence Roberts was alive. "I was convinced he would surface, although I was flabbergasted when he did. Roberts, I realized, was in hock for more than $200,000. His business deals went sour."

Townspeople's sympathies lay more with Geneva than with the ex-sheriff. "Geneva was a haunted woman. She just appeared to dry up after the first fire. If I saw her unexpectedly on the street, she would put her head down and avoid making eye contact," one of her friends confided.

Some townsfolk were convinced that Clarence Roberts' financial troubles stemmed from being too greedy. They said he wanted the big bucks and was willing to walk over a lot of people to get where he wanted to be—on the top of the pile. As one businessman suggests, "He had his own personal goals and he pretty much didn't care who he pushed aside to get what he wanted. Let's face it. Clarence Roberts wasn't the most popular guy in town."

Area lawmen are certain that the Roberts case may linger on for years. The identity of the man who died in the first fire will probably never be known. Other mysteries remain.

The man who directed the grand jury on the Roberts case, Prosecuting Attorney William Fawcett, says there may never be a clear-cut solution to the mystery surrounding the deaths of Geneva and Clarence Roberts and the unknown third party. Fawcett subscribes to the theory that some mysteries tend to remain mysteries forever.

"Perhaps we were too close to the Roberts story. One five-page grand jury report delivered to me recommended that there was insufficient evidence presented in the case to involve anyone else. Unless more evidence surfaces, jurors reasoned that further probes into the three deaths should be closed."

Just when the community thought it had heard the last of the Roberts' mystery, a national television network announced that they would recreate the strange and complicated story for its mystery-loving viewers. Presented on NBC's *Unsolved Mysteries* series last year, a number of Brown County residents appeared as themselves, including Anderson. Filming was conducted along Nashville's streets and alleys and both fires were recreated by technical crews.

Professional actors played the parts of the Roberts, the vagrant, and the county coroner, who died before filming was completed. One of the film producers suggested that Roberts might show up and play himself. He didn't.

After reversing himself on the identity of the fire victims, pathologist Pless is in demand as a speaker at medical conferences and seminars throughout Indiana. In his talks, he stresses the fact that he has learned something from every death and that autopsies involve visual examinations as well as chemical and microscopic work—all of which takes time.

Pless is now involved with setting up a state medical examiners' system—a system that has received enabling legislation and has, just recently, established rules and regulations. The system would divide the state of Indiana into five districts with a forensic pathologist in charge of autopsies in each district. He says this would enable pathologists to set up standard formats for all autopsies.

The pathologist who figured prominently in the Roberts case would like to see the state fund the cost of autopsies, which average in cost from $500 to $1,000. "If the state gets into the picture, we would be able to guarantee the quality of the autopsy. Under the present system, we cannot do this, and this weakens the procedure," he states.

Pless would also like to see more use of the emerging forensic technique known as DNA fingerprinting. It was not used in the Roberts' case, but it has been used during a recent murder trial in Fort Wayne. DNA, or deoxyribonucleic acid, is contained in every human cell, including those in blood, semen and hair roots. Because everyone's DNA is unique (with the exception of an identical twin), it can establish identity with pinpoint precision.

Researchers at the nearby Indiana University medical school and Indiana State Police investigators say that given an adequate sample of DNA—from blood on a knife, for example—and proper testing procedures, the high-tech analysis can inextricably link a suspect to a crime scene. Or exonerate someone who's been unjustly accused.

The Roberts case may not be what the folksy Hoosier community wants to be best known for, but the glare of wide-spread publicity is not likely to stop with the presentation of the television show. Other news and mystery groups report that they are presently doing stories or review of the intriguing Roberts case.

"FLORIDA'S EASTER SUNDAY MURDER MYSTERY"

by Julie Malear

It was Easter Sunday, April 3, 1988. All day the weather had been beautiful in Delray Beach, Florida. The few on-again, off-again clouds that occasionally covered the sun had not marred the postcard-pretty scenes at the beach, nor kept local youngsters from hunting colored eggs in Lake Ida Park.

Now, as dusk approached, a young Delray Beach woman stared at the wall clock with worry on her attractive face. Where was he? It was so very late. After drying her hands on a kitchen towel, the young woman walked into her living room to peer out the front window one more time. They'd called and called. Where was David Steen? David was usually so prompt, it wasn't his nature to have missed the holiday dinner and not even phoned. Now, it was time to eat again. Perhaps David thought she'd meant the evening meal. Perhaps he'd soon appear. But she couldn't help worrying. Where *was* he?

The young woman expressed her concern to Betty and Ed Taggart, who were like members of the family. The Taggarts told her they'd drive over and check on David Steen. They liked him, too. Perhaps he was sick, they suggested, or maybe company had come at the last moment. The tall, slender man always had lots of company. He was so friendly — such a nice guy.

It didn't take long for the Taggarts to make the trip to Steen's small home on Northeast Third Avenue. The narrow, quiet road, which stretched behind a row of stores and small businesses near the Delray Post Office on the next street, was deserted when the Taggarts parked in front of the tree-shrouded house.

The couple laughed as they hurried up the walk. Steen's black mutt, Suzy, was outside in her doghouse. The usually friendly mongrel greeted them in a frenzy, as if she wanted to show them something but was unable to reach them through the fenced-in enclosure. They spoke to the mutt momentarily before stepping up to the door.

When no one answered their knock, they turned the knob. It was unlocked. The couple entered, calling out to the 50-year-old man as they looked around inside.

It was when they walked into the kitchen that the Taggarts saw blood on the floor. Lots of it. Something was wrong, very wrong. Afraid of what might be lying beyond the door, Ed pulled Betty with him as he ran outside.

Hurrying next door to a new light-colored building that belonged to David Steen, the couple called out to an employee who worked for Steen at his aluminum-shutter business there and lived in a room on the second floor. As soon as the employee heard about the blood, he rushed back with the Taggarts to his boss' house.

Although each of them feared the worst, they were completely unprepared for what they saw in the kitchen. The scene was so gruesome, so cruel and sudden, they would never completely erase the sight from their minds.

There on the floor lay David Steen, his balding head bashed, as if he'd been attacked by a maniac. Blood was everywhere; a great pool of it had coagulated under his body.

The trio stared for a moment, unable to accept what they were seeing. Then, as with one accord, they ran back to the plant and immediately phoned the police.

Elsewhere, relaxed and happy after a restful holiday, Detective Craig Hartmann of the Delray Beach Police Department had just finished the last bite of a hardy Easter dinner when the phone rang. It was the homicide unit, he told his family after speaking with the dispatcher. He was needed immediately.

As the dark-haired, well-built investigator said goodbye and hurried out the door, he noticed the time — 6:30 p.m. Responding to the Third Avenue residence a few minutes later, Hartmann was met by Sergeant Mike Swigert and several Delray Beach police officers.

As road patrol supervisor that afternoon, Sergeant Swigert, a young, wavy-haired lawman with blue eyes, was first on the scene after headquarters received the Taggarts' call. Swigert filled in the detective: "Friends had come over here to check on the victim because he was long overdue [at a family member's house] for dinner and he was usually on time. So the male went in." That, he told Detective Hartmann, was when the Taggarts called 911.

"I've seen a lot of homicides," Hartmann told Swigert, "but nothing this brutal, violent! Lots of blood, lots of blood and castoff scattered in every

170

direction. No saying how tough this case is going to be!" Hartmann shook his head. The Easter dinner felt heavy in his stomach.

"Nine people responded from the fire-rescue department," the road patrol supervisor added. "I had everyone wait outside." He wanted to protect the crime scene, he told Detective Hartmann. "I drew my gun and went in. It was a real mess! I couldn't tell if it was suicide or not." The victim, dressed and wearing jewelry, had one arm folded under him, Swigert explained, which hid whether or not Steen was holding a gun.

A short time later, the first clue came in, Swigert continued. While one of his police officers, Charles Hoeffer, stood outside the house for the duration of his shift to guard the crime scene from concerned friends and curious bystanders, and Sergeant Ken Herndon checked for signs of forced entry inside, Sergeant Swigert answered the phone, which was ringing in the next room. The caller was a male who identified himself as Leroy Barnes. He wanted to "speak with David Steen," Swigert said. Barnes claimed that earlier in the day he'd found a wallet belonging to Steen on an exit ramp off of Interstate 95 on Pompano Beach and was calling to return the wallet to him.

Was Barnes the perpetrator? Was he calling to see what had happened to the victim he may have robbed and murdered? Was he hoping for a reward? Or was he merely calling to be helpful? All these questions came to Swigert as he took that telephone call.

As a result of the call, Delray police contacted the Fort Lauderdale PD. Detective Mike Anzalone of that department met with the caller, recovered the wallet, and took a taped statement from him.

As soon as they could, Detective Hartmann and Detective-Sergeant Bob Brand, a tall, mustached veteran of the Delray PD, drove to Fort Lauderdale, a larger city 25 miles south of Delray Beach. They then interviewed Leroy Barnes themselves after learning he had five "firearms" against him.

The man told them he'd been out all night with some friends and was walking back to his home. He got on the interstate and was "going to walk home" when a state trooper told him to get off I-95. As he was going down the exit ramp at Atlantic Boulevard in Pompano Beach, he found the wallet off the shoulder. Then, Barnes said, he took the wallet back to the tree where he'd spent the night with other friends. They were all looking through it to find identification. Finally, Barnes told the lawmen, he took it to his boss and they "tried to get ahold of David Steen." Hartmann and Brand realized that during all the time Barnes had been ringing the victim, Steen had been lying dead near the phone. Finally, Sergeant Swigert had lifted the receiver and talked to him.

At that point in the interview with Barnes, the two Delray sleuths took the victim's wallet. It contained no money, but they did not know at that time if anything had actually been taken from it.

Meanwhile, back in Delray Beach, where the crime scene investigation had been completed, Sergeant Herndon reported to Detectives Hartmann and Brand that there were no signs of forced entry, nor did the house appear to be ransacked. Apparently the only item missing was that wallet. So what was the motive for the homicide? Hartmann asked himself.

172

The Sunday *Palm Beach Post* was in the victim's living room. Detective Hartmann called to find out when the newspaper was delivered on Northeast Third Avenue and learned that the carrier always brought it on Sundays between 6:30 and 7:00 a.m.

"Okay," Hartmann said to the officers at the crime scene, "it looks like the newspaper's been read. So it happened sometime after six or seven in the morning—right?"

Stepping outside to question the curious crowd that had gathered, Detective Hartmann interviewed Janet Simon, the mother of Betty Taggart—the woman who had discovered the body. Simon said she drove eastbound on Northeast 4th Street—only one house was between David Steen's house and 4th Street—around seven o'clock that morning. She'd seen David's car in the driveway, she told the officers, and noticed that the front door to the residence was open.

Probing further, the sleuth learned that Janet Simon had been the victim's girlfriend for several years. In fact, they had just broken up a month ago. In spite of their breakup, however, Simon apparently still checked on David from time to time. She lived less than a mile farther north. Simon seemed genuinely upset about the victim's death. Surely, the breakup hadn't caused her to do in her former boyfriend? Detective Hartmann thought it highly unlikely.

The detective conducted a neighborhood canvass in hope of finding someone who had seen or heard something. No one had. Friends and family members at the scene seemed extremely surprised and upset by the homicide. No one could understand why anyone would want to do something like that to Steen. The victim's family told the sleuth that Steen lived alone and was the owner of Viking Aluminum, the company and building adjacent to Steen's home. Steen's hobby was tinkering with old autos. He'd often bought '50s and '60s Cadillacs to fix up.

The next morning, Detectives Hartmann and Detective-Sergeant Bob Brand went to the Palm Beach County Medical Examiner's Office and watched Dr. John Marraccini perform the autopsy on David Steen. The M.E. noted numerous blows to the victim's head, although he couldn't determine the type of murder weapon used. Cause of death was listed as "injury due to blunt trauma."

On April 5th, Hartmann and Brand began checking places frequented by the victim. At a chain restaurant in the Delray Beach Mall, the two lawmen interviewed a waitress who identified the photo they showed her as a customer whom she knew only as "Dave." The man often came to the restaurant, she said, and was definitely there the night before Easter. He'd been in around 10:00 p.m., she recalled, and had been sitting with two other men whom she did not know. She wasn't sure what time Dave left.

Around noon, Hartmann interviewed Betty Taggart, who repeated that David Steen was supposed to have been at his relative's home for Easter dinner and she'd made several attempts to contact him in vain. As the detective pressed for details, the woman recalled that the electric roll-up shutters in the victim's house had been in a down position.

Later in the day, Sergeant Morrison of the Palm Beach County Sheriff's Office phoned to tell the Delray Beach investigators that a female jail inmate was requesting to speak to the detectives in charge of the David Steen homicide. Could this be the break they were hoping for? Detectives Hartmann and Brand drove to the Palm Beach County stockade in rapid time.

The woman, in jail for prostitution, seemed quite upset at Steen's murder. She informed the two officers that David had dated "numerous prostitutes in the Boynton and Delray Beach areas." She suggested that they interview a woman named Dara Bonanno, who had dated the victim in the past. It was all she could think of to suggest that might be pertinent.

After thanking her, the two lawmen left and attempted to find Dara Bonanno to question her. It was a far more difficult task than they'd expected. "It's frustrating," Hartmann said about the case, "when you don't have a home address and you don't have regular business hours so you can pick up a phone and call them."

Finally the sleuths learned that Dara had gone to the Fort Lauderdale area, over 25 miles away. Since they already knew the woman had a misdemeanor warrant out for her, the sleuths let the police department of that city have pictures and information on Dara Bonanno so they could help find her, since she was in their territory. Brand and Hartmann spent days working with the Fort Lauderdale police to track down Dara. One night, the other department called the Delray duo to say they'd arrested her in a crack house.

"At last!" the Delray Beach detectives thought as they drove down to interview the elusive prostitute. A whole month had gone by since they'd started looking for her.

But when they questioned Dara Bonanno, she said she didn't know anything about the Steen homicide. They found no reason not to believe her.

"All that time wasted," the probers said to themselves. Dara was just one in a series of prostitutes Dave Steen had known, all of whom were on the move and hard to locate.

But back on April 5th, before the meeting with Dara Bonanno, the sleuth duo again contacted Betty Taggart's mother, Janet Simon. The woman told the detectives that she'd broken up with Steen because of problems they'd been having with her son. She admitted that she often drove by Steen's house to check on him. Her daughter, too, had driven by on Easter morning around eleven o'clock. At that time, the victim's car was in the driveway and the front door was closed, not open as it had been at seven o'clock, when Janet herself had driven past the nearby intersection.

The woman also told Detectives Brand and Hartmann that Steen kept a large amount of money in an envelope hidden in the right side of his waterbed. Upon hearing this, Hartmann drove back to the victim's house and found $1,500 in U.S. currency in a white envelope in between the frame and the mattress. The money was placed into evidence for safekeeping. Had someone who'd known that Steen kept large amounts of cash killed him for it but been interrupted before finding the cache? This was just another one of many questions sleuths had to answer.

Knowing that time is essential in a homicide investigation if they were to find the perp, the detectives continued their interviews. They located the manager of Steen's aluminum awning business as well as Darrin Daly, a younger relative of the victim's. Both men said Steen had been involved with one of his secretaries. Steen had hired her for the business in early 1986. They also told the sleuths that the secretary's husband knew that his wife was cheating on him with Steen and at that time became very jealous. So, was Steen's murder a crime of passion then—of jealous rage? Lawmen knew they would have to delve into this angle as soon as possible.

The following day, the Delray Beach detectives learned the identities of—and separately interviewed—the two friends who were with Dave Steen at the chain restaurant on the night before he died. The first, a 38-year-old man, told the sleuths that all three of them left the dining spot at the same time—between 10:30 and 10:45 p.m. Each of them went off in a different direction. The witness said he had just seen the victim heading north on the South Federal Highway (U.S. Highway 1), a route bisecting Delray Beach. He also gave Detectives Hartmann and Brand names of people Steen had known. The list included prostitutes and alcoholics whom the victim had befriended. Unfortunately, the friend knew most of them only by first names. He said Steen was wealthy but cared more for people than money. "He just cared. . . . He was just a wise man."

After a little probing, the sleuths also learned that the victim had an appointment with a woman at 11:00 p.m. This woman, the witness told them, had formerly been in a "way side program." Steen, a former alcoholic who'd been dry 18 years, worked continually with others who drank and needed help. He didn't tell his friends where he was to meet his date. When the lawmen interviewed the other friend who'd been with the victim that night, he gave them essentially the same story.

Did this pre-midnight "date" have something to do with David Steen's death? Was she a recovering alcoholic who took one drink and became berserk? Had she gone home with Steen, spent the night, and then quarreled with him the following day? Sleuths had to find the elusive woman. But in spite of their questioning of anyone who might know her identity, it was as if she'd never existed.

As they continued seeking Steen's friends, the sleuths learned only good things about the victim. They heard over and over that Steen was a member of Alcoholics Anonymous and had been sober for many years. Witnesses said that he was very active as far as being a sponsor and counselor with AA.

The detective team discussed the situation. "Obviously, when someone felt they had to talk," observed Detective Hartmann, "or they wanted to take a drink or something like that, he was always available like that. Nobody at all had anything bad to say about him." In fact, the investigators learned, after Steen constructed the building next to his house, he had supposedly placed as many of the recovering alcoholics as he could into temporary positions with his aluminum business to help them get on their feet. "He was very helpful that way," Hartmann noted. "A very considerate man." Could Steen have been *too* helpful—taking someone into his house or business who wasn't quite stable?

On April 8th, Detectives Hartmann and Brand went to Pompano Beach, where they located Steen's secretary who had the jealous husband. The woman expressed surprise at her former lover's death. She told them that the last contact she'd had with Steen was five weeks before, when she'd "borrowed fifty dollars from him." At that time, she said, she and her husband were separated and she was living with her mother in Delray Beach. A couple of weeks later, however, the couple made up and moved in back together.

Delving further into the couple's actions, the lawmen asked where they were on Easter morning and the night before. The secretary assured the sleuths that she and her husband were at a neighbor's party that night and in the morning were hiding Easter eggs with other neighbors at their apartment complex. This alibi was quickly confirmed by fellow residents of the complex.

That done, the lawmen returned to Delray Beach to attend David Steen's funeral. Although they conducted a surveillance on the guests, they noted no unusual activity.

On Monday, the detectives began again to interview known prostitutes, all of whom spoke highly of the victim and expressed outrage at his murder. Most of the young women were very cooperative, including the first one on their list who told them that she'd dated David Steen in the past but had not seen him recently. She named another prostitute, a tall blonde, whom she felt they should question.

It was close to impossible for the sleuths to track these women down, and as before, it was several days before they finally found the blonde hooker. The young prostitute said she had indeed dated Steen, but only once, and that was when her boyfriend was in the county jail. She couldn't recall the exact date, but she said she hadn't seen Steen since then.

The frustrated lawmen interviewed woman after woman, tracking down names given to them by Steen's two male friends at the restaurant. Some of the interviews were dead ends; others gave the sleuths more names to pursue. All the interviewed individuals praised the dead man.

That same week, the detectives interviewed Steen's ex-wife, who had been married to him for a year and divorced from him for 12 years. Her ex-husband, she told them, had threatened Steen years ago, blaming him for the separation between him and his wife. This man, Steen's ex-wife told the sleuths, lived in New Jersey. After a dozen years, could he still have harbored a grudge? lawmen wondered. Delving further into the victim's past, the lawmen learned that he'd been divorced three times.

On April 12th, the detectives were elated when a suspicious clue emerged: apparently, neighbors just to the north of Steen had left their apartment right after the homicide. This news seemed a true breakthrough, until further investigation turned up a woman from a Delray church who claimed she knew the couple, having been the one who'd located the Third Avenue apartment for them next door to Steen. She explained that they'd moved out because the man had gone to see his sick father in Kentucky. His wife and children had followed several days later.

Turning back to Steen's secretary and her husband, Detective-Sergeant Brand contacted the Florida Department of Law Enforcement (FDLE) and requested all vehicle information under the husband's name. The reply listed a 1979 four-door Chevy on which Detective Hartmann immediately requested an off-line search in addition to one on the couple themselves. Sometime later, reports came back "negative."

Why, the sleuths wondered, was every clue a dead end?

Perhaps the killer had used a taxi? Sergeant Brand checked with all area taxicab companies to see if any of their cabbies had taken a fare to the victim's residence on the day of the homicide. Again, the report came back negative.

The investigation suddenly veered in another direction when, on April 19th, the detectives received a call from the manager of Steen's awning business. His late boss' Visa card had been used, he told the lawmen, "twenty-three different times since the homicide."

The sleuths went to Miami to the bank that had issued the card. The representative told them that when a card has been used for excessive charges, it is company policy to notify the business in question. As soon as they obtained the list of charges, Detectives Hartmann and Brand drove to a motel on State Road 7 to ask who had charged a room there to David Steen's card.

The clerk who'd been on duty April 9th, when the Visa was used, furnished the detectives with the original desk registration form. It was signed "David Steen," with a Chicago address. The car was a 1979 Chevy with an Illinois tag. When they did a computer check on the tag, it came back listed to a 1986 Buick coupe registered to a Joliet man. Although the clerk could not remember anything about the person who had stayed in the motel room, the guest registration showed that two people had spent the night.

Checking other charges on the itemized list from the bank, the lawmen found that $132.59 was charged on April 9th to a service station in Pompano Beach. Heading there at once, the detective duo soon questioned the owner-manager about the "130 gallons" that had been purchased. The owner said it was "not an unusual amount" to be purchased when dealing with construction companies or large mobile-home vehicles. Although the owner questioned his clerk on duty at that time, the clerk could remember nothing.

Detectives Brand and Hartmann recalled that Leroy Barnes had shown the wallet to a group of his friends under a tree when he first found it. Had one of them slipped the credit card out at that time?

When the detectives returned to Delray Beach after interviewing those on the Visa list, they learned that there'd been a burglary two days before across the street from the Steen home. They met with the victimized resident, a young woman, who had filed a report. The young woman accused her brother-in-law of burglarizing her place. He could easily be considered a suspect in Dave Steen's murder, she claimed. At the woman's words, the lawmen who had persevered so long, had a surge of hope. Was she finally pinpointing the perp?

Checking into her suspicions, Hartmann and Brand found that the man had about $200 in his possession after Easter which he had not had the night before. The dark-haired woman continued to vent her reasons, telling the probers that the day after the homicide she saw what she believed to be blood on the shirt her brother-in-law had tied around his waist. The reddish substance was also on his nunchaku, a martial arts weapon composed of two sticks with a chain in between. When the young woman confronted her brother-in-law about the shirt and nunchaku, he turned to his girlfriend and told her to throw away the shirt.

Before the detectives made contact with him, his sister-in-law again phoned the police. When Hartmann and Brand responded to the call, she told them that earlier in the day, her brother-in-law had again broken into her apartment. This time, he walked up behind her, grabbed her around her throat, and started choking her. When she managed to scream for help, he let go and fled. The young woman told the detectives they could find her brother-in-law's girlfriend through a counselor. They did.

After driving about 20 miles to the girlfriend's home in West Palm Beach, they interviewed her about the Steen homicide. She swore she knew nothing about it. The lawmen then confronted her with the information given to them by her boyfriend's sister-in-law concerning his shirt and nunchaku.

"She's lying," the girlfriend said. "She's purposely trying to get him in trouble because he refused to have sex with her." The young woman added that her boyfriend was to call her at 8:00 p.m. from a public phone located at the public boat ramp in Boynton Beach, another resort town just north of Delray Beach.

Before leaving to intercept the suspect, the lawmen asked the whereabouts of his nunchaku. The girlfriend got it for them willingly and they took it with them for a lab exam.

Around nine o'clock, the sleuths found the suspect at the boat ramp and with his consent drove him back to the Delray Beach PD for questioning. During his interview, the man claimed he awakened at nine o'clock on Easter morning; he heard or saw nothing unusual in the street. When Hartmann and Brand confronted the man with his sister-in-law's statement, he swore that *she* was lying. Obviously, he said, his sister-in-law was trying to get him in trouble because he wouldn't have sex with her. Regarding the April 18th burglary report, the suspect admitted that he went to his sister-in-law's apartment to retrieve his bicycle and met her. When she refused to give him his bike, he left.

After the lab test proved negative, the determined sleuths went back to tracing credit-card purchases. On April 20th, they interviewed a clerk at a sports shop in Delray Beach who recalled two black males coming into the store on the 9th and buying several pairs of sneakers. They paid for the $140.68 purchase with a credit card in the name of "David Steen." The woman described one of the subjects as a "black man in his forties, five-foot-nine, with dark skin and a medium afro with a little gray." The second subject, she remembered, was a black male in his 20s who was "tall, had dark skin, a 'low' haircut, and bloodshot bulging eyes." Her opinion was that both men were "drug users."

Pulling out a picture of Leroy Barnes, the finder of the wallet, Sergeant Brand showed it to the clerk. "No," she said, shaking her head, he was not one of the suspects.

The following day, Brand and Hartmann went to

a jewelry store in the Fort Lauderdale flea market. At first, the employees they interviewed were not cooperative, but when they understood that the suspects had illegally spent $321.08 at the store, the clerks opened up. Collectively, they described the black males as "thin, around thirty years of age." The pair had purchased an 18-karat gold chain and charm, the employees remembered.

In turn, the investigators contacted other businesses where purchases had been made on Steen's credit card. The results were negative in each case. The probers ended up with descriptions of the buyer, but little else.

On April 21st, a bank official called to report that the credit card had been turned in to them by a pharmacist in Lauderdale Lakes. The sleuths contacted the pharmacist at once. He told them that he'd confiscated the card 11 days earlier. He described the man who was using it as a black male, 5-foot-7 to 5-foot-8, in his late 20s, with short hair.

Detective-Sergeant Brand then questioned the security guard on duty at the time the card was confiscated. The guard's description of the suspect was slightly more detailed: black male, 5 feet 11 inches, 150 pounds, dark skin, low haircut, no facial hair, spoke with a slight accent. The guard claimed the man got into a "possibly white Chevy, 1974-75 with an unknown state tag that had a dark blue background." He further noted that a white woman was in the car. All he recalled of her was that she had "shoulder-length blonde hair."

Meanwhile, a confidential informant told the lawmen that a man and a woman, both black, had recently beaten and robbed an older white male. They found the woman on April 23rd. She told them that she'd been at the base house in the 1000 block of Northwest 4th Street in Delray Beach on Easter morning and had not been on the North Federal Highway (where some of the prostitutes hang out) for at least one month.

When the sleuths confronted her with what they knew of the beating-robbery, however, the woman confessed that she and two men, including the one mentioned by the informant, had indeed robbed one of her dates. The victim, she said, was in his car in the 900 block of Northeast 4th Street.

This was confirmed by a friend of the robbery victim's who had never reported the incident to the police. Because of this friend's active involvement with known prostitutes whom the two detectives were interviewing, they also questioned him. The man said he might have been with a prostitute—a buxom woman with frosted hair—on Easter, but he was *not* at Steen's house. To check his credibility, the sleuths had Jack Land of the Delray Beach PD give the friend a polygraph exam. It indicated "no deception" on questions referring to the homicide.

On questioning the buxom, frosty-haired prostitute he'd been with on Easter, Detective Hartmann and Brand learned that she'd been with David Steen on Good Friday, April 1st, and had sex with him at his house. The following day, she said, she went with another man and stayed with him all day Easter. She did recall going over to the victim's house sometime on Easter to borrow money. He didn't seem to be home, she told the detectives.

After leaving the prostitute, the lawmen interviewed the 49-year-old man she'd named as being her bedmate on Saturday night. He confirmed her statement, adding that he left her sometime Sun-

186

day. He knew nothing of the homicide, he insisted.

A few days later, the buxom, frosty-haired witness phoned the detectives. "Look for a redhaired hooker and a Puerto Rican," she said, giving them a couple of names.

It was several days before the sleuths could locate the Puerto Rican she'd accused. While they were searching for him, the frustrated lawmen continued to question other known prostitutes, many of whom had borrowed money from David Steen or had otherwise been helped by him and had only good to say about the man. Some of the women went by aliases; most were extremely difficult to track down. At least two were in the Palm Beach County Stockade. One of them said she'd "borrowed thirty dollars from David Steen over a month ago and hadn't seen him since." Another told the sleuths that a redhaired prostitute was involved in Steen's death. After much searching, the probers located the redhead. She, too, named the same Puerto Rican.

It was May 13th when Hartmann and Brand found the 26-year-old Puerto Rican the witnesses had accused. He was living in the Germantown Road area of Delray Beach. Because he'd been pointed out more than once, the lawmen hoped he was the perp and that an interrogation would prompt a confession, especially after he told them that he'd worked for Steen two years before and had been fired. No confession was forthcoming, however. The 26-year-old man said he'd been let go because he'd gotten a friend a job who in turn stole property from the business. He told the sleuths he could not remember where he was on Easter and had no further information in regards to the Steen homicide.

After that, the detectives interviewed several male prostitutes, plus a man in jail who'd been involved in selling drugs to known prostitutes in Delray Beach. They interviewed the husband of the secretary, as well as several of her relatives who lived with them. All said they had no knowledge of the Steen homicide. By this time, so many people were implicated in the case, the homicide team wondered how they'd ever untangle the web.

To help sort truths from untruths, Detectives Hartmann and Brand began giving polygraphs to *everybody*—close friends, family members, business manager—whether they were suspects or not. On May 19th, they tested the employee who lived on the second floor of Viking Aluminum and who had helped find the body. In reference to questions asked about the homicide, the man showed "no deception." That same day, the sleuths interviewed another former employee of the victim who willingly consented to be tested.

A few days later, when Steen's girlfriend, Janet Simon, was given a polygraph, she showed "no deception." She told Land, the polygraph operator, that she "had a gut feeling" it was her son. Later in the week, they gave a polygraph to the son, as well as the daughter who had helped find the body. Both results were negative.

The next day, Darrin Daly, the victim's young male relative, failed his polygraph examination. Deception was evident in the responses to the following questions:

(1) Did you deliberately lie when you stated you were not in David Steen's home during the morning he was killed?

(2) Are you now withholding any information on the murder of David Steen?

(3) Other than discussed, do you know the names of any other suspects who may have killed David Steen?

When Land confronted Daly about the deception, his response was that when being asked those serious questions, he felt a "pang" of fear. Daly could not explain why the polygraph exam would show deception when he stated that he had nothing to do with the homicide, and he maintained that he was not withholding any information.

"Strange," Detective Hartmann observed when given the results of Darrin Daly's test indicating deception. "Now, he *passes* the part where he's asked, 'Did you kill David Steen?' "

As the two detectives talked about it, Hartmann added, "That's the thing—it's hard to know how various people react to these questions and situations. Darrin gave us the name of one or two people who worked for Dave Steen that had problems. You don't know whether in that person's subconscious—whether they believe: 'I know this person had to do this to my relative. I know they must be responsible for it.' But they don't want to come out and say, 'That's the guy who did it.' He's suspecting, is all."

Perhaps, the lawmen decided, those suspicions had affected Daly's test. Besides, they knew the polygraph exam is not foolproof; they could not use it in court. It is only an investigative tool they tried to use. Daly, a member of AA like Steen, apparently had a good relationship with Steen.

Two days later, Darrin Daly consented to take another polygraph examination—this time given by an outside expert rather than the department's in-house operator. Again Daly showed deception on the same questions, and again he insisted he had no knowledge or involvement in the homicide.

Although the sleuths did not suspect the manager, who was a longtime friend of the victim's, they still brought him in to take his lie-detector test. He showed "no deception."

The young woman relative of Steen's who'd cooked him Easter dinner took the exam willingly, as did her husband. For her and her brother, both of whom would inherit Steen's money, the tests showed "no deception."

On June 7th, Hartmann and Brand met with Pompano Beach detectives and obtained information on a black male of about 50. The man was suspected in the homicide of an elderly white male who'd been beaten in the head with a two-by-four piece of wood on which the suspect's fingerprints had been found in blood. Detective Hartmann requested the Florida Department of Law Enforcement (FDLE) to do an off-line search on the black male. It turned out negative.

Almost a month later, Detective Hartmann learned that the black male had been arrested on the homicide charge and was incarcerated in Fort Lauderdale. It was an attack somewhat similar to the one on David Steen, except that it happened in the Pompano area. Actually, the investigators learned, there had been several such episodes down there. In this one, the suspect was alleged to have attacked his victim in a public restroom in the beach area. The murder had occurred on June 30th—three months after the Steen homicide.

Detective Hartmann and Sergeant Brand sped to

Fort Lauderdale to interview this man at the Broward County Jail. The suspect agreed to talk, but he wouldn't permit them to use a tape-recorder.

On Easter, he told the lawmen, he was "at home all day" in Pompano Beach. Until March 28th, he was working for a florist shop. The detectives were able to confirm both statements, but the suspect, who said he'd never been in Delray Beach, refused to take a polygraph exam, saying the "police are trying to frame" him and that he was innocent.

Talking it over, the detectives noted that in one of the other cases in which the Fort Lauderdale police believed the suspect to be guilty, an assailant had entered an old man's home and had beaten and killed the victim. The police were unable to prove he did it, but he was a strong suspect, nonetheless.

And, of course, the lawmen told each other, Steen's wallet was found in Pompano Beach. So, did this suspect murder Steen and steal his wallet? There were other items on the victim which had *not* been stolen. Was it a robbery or not? Perhaps the wallet had nothing to do with the murder. There was no actual evidence to link the suspect to their homicide, in any case.

Besides, the sleuths agreed, there was "such violence in the bludgeoning." Detective Hartmann summed up their impressions: "The crime was so brutal, you'd really have to say he knew his attacker. The attacker didn't want him to identify him later on. If I'm robbing you, I might just want to rob you, take your valuables, and get out. Maybe I'd have to knock you unconscious. David Steen had possibly twenty blows to the head — just the head. Few defense wounds. If it's robbery, I

191

don't believe it would be this violent."

Still concerned about Darrin Daly, the victim's young male relative who'd failed his polygraph exam, the sleuths interrogated him further. He told them that after attending church from nine to ten o'clock on Easter morning, he'd gone to a chain restaurant in nearby Boynton Beach before going home. At noon, he went to an AA meeting. When it was over, he went home, where he stayed until he was contacted about the murder. Daly was still shocked that "deception" showed on his examination.

A couple of months passed during which the detective team kept the Steen homicide in their minds. Then they interviewed a 22-year-old black male after an informant told Delray Beach Police Officer Fred Parker that the man was bragging at the Gulfstream Mall about having murdered someone named David Steen. The 22-year-old suspect denied having made the statement and refused to take a lie-detector test. Officer Parker was unable to determine if the informant was telling the truth or not, for he refused to give further information and would not identify himself.

About this time, another prostitute came forward. She said she'd talked to Dave Steen the night before Easter because she was supposed to come over on Easter Sunday to do some typing. She phoned the victim around 12:50 a.m. Someone picked up the phone, she told the detectives, and hung it up right away. She called back and there was no answer.

Detectives Hartmann and Brand were stymied. There'd been so many leads, none of which had taken them anywhere. Now, other cases needed their attention. Much as they hated to do so, they had to put the Steen homicide on hold.

A year went by with no new developments, except an occasional polygraph exam given to individuals among the scores of people already interviewed. Despite the inaction, the grisly puzzle was never far from the detectives' minds.

Then, on January 21, 1990, the sleuths learned that police in nearby Ocean Ridge had arrested a man named John Raymond Wall and charged him with three counts of aggravated battery. The Delray Beach team first heard of the arrest on the news. Part of the perpetrator's M.O. was so similar to that in the David Steen case—a bludgeon attack, and only a few miles away—that even though two years had passed since their homicide, it caught their attention at once. They wanted to know exactly what had happened.

Detective Hartmann phoned the manager who'd been running David Steen's business in 1988 to see if by some chance he knew a John Wall.

"Funny you called," the manager answered the sleuth. "I was going to call you."

"How come?" Hartmann asked.

The manager answered, "This guy, John Wall, that was arrested in Ocean Ridge, used to work for David Steen." At this point, Hartmann thought it was merely a coincidence. "He was a strange man," the manager continued. "Quiet. He never really gave a problem or anything. He just left—you know, just kinda left the job. Never really quit or anything. No problems with him when he left."

Delving further into the circumstances, the detectives found out that Wall had worked for Steen from November of '87 to January of '88, just three months prior to the homicide. Talking it over, the sleuths found it very suspicious. Still, they learned that Wall was working at the time of the Steen murder and was living in nearby Boynton Beach.

On January 24th, Detective Hartmann contacted Lieutenant James Haugh at the Ocean Ridge PD, who was the lead investigator in this case. The lieutenant told Hartmann that the 39-year-old Wall had attacked an elderly woman at the front door of her residence. When an elderly neighbor and his wife came to the victim's aid, they, too, were violently attacked by Wall. Haugh told Hartmann that the retirees were struck several times in the head with an unknown blunt instrument.

When the police arrived, the attacker was gone, Lieutenant Haugh said. "But while the police were still at the scene, Wall came walking back to the scene, carrying a hammer and screaming, 'They have to be saved; I have to save them!' At this point, Wall was read his rights and placed under arrest."

Lieutenant Haugh said it was unknown if the weapon used in the attack was the hammer or possibly a hatchet that was found at the scene. He added that at the time of the arrest, Wall was a "raving maniac." Approximately 45 minutes later, Haugh interviewed Wall. The man, now calm, asked what he was being arrested for. When the lieutenant told Wall what he had done, the suspect replied that he "didn't remember." He then asked to talk to an attorney. Haugh told Hartmann the attacks were "unprovoked and for an unknown reason."

While Wall waited in jail for his trial, the Delray sleuths probed deeply into his background. Al-

though they had no physical evidence to link Wall
to their victim, David Steen, and he was not a
"suspect" per se, there were too many similarities
for the sleuths to ignore Wall. Remembering how
he'd ranted and raved at the time of his arrest, Detectives Hartmann and Brand thought of him as a
mentally disturbed type of person.

What's more, Wall had been part of the local Alcoholics Anonymous group, so he'd undoubtedly
known Steen as a counselor as well as an employer.
In trying to contact various AA members for further information, the detectives again ran into the
problem of knowing only first names, so they had
to rely on word of mouth. The members were cooperative but passionately protective of their anonymity. Many considered their jobs at risk if the
media learned their identities.

Through interviewing a number of people who
knew John Wall—this included Darrin Daly—the
lawmen found out that the suspect would "just
kinda flip out at times." The sleuths told each
other that this was something to be considered in
an attack which was so very brutal. "Somebody in
a strange state of mind," remarked Hartmann.

The next day, when the investigators interviewed
a businessman who'd formerly roomed with Wall,
the businessman not only agreed that the suspect
was an alcoholic, but he also told them he'd heard
a rumor that Wall "killed his commanding officer
in Vietnam." The businessman could furnish no
further information.

That afternoon, the two detectives interrogated
Wall's ex-wife, who'd been divorced from him since
1986. She said that her ex had served eight and a
half years in a federal prison in Port Smith, New

Hampshire, for the military killing. She also said that Wall had been violent to her in the past, but she'd never heard him talk about the murder of Dave Steen.

The lawmen next spoke to Wall's employer, who told them that Wall was working as a delivery truck driver at the time of Steen's homicide. Wall was a "quiet worker," he added. He mentioned that Wall rode a bicycle to work from Boynton Beach when he didn't have a car. He'd been fired in May 1988 for "excessive tardiness."

On January 26th, Detective Hartmann contacted Wall's AA sponsor, who'd been listed as a reference on Wall's job application. The sponsor said Wall told him, "Everyone's going to think that I had something to do with it," referring to the murder of Dave Steen.

The lawmen also interviewed Wall's roommate during Easter 1988. The roommate said the suspect had "mental problems" and was "always paranoid." He recalled Wall telling him that people were accusing him of killing Dave Steen. He told his roommate he did not do it, that Dave was "his boss."

Still suspicious of John Wall, the detectives called a gunnery sergeant in criminal investigations from the U.S. Marine Corps to check into the suspect's records. The sergeant told them that Wall had served time.

Research revealed more. In a Vietnam barracks at a place called "Monkey Mountain," a 19-year-old John Raymond Wall had gone berserk, grabbed a rifle, and started shooting.

As the Delray detectives probed, a peculiar coincidence struck them. The date in 1969 when Wall killed his commanding officer in the Vietnam war while wounding several other people, was April 3rd—the exact day of the year as the Steen homicide 19 years later.

Did these strange similarities mean that John Wall had killed David Steen? It could be, the lawmen thought. Still, there was no physical link to the homicide. No witnesses. And they could not find out where Wall spent Easter of '88. Nonetheless, they were anxious to interrogate Wall to see if he was hiding anything.

The duo waited until he was tried and convicted for the bludgeoning case in Ocean Ridge. By the time he was imprisoned in Miami, it was 1991. Unfortunately, when some of the press found out that the Delray Beach detectives planned to interrogate John Wall, they created problems. Someone from the media contacted the suspect's attorney and told him that Detectives Hartmann and Brand were on their way to Miami for an interview.

When the pair arrived to see Wall, he and his attorney said the police had already put him "in enough trouble." He had "nothing to say" to the lawmen. He wouldn't talk to them at all. Legally, that tied their hands. They could not force the interview. On the drive home from Miami, the two detectives vented their irritation. "It's so frustrating," Hartmann noted, "because it's possible that this man committed the murder, but in this particular case there's no physical evidence to prove that. No eyewitness, no murder weapon. So, with no statement from him, it's almost . . . it *is* impossible!"

Whether John Wall murdered David Steen or not may never be known. At present, the suspect is serving a life sentence for the brutal attack on the elderly retirees in Ocean Ridge.

Of course, it could have been someone else. The lawmen never found Steen's date for that Easter evening. Maybe there was no such person. So many questions were left unanswered. There were so many suspects—Leroy Barnes, Dara Bonanno, Darrin Daly, the secretary's husband, the Latin with the nunchaku, the basher in the Broward jail, an ex-wife, their ex-husbands, a girlfriend . . . or perhaps an unknown prostitute or pimp the lawmen never knew about.

To the two Delray Beach detectives, who had spent so many hours on what they considered a "very major project," it would be a great relief to solve the homicide. Perhaps someday someone will confess. But, for now, although the David Steen file is still marked "open," there are no new clues. Unfortunately for the lawmen, the baffling murder remains an "unsolved case." If any of our readers has information that could help solve this mystery, please get in touch with Florida's Delray Beach PD immediately.

EDITOR'S NOTE:
Betty and Ed Taggart, Janet Simon, Dara Bonanno, Darrin Daly, and Leroy Barnes are not the real names of the persons so named in the foregoing story. Fictitious names have been used because there is no reason for public interest in the identities of these persons.

"LISA GIBBENS MURDER—HALF HER HEAD WAS BLOWN OFF!"

by Loretta Linser

"We have a problem," said Westchester County Police Commissioner Anthony V. Mosca, "and the problem is, we're at a dead end."

The dead end in question had its lethal beginning on a summer morning in 1990—and now, nearly two years later, police at the Westchester County Department of Public Safety remain stymied. For on that deadly date, a young woman was brutally raped and murdered. The circumstances surrounding the crime—and the identity of the perpetrator—remain murky.

As a result, explained Commissioner Mosca, "Right now I want to reach out through any [available medium]"—in this case, *Official Detective*—"and hopefully somebody can come up with something, anything. . . ."

Commissioner Mosca is all too well acquainted with violent crime. He spent 20 years with the NYPD before serving as a police commissioner, first for the town of Mount Vernon for three and a half years, then Westchester County for the past eight. But even the commissioner, with all his years on New York's embattled streets, regards this case as particularly gruesome — and uniquely perplexing.

At about 8:40 a.m. on Tuesday, July 17, 1990, a man was riding his bicycle along a path near a four-building apartment complex in the quiet residential community of Tuckahoe. The cluster of multiple-story buildings, flanked by parkland adjacent to the Bronx River Parkway on one side and by railroad tracks on the other, is somewhat isolated. The dirt footpath along which the man was piloting his bike was traversed frequently by apartment dwellers en route to the railroad station, where commuter trains would hustle them off to jobs in Manhattan and in neighboring towns.

About 30 feet away from the apartment complex, the cyclist was forced to dismount his bike so that he could clear away some branches that lay across the path, impeding his progress. As he did so, he glanced into the woods that lined the path. What he saw there prompted a hurried and horrified call to the Tuckahoe Police Department.

At 9:20 a.m., minutes after the cyclist's frantic phone call, Tuckahoe police led by Detective-Sergeant Hank Bellis arrived at the secluded apartment complex. In the woods, about 20 feet off the footpath and 50 feet from the buildings, lay the body of a woman who looked to be in her early to mid-20s. A medical examiner would subsequently determine that her head had been shattered by a blast from a shotgun. A substantial part of her skull was blown away. The skirt of the blue print dress she was wearing had apparently been smoothed back down after her assailant had torn her pantyhose from her body and scattered her high-heeled shoes into the woods. Police found the victim's house keys at the scene, but no handbag or other personal belongings.

Realizing at once that the rape-murder had occurred on county property, the Tuckahoe police were quick to call in Westchester County lawmen. Less than 10 minutes later, a county patrol supervisor and patrol officers arrived to secure the crime scene while they waited for personnel from the General Investigations Unit.

At 9:40 a.m., a quartet of lawmen from General Investigations arrived to finish securing the murder scene and initiate the gathering of evidence. Detectives Russell Lowenstein, Jerry Schiavo, Paul Grutzner, and Jeffrey Hunt were soon joined by other investigators who would assist in canvassing the area and interviewing potential witnesses.

About an hour later, the crime scene van drove up, bringing a coterie of forensic experts who were prepared to process and photograph the site and to collect evidence. Among those arriving at this time were Dr. Ashar, the medical examiner; Officers William Mackey and Roger Piccirilli from the Identification Unit; and Ballistics Technician Frank Nicilosi.

By this time, a number of tenants who lived in the apartment complex, their curiosity piqued by the police activity that was virtually on their doorstep, had gathered around the crime scene. One of those present, however, was someone whose interest was inspired not by any morbid inclination, but by an ever-mounting fear. Earlier that morning, this tenant had received a phone call from a medical clinic in the nearby town of Hartsdale. It seemed that the man's relative, Lisa Gibbens, an employee at the clinic, had failed to show up for work that day. Aware that the relative lived just two buildings away from Lisa, her employer thought that perhaps he would know whether anything was wrong.

Something was indeed wrong—tragically wrong. For when he went downstairs to investigate the commotion, the relative discovered that the lifeless body left in the woods belonged to 25-year-old Lisa Gibbens.

As lawmen continued to gather evidence and began canvassing the buildings, the victim's body was transported to the Westchester County Labs in Valhalla, New York, for autopsy. As Dr. Ashar conducted the postmortem examination, it became clear that the procedure would yield but few physical clues. Except for the fatal gunshot wound to the victim's head, the only visible injuries were some abrasions on the knees, which were probably sustained when the victim was knocked down or dragged along the dirt footpath. The presence of semen confirmed that the victim had been raped, but it was unclear whether the sexual assault had been committed before or after the shooting. Some blood was scraped from beneath one of the victim's fingernails, but it could not be typed. Likewise, some foreign hairs removed from the body defied a conclusive determination of their origin.

Dr. Ashar fixed the time of death as no earlier than six o'clock that morning, and probably closer to eight o'clock—in other words, not long before the body was discovered.

The investigators who were continuing the probe at the crime scene weren't having much luck, either.

The condition of the wooded area where Lisa Gibbens' body was found indicated that she had put up a fight, but the struggle appeared to have been neither severe nor sustained. This finding did, however, serve to rule out the possibility that the victim had been killed elsewhere, then dumped in the woods.

Sleuths learned that Lisa had not carried a purse, just a billfold-type wallet and her house keys. Her keys were found, but her wallet was missing. Nonetheless, the investigators were skeptical that robbery had been the killer's primary motive. Muggers don't customarily tote along a shotgun when setting out to rob an unwary pedestrian—particularly when the locale is a densely populated apartment complex with numerous windows overlooking the path leading to the train station.

The sexual assault on the victim also suggested that the theft of her wallet may have been little more than an afterthought. If robbery had been foremost in his mind, the assailant would probably have fled the scene as soon as Lisa relinquished her money. Raping the victim would require additional time, during which the perp's chances of getting caught—especially considering that the crime took place near a much used path during the morning rush hour—would be greatly increased.

Another early speculation among lawmen, that the slaying may have been a contract hit or motivated by revenge, seemed implausible as well. Both logic and prior investigative experience dictated that a contract killer, having gunned down his target, would have left the scene immediately. As in the robbery scenario, it seemed unlikely that the perpetrator would diminish his escape time by engaging in a sexual assault.

But at this point in the investigation, any theory as to who had killed Lisa Gibbens, and why, could only be regarded as premature. The detectives assigned to the case still had to undertake the arduous task of canvassing the area, interviewing the complex's many residents—as well as the victim's family and known associates—and waiting to see what information forensic and ballistic analysis would provide.

The sleuths learned that Lisa Gibbens and her boyfriend had moved into the apartment complex about a year and a half previously. Conversations with neighbors indicated that the couple had stayed pretty much to themselves. Consequently, no one in their building was able to provide much insight into their lifestyle, beyond the observation that Lisa and her beau had not been known to throw wild parties, engage in loud arguments, or otherwise cause any disruption that the other tenants would notice—and that would indicate some sort of domestic problem that could have erupted into violence.

Inquiries into what the complex's occupants may have seen or heard on that blood-spattered summer morning were equally unproductive. Strangely enough, no one reported having witnessed anything unusual in the three-hour time frame—from approximately 6:00 to 9:00 a.m.—during which Lisa Gibbens was murdered. Not one of those who had walked along the footpath that day had seen anyone who looked or behaved suspiciously. Except for one person who had a vague recollection of "hearing something," not one of the many tenants preparing to start another ordinary workday heard anything extraordinary going on outside.

Not one resident in the four-building complex on Consulate Drive could provide any leads that would bring lawmen any closer to determining who was responsible for the ambush and lethal assault on the pretty young clerical worker.

But Detective Russell Lowenstein and his colleagues still had plenty of investigative ground to cover. True, their preliminary canvass had failed to produce an eyewitness to the slaying; however, they had not yet spoken with the victim's boyfriend, her family, or her friends and co-workers. Perhaps those interviews would give the detectives from the General Investigations Unit something to go on.

It seemed that every scrap of information furnished to the lawmen, rather than giving them answers, was merely generating more questions. This would, as the investigation progressed, become a familiar — and frustrating — theme.

The relative who identified Lisa's body told police that he had talked to her the previous Sunday afternoon. Apparently nothing was amiss at that time, as Lisa did not hint at any problems that might have precipitated the Tuesday-morning slaying. There was no indication that someone was following or otherwise harassing her, or that there was someone in her life whom she feared.

Police also ruled out two other factors that frequently constitute a motive for murder: money and drugs. Nothing in Lisa's background suggested that she was having financial difficulties or that she was in debt to some unsavory creditor. Likewise, they found no evidence that Lisa had had any involvement in the use or sale of drugs.

A talk with Lisa's co-workers at the medical clinic proved more enlightening. Apparently, Lisa's relationship with her live-in boyfriend had been somewhat less than idyllic for the past six months, and she had told her workmates that she was planning to break it off. Lisa had also disclosed that there was a new man in her life, sleuths were told.

Following up on these intriguing new developments, the investigators spoke to people at the local nightspot where Lisa and her new romantic interest had met. It was subsequently confirmed that Lisa had begun seeing this man about two weeks earlier. Was it possible, lawmen wondered, that Lisa's live-in boyfriend had learned of her involvement with the other man and, in a jealous rage, exacted his revenge for what he perceived as her infidelity? Detectives Lowenstein and Schiavo were determined to get an answer to that question as soon as the boyfriend arrived home.

At approximately 6:00 p.m. on the day of the murder, Lisa's boyfriend got home from work and was promptly intercepted by the two detectives. In order to gauge his initial reaction, he had not been notified about Lisa's murder earlier in the day.

If the sleuths believed an arrest to be imminent, they were in for another disappointment. Lisa's boyfriend acknowledged that their relationship had been troubled of late and that he suspected she had been seeing another man. However, he also told them that he had left for work that morning between 6:00 and 6:30; he said Lisa was still in bed at that time. He arrived at his office around 7:00 to 7:10 a.m. His co-workers verified that he had come to work at that time and had not left the office for any extended period.

If the victim's time of death, as established by the medical examiner, was indeed no earlier than 6:00 a.m., Lisa's boyfriend would have had only a narrow "window of opportunity" in which to commit the crime and still get to his office by seven o'clock.

As the sleuths digested this information, they recognized that other elements of the crime also pointed away from Lisa's boyfriend as a prime suspect.

Admittedly, the man had a motive; he'd confirmed that over the weekend Lisa had told him she wished to terminate their relationship. Now, just a few days later, she was dead. A macabre coincidence?

Perhaps, the lawmen reasoned. The chronology was suspicious, but the M.O. didn't make sense. Even if the proposed breakup had propelled him into a murderous frenzy, sleuths reasoned, why would Lisa's boyfriend wait for her to walk out of the building, then gun her down in broad daylight? He did, after all, live with the victim; if he wanted to kill her, there were less risky ways of accomplishing that malign goal than to opt for a public assassination.

The detectives working the case were not yet prepared to rule out Lisa's boyfriend as a suspect—not entirely. But it was apparent that other avenues of investigation would have to be explored.

It was time for the sleuths to talk with the other man who had figured in Lisa Gibbens' life—and who could have engineered its abrupt and brutal end.

Lisa's new beau didn't have as solid an alibi as her live-in lover. When police spoke with him around 10:00 p.m. that night, he claimed to have been in a distant part of the county at the time of the murder. The detectives noted, however, that his work schedule was considerably more flexible than Lisa's boyfriend's. He could have committed the crime and then gone to work. Alternately, he could have first gone to work, slipped away long enough to complete the grisly task, and then returned to his job. Both of these theories were flawed—as with Lisa's live-in boyfriend, the "window of opportunity" was small— but neither was inconceivable.

On the other hand, neither theory supplied one crucial ingredient that continued to evade the investigators: a motive. Why would Lisa's new boyfriend want her dead? They had only begun seeing each other about two weeks earlier, and there was nothing to indicate that any dispute or rancor had arisen in this short time. Furthermore, witnesses had confirmed that Lisa was planning to break up with her current boyfriend; consequently, it seemed both illogical and implausible that her new lover would be jealous.

No amount of speculation has yielded a satisfactory answer to this question—and until it does, the investigative team's second most promising suspect must be regarded as just another witness.

Faced with these discouraging developments, the detectives continued their probe with even greater diligence. The crime scene, the victim's apartment, and other likely locales were laboriously searched for physical evidence. More than 200 witnesses were questioned. Calls from tipsters were painstakingly documented and followed up.

In addition, the case was entered into VICAP and into New York City's Ballistics and Sex Crimes computers. The rationale was that the Lisa Gibbens slaying might not have been her killer's only such crime; if so, it was possible that the computer network would reveal similarities between her murder and other seemingly unrelated homicides, thus generating valuable new leads.

The upshot, thus far, of this exhaustive—and exhausting—effort? No additional physical evidence. No promising new leads. And, perhaps most maddening of all, still no clue as to what the killer's true objective might have been in killing Lisa.

The murder of Lisa M. Gibbens continues to defy any unequivocal categorization. As Commissioner Mosca recently remarked, "It's difficult to tell if it was a robbery, if it was a rape, or if it was a deliberate homicide." Obviously, the crime encompassed all of these elements—but what was the killer's primary impetus? The use of a shotgun suggests premeditation; the rape, impulse. The time and location would necessitate expediency, once again indicating premeditated murder—and once again confounded by the extra time taken for the commission of the sexual assault. And the stolen wallet—an additional motive, an afterthought, or just a red herring? Or maybe the killer was trying to throw police off track?

Answers to these questions might very well provide the break that Westchester County lawmen need to solve this tragic and enigmatic case, the first murder the little commuter town of Tuckahoe has seen in 10 years. They're convinced that someone out there is holding a vital piece of the puzzle—and, as one high-ranking officer phrased it, "Until we find a piece that tells us where to point," the cold-hearted killer who ruthlessly extinguished an innocent young life will continue to go unpunished.

Readers of who have any information regarding the Lisa Gibbens homicide are urged to contact Detective Russell Lowenstein of the General Investigations Unit at (914) 741-4267. All calls will be kept confidential.

"WHO LACED THE BRUNETTE'S TYLENOL WITH CYANIDE?"

by Bud Ampolsk

It might have been a spot produced by a top ad agency. It had all of the components of a typical patent pain killer promo seen innumerable times on countless American television sets.

The woman was young, beautiful, and obviously in glowing good health. But at this moment, her face was slightly contorted by the nagging pain shooting through her body. She was suffering from the most common of life's little upsets.

Not to worry. She had already opened the medicine cabinet. Even now she was reaching for the pristine white plastic container with its red label and white and yellow trade name emblazoned in large letters. In a moment would come the blessed relief she sought, and a happy smile would climax the 30-second story.

Tragically, this was no copywriter's effort. Nor would it end in 30 seconds. This was real life — and death — and at this writing, more than five years later, there is no end in sight to the mysterious saga.

It was just after 1:00 a.m. on Saturday, February 8, 1986, when 23-year-old Diane Elsroth opened the medicine package in the home of Yonkers, New York, friends whom she was visiting for the weekend. She had been given the Tylenol capsules by her host. Extracting one from its container, Diane had every reason to believe that the combination of the analgesic and a good night's rest would soon cure the pain that gripped her. After all, a common little upset was no reason for major concern.

Without further thought, Diane swallowed the proprietary medicine and prepared for bed.

It was some 12 hours later when the young woman's host, a friend Diane had met when they were students at C.W. Post College, looked in on her to see how she was faring.

It was then that he was confronted by the stunning horror of what had occurred. It was shown in the terrible stillness with which Diane Elsroth's body lay on the bed. Her panic-stricken host and his parents, with whom he shared the Yonkers home, became immediately aware that for some reason beyond their comprehension their weekend guest was not breathing.

An immediate call was placed to police and medical units of the Westchester community. As is the usual procedure in the unattended death of a person with no apparent medical history, the Westchester County Medical Examiner's Office took over responsibility for searching out the whys and wherefores of the mysterious demise of the Peekskill, New York, woman. On Sunday, February 9th, a routine autopsy was carried out in the medical examiner's facilities. However, no cause of death could be determined at that time.

Perhaps the cause of Diane Elsroth's death

would have remained unestablished had it not been for the expertise of a toxicologist who served as a consultant to the medical examiner's staff.

It was this scientist, working with a small container of tissue excised from the victim's body, who detected the faint odor of bitter almonds, a smell often associated with cyanide.

Alerted to the fact that one of the most deadly poisons known to man might have been ingested by the lovely young real estate secretary, staff investigators undertook an exhaustive study of the contents of Diane Elsroth's stomach. They also checked samples of her blood.

According to Millard Hyland, the county medical examiner, the examination showed that Diane Elsroth had taken two Tylenol capsules, one containing the poison and "perhaps one" with just acetaminophen, the active ingredient of Tylenol.

Officials had also tested the other capsules in the 24-capsule bottle and had discovered that three of them contained that cyanide compound. The mixture was said to have been 60 percent potassium cyanide and 40 percent inert materials, including silver and iron.

At a press conference in which he shared the lectern with Dr. Hyland, the Westchester County executive revealed that Diane Elsroth's host had opened a brand new Tylenol bottle, which was "apparently sealed," and had given the young woman two capsules. The bottle had been purchased two weeks before. However, police were keeping a tight lid on information concerning who the purchaser had been.

Reporters also were told that on the fatal night,

213

four persons had been in the Yonkers home. In addition to the young host and Elsroth, the young man's father and mother had also been present.

The older woman had been much luckier than her guest. When she had learned of Elsroth's death, according to detectives who were now briefing the press, the woman had become so distraught that she, herself, had taken a capsule from the tainted container. Fortunately, that capsule had not been contaminated with the lethal dosage. The host's mother therefore suffered no ill effects.

Experts in the packaging field were quick to point out that the makers of the popular over-the-counter drug product had made every effort to protect the public from just such a maniacal poisoning as that which had been suffered by Diane Elsroth. They said that the steps taken had far exceeded federal regulations governing such matters.

The outer carton was sealed with what the trade called a "hotmelt" adhesive. The cardboard was thin gauge so that the flaps, sealed with the adhesive, could not easily be opened without ripping the box.

Inside the carton, the cap was sealed to the bottle with a plastic band that was "heat shrunk" for a tight fit so that it had to be broken to open the bottle. Underneath the cap, an aluminum foil seal was laminated to the lip of the container.

Despite the outstanding precautions taken by the manufacturer, one packaging expert commented, "Suffice it to say, there is no package on the market today that cannot be compromised if an individual has the time and the will."

Even with the reassurance of police and private

experts, the new case of murder by poisoned over-the-counter medicine brought back harrowing memories of a serial killer responsible for seven homicides in the cyanide poisoning of Tylenol capsules four years before. The 1982 series of murders had taken place in Chicago, and the perp or perps remained at large. This, despite the valiant efforts of 35 members of federal and local law forces who had been assigned full time to the probe of the Illinois slayings.

For their part, Yonkers, Westchester, and federal lawmen who were now probing the Diane Elsroth case were following the best possible techniques in working on seemingly inexplicable murders.

They had started out with a thorough canvass of family members, friends, and associates of the dead woman to eliminate them from suspicion.

The more the lawmen checked into her background, the more convinced the investigators became that Diane Elsroth was the type of person who had been universally loved and respected.

Photographs taken of Elsroth when she was a member of the cheerleaders' team at Peekskill High School showed a happy and attractive youngster filled with self-confidence and the love of being alive.

Typical comments about her from those attending a memorial service for her attested to Diane Elsroth's popularity.

A close relative said, "She was such a nice girl. She was always joking. She was the kind of girl who always wanted to help, to bring us tea and crackers, things like that."

A young man who had known Diane well commented, "She was dynamite. She was my sister's best friend. They were sisters by choice. What did she do to deserve to die so young?"

A girl who had been Diane Elsroth's classmate and close friend stated, "She was a lovely, popular girl. That's how I'll always remember her."

A teacher who had had Diane Elsroth as a social studies student remembered, "She was one of our better students, the kind of student a teacher likes to have."

The flood of positive remembrances of the dead woman caused Yonkers Deputy Police Chief Owen McClain to report, "There doesn't seem to be any reason for this death. We don't believe she had any enemies." The deputy chief added that he had been in touch with Chicago police checking out the seven poisoned capsule slayings that had taken place there in 1982. "We have received some information there which might prove helpful," he added.

But McClain expressed doubts about the possibility of a link between Diane Elsroth's slaying and those of four years before. He emphasized, "I don't think it's a national thing. I believe it's an isolated case."

When asked whether there had been any recent reports of Tylenol having been stolen from Westchester stores, as had been the case in the Chicago capsule tamperings, McClain replied, "We have no information about any.

"We don't intend to start a national scare; we don't believe the nation's smothered with tainted Tylenol."

Bruce Bendish, chief of the homicide squad of the Westchester County District Attorney's Office, noted that the 10 local detectives, county police officers and federal agents assigned to the poisoning mystery were still sorting out basic details concerning the crime.

"We have to find out if the tampering occurred pre-selling or post-selling before we decide our next step.

"We have no reason to believe Ms. Elsroth was a target, particularly." However, the homicide specialist added, "But while there are no suspects, we are not ruling anybody out."

Other police sources revealed that they were receiving the full cooperation of everybody who in any way had been connected with Elsroth during her lifetime.

One theory that had been checked out and soon abandoned concerned the possibility that the capsules were laced with cyanide at the manufacturing level. Federal officials held that it was very unlikely that any lethal adulteration had taken place in sites where Tylenol had been made or stored before being shipped to stores.

A Federal Food and Drug Administration (FDA) spokesman noted, "Everyone involved believes this is a local situation."

He said federal officials based this opinion on two main elements. First, the spokesman pointed out, the bottle that contained the capsule which caused Elsroth's death was part of a lot of 200,000 bottles manufactured in May 1985. Second, the lot had been shipped in August of that year and because of the popularity of that particular pain killer, it was likely that most of the lot's units had been sold within a month's time.

Thus, the spokesman reasoned, if other bottles in the shipment had been tainted, officials probably would have known about it long before the Elsroth death.

A spokesman for MacNeil Consumer Products, which produces Tylenol, reported that the company was doing everything possible to aid the probe. It was checking with its distributors to track down bottles in the lot, marked ADF-916. So far, only a few had been found.

It was learned that the three cyanide-impregnated capsules, one of which had taken the life of Diane Elsroth, had been purchased in a Bronxville supermarket.

Lending weight to the contention that the capsules had not been tampered with during production was expert opinion by company executives.

Said one highly placed company officer, "We have a conviction that none of the poison was put in the capsules by a worker at the plant." He added that this conviction was based on the knowledge that while a certain amount of cyanide was kept at the plant "for testing and quality control of our products," cyanide breaks down the gelatin capsules with which the medicine is inserted. The deterioration of the adulterated tablets becomes evident "in less than a month."

A financial analyst for a top investment firm supported the position of the manufacturing executives. He commented, "Right now the company is treating it as an isolated incident, and until it's determined exactly how the woman died, I don't think one should jump to the conclusion that the capsule was poisoned at the retail level. It's clear

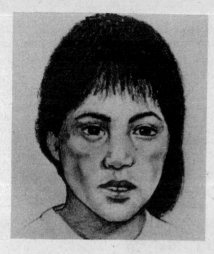

Sketch resembling "Baby Hope," the little girl police found dead in an ice cooler.

The thirty-quart ice cooler in which "Baby Hope" was discovered.

"Pixie" Grimore, found strangled to death with a clothesline.

Krissie Povolish disappeared on July 25, 1987 and was found murdered three days later.

Teresa Butler, missing and presumed dead.

Eunice Karr, 74, was strangled to death in her own home.

Geneva and Clarence Roberts are thought to have burned alive under mysterious circumstances.

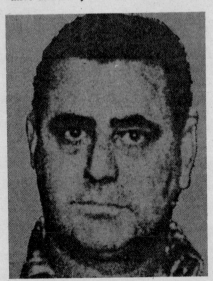

Russell Keith Dardeen, his wife, Ruby Elaine, and their three-year old son, Peter Sean in happier times.

Edward Andrassy and
Florence Polilo, victims
of Cleveland's Mad
Butcher.

Playboy Bunny Eve Stratford was brutally tortured before her throat was cut.

Lynda Farrow was found in a pool of blood by her young daughters.

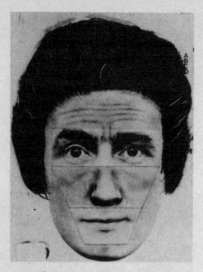

Photofit composite of the man thought to have killed Stratford and Farrow.

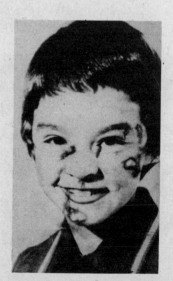

Genette Tate, 13, missing and presumed dead.

Maureen Smith, a New York City teacher, was murdered and found in the trunk of her own car.

Diane Elsroth, 23, died after taking two Tylenol capsules poisoned with cyanide.

David Steen, victim of Florida's Easter Sunday Killer.

David Steen's home in Delray Beach, Florida.

John Raymond Wall, an employee of David Steen.

Lisa Gibbens was raped and murdered near her Tuckahoe, New York apartment.

William Desmond Taylor, Hollywood director, found murdered in his mansion.

hat the company is indicating that it doesn't antic-
pate a major full-blown recall, and I think that's
he big difference."

The analyst also cited steps likely to be taken in
he wake of the Elsroth killing, which he thought
would be less drastic than the massive nationwide
recall launched in the wake of the seven 1982
murder-by-poisoning cases.

However, on the day following these pronounce-
ments, there was a development that increased officials' fears of possible peril to others. This came
when it was reported that two more bottles of
cyanide-laced Tylenol capsules had been found in
Westchester County on Thursday, February 13th.

The discoveries had been made in laboratories,
where the count of capsules screened had reached
the 100,000 mark.

Coming just five days after Diane Elsroth's
death, the fact that two more tainted bottles had
surfaced prompted FDA officials to widen their
search for the poisoned medicine.

The first contaminated bottle found on February
13th contained five spiked pills. It had been taken
from a variety store on Pondfield Road, just two
blocks from the store where the tainted bottle that
led to Diane Elsroth's death had been purchased.

The chemical content in the spiked capsules from
the Pondfield Road store was exactly the same as it
was in the samples taken from the tainted bottle
that killed Diane Elsroth. The percentage of cyanide among the alien substances again stood at
60%.

What did not check out was the lot number of
the Pondfield Road bottle. This was AHA-010, in-

dicating that the lot had been manufactured and
shipped from a plant in Puerto Rico rather than
from the lot in the Elsroth case, which had been
coded ADF-916 and had originated in a Pennsylvania plant.

The second recovery of poisoned capsules to occur on February 13th, according to the FDA commissioner, was in a bottle of regular-strength
Tylenol taken from a supermarket in Shrub Oak,
New York, some 30 miles from Bronxville. The lot
number on this bottle was AJR-358. According to
the government officials, the amount of cyanide
found in the single capsule was minute.

Perhaps the most puzzling aspect of the find by
the FDA was the fact that both contaminated bottles and their packages showed no outward signs of
tampering. It was reported that all glued flaps were
intact and apparently the security seals were untouched.

So what had been only a countywide sales ban
on the suspect product now became statewide.

New York State Governor Mario Cuomo ordered
an embargo on all Tylenol capsules, saying, "I urge
every resident of the state, and especially all residents of Westchester County and the New York
metropolitan area, to refrain from using Tylenol
capsules already in their possession."

The governor's action was quickly followed by a
statement from the chairman of MacNeil. He said
that the firm had issued a nationwide alert on the
Extra-Strength capsules "in the interests of giving
the public the widest protection." However, there
was no immediate word of warning from this
source on the regular-strength capsules.

The State Health Commissioner cautioned that the earlier reports saying the Elsroth death was an isolated tragedy might have been premature.

A roller-coaster of emotions triggered by the possibility that a possible crazed killer was once again on the loose, not caring who died as long as his perverted needs could be satisfied by the act of introducing lethal doses of cyanide into the widely distributed over-the-counter preparation.

At the back of the minds of lawmen and the public alike was the chilling thought that whoever was responsible for the seven 1982 Chicago cyanide killings was still at large. Was it possible that after a four-year hiatus, the perp or perps had once again become active and had merely moved their operation from Chicago to the metropolitan New York area?

The question caused ever more intensive efforts from personnel at the FDA's headquarters office in the nation's capital.

After stepped-up lab testing, the FDA experts had satisfied themselves that they had ruled out any connection between the Yonkers slaying of the pretty young secretary and the deaths in Chicago.

Reasoned the spokesman for the federal agency, an analysis of the Elsroth case showed that the cyanide in the capsules had not come from the plant where the Tylenol capsules had been manufactured.

He added, "The chemical profile is not the same as the profile of the substance in the Chicago poisonings, nor is it similar to anything that is in the area of the McNeil plant in Fort Washington, Pennsylvania."

The spokesman said the federal agency's "negative findings, added to a number of others" suggested there "was not a broad problem" with tainted Tylenol elsewhere or "any manufacturing problems" with the drug. The government official contended his agency's chemical analysis of two capsules contained to "confirm that this [the Elsroth murder] was an individual, isolated crime."

Meanwhile, in Yonkers, the intensive search for the poisoning killer continued. Deputy Police Chief McClain reiterated his department's position that nothing conclusively indicated that Diane Elsroth was the specific target of the killer. But they were not ruling anything out.

"We're obviously exploring the relationship between anyone who was involved with either of the two families [Diane's, or the family she had been visiting on the weekend of her death]," McClain said.

McClain also added that police were checking local suppliers of potassium cyanide. The white or off-white powder is used in the electroplating of jewelry, computer components, and other products. "I've been led to believe it can be bought quite easily," he added.

Other county officials continued to feel that Diane Elsroth's death had been the result of her being in the wrong place at the wrong time. They stressed that they were faced with the most difficult and frustrating of all cases to be handled by dedicated crime fighters—the senseless and depraved random slaying in which whoever happens to get in the way becomes the murderer's target.

Said one detective, "There's nothing tougher than a situation where there is no logical relationship between the perp and the victim. That's when you get into the 'needle and haystack' mode. That's when you begin asking yourself the same damned questions that those who mourn for a dead young woman who had everything to live for ask: 'Why her?' " The veteran cop added, "You can find yourself climbing walls just trying to make some sort of sense out of a crime which has no apparent sense nor motive."

Such is the feeling of many who over the course of the last five years have taken part in the exhaustive and exhausting search for an explanation of why a vibrantly healthy and beautiful young woman, one with hundreds of friends and admirers and no enemies, swallowed two capsules because of a minor complaint and died within minutes.

There is the possibility that the person who added a concoction of 60-percent potassium cyanide to the contents of three over-the-counter painreliever capsules had some insane need to get even with the manufacturer of the product because of his fancied grievances. Certainly, if he did, he created enough havoc to satisfy himself.

Perhaps, despite all the evidence to the contrary, somebody had a personal motive for poisoning Diane Elsroth. Even now, that possibility can't be totally ruled out.

There is also the possibility that the maniac who had taken the lives of seven Chicago people, not caring who they were or what grief their deaths would cause, had somehow struck again. Had that maniac picked a new venue, it was one that resembled Chicago and its environs. He could have singled out a suburb close to the metropolitan area where his comings and goings would cause little concern and no suspicion.

Or it might have been a copycat lunatic who had been inspired by the fact that the Chicago cyanide killer was still at large some four years since he had struck. Such a person might have been driven by his own twisted ideas of the ego-building potential of keeping at bay the nation's top law enforcement agencies.

Many a random serial killer has disappeared for a time only to show up and start his terrible work once more at some future date.

All this is conjecture, however. All that can be said with a degree of certainty is that the search for the person who laced a helpful home remedy with a deadly concoction of potassium cyanide and other chemical substances goes on.

Armed with the knowledge that there is no statute of limitations on murder, lawmen keep the events of February 9, 1986, firmly in mind. They still live in the hope that some day, something will break and all the pieces of the haunting puzzle will be fitted into place. Until such an event takes place, they know there can be no rest.

The fading picture of lovely, 23-year-old Diane Elsroth is too much before them. They recall what it was like at the memorial services held on a cold winter day in 1986, where the tears of those who loved Diane added to the sense of pain.

They recognize that had she been given a better break, she would now be 28 years old. Perhaps she would be the mother of young children. Perhaps she would now be a successful real estate executive. Who can say for sure?

But there is one thing all the law personnel who worked on her murder agree upon. Whoever denied Diane Elsroth's future should be made to pay for what was done to her!

"DOES A SEX MONSTER PROWL FOR LITTLE GIRLS?"

by Richard Walton

Genette would have been 23 years old this fall, perhaps herself the mother of a young daughter. She was a beautiful and gentle child, and certainly she would have grown up into a remarkably attractive woman.

And that, apart from a few photographs and mementoes, is all her parents have to remember her today—poignant memories of her too-short childhood and dreams of a future that never came, because gentle Genette Tate is either dead, a victim of murder, or, if not, then she is a prisoner somewhere in a living hell from which death would be a release.

Many theories have been advanced over the last 10 years since the 13-year-old girl vanished into thin air one sunny afternoon in a tranquil picture-postcard English village.

They ranged from the improbable theory of a ransom kidnapping, to her having been snatched up and transported to outer space by a UFO which a surprising number of local people reckon they saw hovering in the area at the time.

The fact remains—Genette vanished and the police are no nearer to a solution to the mystery than they were when it all began on Saturday, August 19, 1978, in the Devonshire village of Aylesbeare, eight miles east of the ancient city of Exeter.

226

It's a land of strong, silent men, where normally everyone knows everything about his neighbor, and strangers, though always welcome, are shrewdly watched.

Which tends to make the child's disappearance all the more of a mystery . . .

It was just another day in the lives of the Tate family, well-respected local folk on a working-class income. At 2:00 p.m., Genette took a blue bicycle from the shed at home in the Barton Farm Cottage and pushed it along the garden path, ready to begin her routine delivery round with the evening newspapers.

She wheeled her bike through the gate, closed it behind her to keep stray dogs and cats out of the garden, then rode off toward the nearby village center.

She passed several local people on the way, waving to them with a cheery "Hi!" before turning into Within Lane, flanked by hedgerows profuse with wild scented summer flowers and the tendrils of pink and yellow honeysuckle.

She reached the junction with a smaller lane running from neighboring villages of White Cross to Farringdon, and only a few yards from the main A3052 motorway which carries traffic from Exeter to the coastal resort of Aidmouth.

At that time of year, holidaymakers seeking sunshine and sandy beaches would be funneling along the highway at frequent intervals. It would be unlikely for one vehicle to suddenly veer off the highway to stop and pick someone up without being seen by other motorists. Indeed, stopping incautiously on that highway could have caused a traffic accident.

Genette certainly had to cross it on her daily route and had been repeatedly briefed by her parents on the need for care in doing so. She frequently had to wait for a gap in traffic before cycling to the other side, and a 50-yard onward journey to the White House Inn, where the newsboys and girls picked up their papers from a wholesaler's vehicle parked there.

On August 19th, she was a little early because she wished to pick up the balance of money owed by customers she had missed on her round the day before.

She was standing by her bicycle when the delivery van arrived. The driver passed her a bundle of 70 newspapers and he saw what she did with it.

The parcel was too big for the front carrier on her bike, so she cut the binding cord with her pocketknife, which was carried hooked onto her cycle frame, then loaded the papers into another carrier above the rear mudguard.

The leather strap and buckle attached to this carrier was too short to fasten, so she secured the papers to the carrier with the cord she had cut earlier. Then she rode off.

Her delivery route lay along the principal road through the village, the clear view of everyone living there, mainly in bungalow-type houses.

This task occupied her until 3:00 p.m. Then she reentered Within Lane to make deliveries to bungalows and picturesque country cottages there, some with rambling long front gardens, on the right-hand side of the lane.

By the time she reached a hill in Within Lane, she had made 14 drops. The incline was too steep for her to ride up, so she dismounted and pushed the bicycle ahead of her.

While doing this, she passed two school friends. They strolled up the incline with her, a black car passing them in the direction of Aylesbeare village as they did.

As Within Lane flattened out again after the crest of the incline, Genette remounted her cycle, waved cheerily to her friends, and rode off around the bend ahead.

The time, according to one of the two girl friends, was just before 3:30 p.m.

As the two friends strolled on, chatting about school life, they reached the same bend a few moments later.

To their shocked surprise, halfway around that bend they saw Genette's blue cycle on its side in the middle of the road, newspapers scattered around and no sign of the girl.

Was it a mock accident, some kind of joke Genette was playing on them? This was the first reaction of her friends but they instantly dismissed it. Genette would not joke about such things or go to all the trouble of scattering marked newspapers on the highway out of their delivery order.

Hesitantly, then more urgently, they called out her name, but they got no response. They looked behind the thick hedge, scaled a fence to scan adjoining fields, and again repeatedly called her name, but the humming of insects and a distant trill of birdsong broke through the sweltering silence.

Their second thought was that Genette had been the victim of a hit-and-run accident, but the mysterious black car which had passed them in the direction of the village was long gone before Genette cycled on out of view. If it had stopped beyond the bend and started up again, they had certainly not heard the sound of its engine accelerating in hurried departure.

Nor had they heard the sound of a motor coming toward them from the opposite direction which might have struck down Genette on the hidden bend.

If one had done so, and after knocking Genette down had then reversed rapidly, turned round and driven her to a hospital, the driver would hardly have left the cycle lying in the lane as a further traffic hazard.

The girls, pondering the possibilities, were in a quandary. To prevent another vehicle hitting the bike, one of them decided to ride it back to Genette's home to see if she had possibly arrived there by another means of transportation.

So, they gathered up the strewn newspapers, lashed them back onto the damaged cycle, and one of them rode off on it.

The other girl, still searching the lane in wonderment, soon met some other school friends who joined in the hunt with her. They, too, found nothing. They had seen nothing of the missing girl in their approach from the village along the tranquil little lane.

Genette's father and stepmother were equally mystified. Genette, a well-balanced, naturally happy child, had no reason in the world to run away from home. All her personal possessions were still in her room, for that matter.

The pocket money she always carried with her, and the cash collected from the customers on her newspaper round, was still intact in a purse inside the front carrier of the cycle. Other money she was saving for a planned school holiday on the Continent was still in her bedroom.

The police were immediately called in. As they summoned their specialists to comb the village and

230

surrounding areas, the parents and the villagers launched their own hunt over territory they intimately knew across ditches, hedgerows, field and stream.

Nothing was found as the sultry autumn evening descended and the sun slowly sank into the lush meadows. As far as the inhabitants of that Devonian village were concerned, Genette Tate had vanished into thin air.

It rained a little that night as villagers continued the search by torch and lamplight until the greyness of dawn.

Police luckily had already thoroughly examined the surface of that lane where the bicycle was found, looking for tire treads, skidmarks, footprints, or specks of blood. Nothing was there, and even the cycle was not scratched, dented, or damaged. There were no signs of a struggle or any disturbance in the grass alongside the lane.

As sunrise brought birdsong back into the hedgerows, the search intensified. No one in the village that dawn had their customary Sunday morning in bed or in church.

Police, now aided by helicopters and other sophisticated aids, including heat-seeking devices, were glad of the voluntary help. It left some of them free to pursue the search with intensive questioning of everyone or anyone who might have seen Genette on her last ride.

As local women served tea and sandwiches from a mobile caravan to weary searchers, police set up a special "hotline" from the village hall appealing for information, however trivial it might be.

Not far from the village lay a derelict airfield, used by the U.S. Air Force in World War II. Now it was in ruin, rarely visited except by passing vagrants. Nevertheless, the old bunkers, underground shelters, and barrack blocks were all searched with tracker dogs. Again, no clues to the girl's disappearance turned up.

By the end of that first week the local Express and Echo newspaper offered a substantial reward for information leading directly to the safe return of the girl, printing thousands of handbills carrying a photograph of the girl, details of the reward, and a police phone number.

The posters were pinned up in the local post offices and villages stores for miles around, on access routes to and from the coastal resorts, and near bus stops and regional village town halls.

So were similar posters issued by the Devon and Dorset Constabulary, detailing a description of Genette as 5 feet tall with short, wavy brown hair and brown eyes, last seen wearing a white cotton top with her name embroidered in red on the left shoulder, light brown slacks, and white sneakers.

One thing was certain as agonizing time passed for the parents. Genette could not possibly be a kidnap victim. The Tates simply did not have that kind of income to make a snatch a feasibility. And no one came forward trying to claim the rewards offered.

Nor was the theory of a hit-and-run accident tenable. The girls in the lane with her would have heard the screech of brakes or the impact of any collision. There were no marks on the discarded cycle and no marks on the road.

Every hospital in a 100-mile radius had been checked and the only patients admitted from road accidents in the general area that day were an old man knocked down by a car, and an old lady who fell off

232

the platform when trying to board a moving bus.

The edition of the newspapers Genette carried sparked off further speculation. It carried the report of a local UFO sighting, together with a photograph, allegedly of the vessel in questioning.

In fact, during the week before Genette's disappearance, there had been numerous such reports in the area.

There were some scorch marks in a field near the bend where Genette disappeared and there had been an inexplicable temporary power failure in the village that morning — soon tracked down, however, to a fire in a local electricity substation.

The scorched grass was later attributed to the use of a too-powerful or underdiluted chemical fertilizer.

These explanations, however, did not quell the fears of some people that Genette had been spirited into outer space. They reacted by reminding the doubters of a greater number of UFO sightings in the West Country of Devon and Cornwall and neighboring Dorset than elsewhere in Britain, unexplained deaths of cattle from intensive burning, tripod-style landing-gear impressions around deeply burned circles of grass, and mysterious flame-tipped objects zooming along country lanes at tree-top height.

The fact that these sightings coincided with harvest time and the imbibing of vast quantities of scrumpy — a potent, rough apple cider — tended to cast a doubt on their credibility.

What did cause a ripple of unease among the local people was that the Genette Tate mystery brought back a similar puzzling case of three years earlier, still unsolved to this day.

An attractive 40-year-old mother, Patricia Allen,

her 7-year-old son Jonathan, and 6-year-old daughter Victoria all vanished from their apartment in Salcombe, Devon, in the Spring of 1975, again shortly after some reputed sightings of UFOs in the area.

Police, releasing the Allen photographs again in the summer of 1976, were still appealing for help in solving the mystery when Genette Tate disappeared, too. Months of intensive inquiries had failed to produce a single clue in the Allen disappearance.

As a police statement indicated at the time, to all intents and purposes, the trio had vanished off the face of the earth . . .

So, the search for Genette Tate went on, spreading out to include the vast tidal basin of Poole Harbour along the Southern coastline, second largest natural harbour in the world to Sydney, Australia. Yachts and fishing boats were searched in case the child was hidden aboard. Even tombs in deserted old graveyards were pried open to see if the child, alive or dead, lay within.

Lakes, river beds, and swamps were dredged; deep caverns filled with beautiful stalactites and stalagmites were explored with the help of speleologists; railway stations throughout the region were checked to see if anyone had dragged an apparently unwilling child on a rail journey, or if a child, senseless or drugged, had been whisked away by train.

Even the instant-photograph booths on main-line terminals were examined for fingerprints in case someone had hurriedly taken the child's photograph to fix onto a travel document.

Time passed, and to this day the fate of Genette Tate remains a mystery. But a number of theories do exist . . .

Perhaps she was kidnapped not for money, but for the sexual pleasure of a pervert somewhere, and locked up in some isolated location and abused at will—perhaps still so.

It has happened before. Examples exist on record in both North America and Europe; one girl had been held a prisoner for 20 years before a passing stranger happened to see her gaunt face behind a barred window and alerted the local police—who had passed the house of captivity every day on routine patrol without bothering to glance up at the window.

If that was Genette Tate's fate, there is still hope of rescue, if the slightest clue can be found to the location of her prison.

A second theory, not so easily scoffed at, is that she may be a sex slave somewhere in North Africa and Arabian Gulf States or in South America. Again, recorded examples exist that the white slave trade continues.

Thousands of young girls and attractive women disappear in Western Europe each year to destinations police firmly believe are private harems in the above-mentioned countries.

If such was the fate of Genette Tate, it would have needed some coldblooded premeditation to succeed, in view of the shortage of time before police rapidly closed all routine exits from Britain via air or seaport.

There were no reports, incidentally, of any private planes in the vicinity of the village or that deserted old USAF airstrip that day.

Everyone is well aware of the well-worn routine of inviting young girls to partake in cabaret acts abroad, posed by unscrupulous white-slaver touts, much to the anger and embarrassment of genuine theatrical agents. Genette was too young to think of, let alone consider, such a proposition.

But, she was pretty and vivacious enough to catch the eye of other slimy individuals now on the touting scene — the ghouls who snatch children for snuff murder videos. Horrific as the possibility is, it has to be coldly considered as a possibility.

Only two years ago, another bright and vivacious child, 10-year-old Sarah Harper, was found a month after she vanished in the county of Yorkshire, in Northeastern England, floating dead in a river, the victim of a bestial sex murder.

The discovery intensified the search for a sex monster who police believe had murdered up to 16 children over the previous eight years, dating back to the disappearance of Genette Tate. An intensive hunt to try and catch him — still going on today — was codenamed Operation Stranger, from the advice both police and parents constantly give their children of never talking to one.

Sadly, but on the grim balance of probability, Genette Tate may be dead: kidnapped and rushed hastily away from the scene that day by a sex monster who either raped and slew her in back of a car, or committed the crimes elsewhere, and then buried or totally disposed of the body in some other way.

If it's so, a puzzle remains. Genette, well briefed by her parents, was not the kind of girl to dump her cycle in the middle of the road and drive off somewhere with a total stranger. She would have struggled or screamed, and those other schoolgirls just down the lane around the bend would surely have heard her.

If she was not accosted by a stranger, then who

took her away? Someone who knew her well enough to interrupt that newspaper delivery round with a pretext perhaps that she was urgently needed at home or somewhere else in the village, that someone might be desperately ill, or that her own home was on fire.

Urgency of some kind seems apparent by the discarded cycle, placed and not thrown or flung to the ground as it would have been on impact with, say, a moving car.

One can theorize ad infinitum on the mental make-up of such child-rapist-slayers, but suffice to say, they have cunning well above average. Nor in all honesty can the possibility be discounted that a woman might have been involved, too.

Again, it would not be the first time, and there have been many examples since the classic example of Myra Hindley, the Moors Murderess, lured children into the car of her lover accomplice, Ian Brady.

It would have been much easier for a woman to entice Genette off her cycle, resting it momentarily on the ground as she neared the open door of a parked auto to give a woman sitting there travel directions.

Perhaps the solution to the child's disappearance all those years ago lies a lot nearer to that tranquil Devonshire village than the numerous possibilities already discussed.

Could she or her parents at some time have incurred the deranged displeasure of some other rural Devonian soul whose idea of vengeance was to attack the daughter?

Doubtless the police went into this very thoroughly and with utmost discretion at the relevant time, and reviewed it periodically since. Again, it would not have been a unique or untenable theory.

Such a state of affairs was being considered four years before Genette disappeared, halfway across Europe in the rural Slovenian community of Prilipe. Fear had the hamlet folk by the throat there since the death or disappearance of 11 local children since 1972.

The mystery began in May that year when 6-year-old Ann Boscovic left her home to gather lilies in a nearby coppice of trees. She was never seen again by the folk of Prilipe.

Then, Bostian Clemencic, age 2, was playing peacefully in the courtyard of his home as grandmother sat on a bench nearby keeping an eye on him. She slipped inside the house to pick up some knitting wool, but when she returned two minutes later, the toddler had gone.

She searched for him without success. So did the inhabitants of Prilipe, local gendarmes and, finally, the military with forest rangers and tracker dogs.

It was four days before they found the toddler, mutilated and dead on the summit of a mountain three miles from the village. It was clear from the wounds that he had been slain by a human being—and then dumped on the mountain for wild animals and birds to devour.

The villagers hostilely closed ranks, convinced that someone among them was taking revenge on the community through the children.

Then came the Marinkovic twins, 5 years old, found drowned in a weir.

And little Andreas Militic, 7, found dead by the roadside just outside the village, apparently killed by a hit-and-run driver, but the position of the body did not match up with faked skid marks on the roadway.

Then came 4-year-old Jirina Kanladic, found dead in a meadow, still clutching her favorite doll.

Other children who vanished from the village never turned up at all.

Theories included baby-snatchers; one farmer's wife had been approached by a strange woman who offered her $9,000 for a little daughter. The stranger said she had taken a fancy to the child, and the parents, being poor, could make better use of the money than of the child.

The farmer's wife, shocked at this coldblooded attitude, slammed the door in the stranger's face, but later wished she had kept her talking until the police could question her.

And that, in the case of Genette Tate, too, is perhaps the only ultimate hope.

Someone, someday, somewhere, pricked by conscience or forced into a corner by new evidence, may have to talk to the police or to someone else, Genette's fate may then be known. It will clear up an unsolved mystery—but it won't bridge the chasm left in her grieving parents' life.

"WHO STRANGLED THE ALL-AMERICAN BOY?"

by Charles W. Sasser

Peculiar thing about working homicides—you want to solve all of them, but now and then one comes along that just won't open for you. Invariably, it's a case you want to crack so badly it hurts. That you don't bust it is no reflection on your abilities nor on the way you conducted the investigation. You can do everything just right—and still not catch the killer.

Me, I'm a homicide cop. Tulsa, Oklahoma. I've cracked murder cases within an hour; I've also worked three years on cases before catching up with a suspect. I don't like to give up, no matter how long it takes. The victim wouldn't want me to. I especially don't like to give up when the victims are kids. Take, for example, the case of a freckled, red-headed 10-year-old Huck Finn named James Riley Woollum.

There was an abundance of suspects in the case. For years I trod through a sick world peopled by pedophiliacs, childnapers, homosexuals, man-boy love advocates, and assorted other sex freaks trying to run down the right madman. Maybe I even found him but wasn't sharp enough or lucky enough to prove it. I'll let you be the judge of that.

It began on a cool, windy day with a pale sun left over from the final days of winter. Blocks of spent time have stacked up since that Friday evening, March 29, 1974, when the homicide supervisor, Sergeant Larry Johnson, telephoned me at home.

"Get ready for it, Sasser," Johnson warned. "The afternoon shift has just found a little boy's naked body thrown in the woods. The case will be assigned to you. It's going to be your baby."

My first question was: "Who's working the crime scene?"

"Sergeant Roy Hunt and John Hickey."

Frankly, there are some detectives I wouldn't trust with a scene. Hunt and Hickey, however, were thorough professionals. I knew without question they'd leave no stones unturned.

"I'm assigning Bill to work with you," Johnson said.

Bill McCracken was a tall ex-Marine, a fine cop, and a friend. Usually I either worked with him or with grizzled old Austin Roberts. Roberts was still in the middle of investigating the extortion murder of a gay businessman. Bill and I had just finished a case in which the mob had hired a hit-man to wipe out a pair of would-be competitors in a bingo racket. So far, we'd obtained mob-related indictments in 15 states, including two murder indictments in Oklahoma. The case was about wound down. The tone of Johnson's voice and the fact that he called me at home was enough to give notice that the challenge of this newest case might be

241

enough to put the bingo case to shame.

I had earned a rep for successful murder probes. While the national clearance rate for homicides stood at about 70 percent, I was solving more than 90 percent of mine.

Successful detectives get all the tough cases.

Tough cases give you ulcers after a while.

On Saturday morning when I signed in for the day watch, there was a stack of reports on my desk. McCracken and I dived right in to get a background on the case. It was like staring at a blank wall. Hunt and Hickey had covered the crime scene expertly, no doubt about that. The only thing was that they had obtained virtually no evidence. We knew the boy's name, because he had been reported missing a week earlier and his parents had identified his body at the morgue. James Riley Woollum, age 10.

"That's about it," McCracken sighed. "All we know for sure is that a little boy ends up missing and we find him dead and apparently sexually molested a week later."

Reports before us detailed the search for a missing juvenile which began at 4:30 p.m. on Thursday, March 21, 1974. The Tulsa County Sheriff's Department handled it originally, not the Tulsa police, as the boy lived with his family on North Cheyenne Avenue, just outside city limits. According to family members, young James left home to collect soft drink bottles for resale and did not return for dinner.

"He's always been good about coming home," the worried parents contended. "We know something dreadful has happened to him."

Within a few days, hard-working deputies were inclined to agree with the boy's parents. Something dreadful had happened. A nationwide police alert described the missing juvenile as male, 4-feet-ten inches tall, 75 pounds, with reddish hair and freckles. An All-American face. He was last seen wearing blue jeans, a maroon shirt, a black-and-white jacket, and tennis shoes.

The alert produced few reliable witnesses. Two of James' schoolmates from Greeley Elementary recalled having seen James the afternoon he disappeared. One of them said he saw the youth on North Cincinnati Avenue walking north toward Turley Hill. Asked what he was doing, James replied, "Picking up pop bottles."

The other classmate said he saw James leaving with a man driving a red, two-door station wagon.

Canvassing the neighborhood, deputies located an additional two witnesses, both adults, who seemed to add credence to the sighting of the red vehicle. A school guard recalled seeing a small red station wagon suspiciously cruising the neighborhood. A housewife described two white men in a red Chevrolet attempting to pick up young girls at the school. Another police alert issued on a red station wagon prompted patrolmen across the state to stop hundreds of such vehicles to interrogate the drivers, all without success. James remained missing as hopes of finding him well and alive slowly faded.

Hopes revived briefly when a man named Roscoe Eskelund telephoned to report he had picked up a small boy hitchhiking in Jefferson, Texas, before dawn on Friday, March 22nd. The youth he described so strongly resembled the description of James Woollum that an FBI agent drove to Eskelund's home in Eufaula, Oklahoma, to question him. Apparently, the agent decided that a 10-year-old could not possibly have traveled so far in such a short period of time. Hopes of finding the boy dissolved.

For a week, sheriff's deputies and Tulsa police searched the north end of Tulsa County by car, foot, horseback, and helicopter. They found nothing. On the afternoon of the eighth day, March 29th, a teenager walking his dog in a vacant field on the far opposite side of the city made a shocking discovery. He ran home and breathlessly telephoned police. He had stumbled upon a dead body in a woodlot in the South 2400 block of West 73rd Street within Tulsa City limits.

The time was 4:50 p.m. Ten minutes later, Sergeant Hunt and Detective Hickey were rolling onto the scene. I had their reports and crime-scene sketches before me. They described in lean, technical jargon the body in the timber where 73rd Street dead-ended.

The body was that of a young boy. It was completely nude except for a gauze bandage covering the ball of the right foot. The dead boy's clothing was gone. Time, weather, parasites, and animals had ravaged the body. It lay on its right side in a half-fetal position. Judging from the settling of the blood in the body, plus other factors involving bodily deterioration, Sergeant Hunt estimated that

244

the boy had been dead in excess of 72 hours and that he had been slain elsewhere before his body was dumped here.

Although officers and crime-scene experts remained at the murder scene until well after nightfall, photographing, measuring, taking plaster casts, and searching, they uncovered not a single clue as to who might have committed such a reprehensible crime against an innocent child.

"We're not even sure what killed him," was Sergeant Hunt's final observation.

After studying the reports, I telephoned the medical examiner, Dr. Bob Fogel, who should have completed his autopsy analysis by now.

"Bob, what killed him?" I asked.

"Asphixiation. He was strangled to death."

"How long ago?"

"I'd say at least a week."

"Was he molested, Doc?"

"I've submitted rectum smears to the lab, but it'll be Monday or so before we have the results. However, acid phosphates in the rectum was markedly elevated. That probably indicates the presence of semen."

"That narrows it down," McCracken observed wryly. "After all, in a city this size there can't be more than, oh, two or three *thousand* pedophiliacs."

About 80 percent of an investigation is nothing but tedium. Pounding the streets. Asking questions. Running down leads. Interrogating suspicious people. Asking more questions. My partner and I wanted this killer badly. We consumed long days and some longer nights rummaging around in the city's underbelly, trying to pick up a scent.

We re-questioned James' classmates. The one who had seen James in the red station wagon wasn't *really* sure now that it was James he saw, but if it *was* James he was with a man who wore a dark, full beard and was "kind of big."

The boy's story took on added authority, however, when McCracken returned to the area where the body had been found and discovered where a vehicle had been driven through the field to within 50 feet of the death site. There were paint smears on some of the saplings. The smears were *red*.

Patrol officers were only too willing to help in the case. They were stopping every red car that dared venture onto city streets. Newspaper reports about a red suspect car generated dozens of citizen complaints.

"Two men in a red car hid their faces and left at a high rate of speed . . ."

"A man named Fred lives on West Seventy-second Place. He's crazy and drives a red car . . ."

"She says her son had been taken out of state and sexually molested by a white male and a juvenile in a red station wagon . . ."

Publicity also produced certain undesirable side effects: kooks, confessors, detectives, seers, and psychics.

"I must remain anonymous in regards to James Woollum," wrote a self-styled psychic. "I see a boy in a close neighborhood . . . He is totally unaware at this time of his cruel act, though at times the scene flashes through his mind . . . He will soon repeat this act unless immediate attention is given . . . I have never seen wrong, for as you see through a platonic vision it is perfect sight. Proudly, Alpha."

On March 31st, a resident of east Tulsa answered a pounding at his door to find a swarthy, middle-aged man armed with a sawed-off shotgun and a pistol in a shoulder holster.

"Is James Riley Woollum here?" demanded the gunman, looking mildly demented.

"I don't know anybody by that name," replied the startled homeowner.

"Has he been here at your house today? I've got a score to settle with him."

"I don't know him."

"Oh. Well, I've got a score to settle and I'll find him."

Two days later, a neighbor's child received a telephone call.

"Do you want to make some money?" the caller asked.

"Yes. How much?"

"Twenty-five dollars. How old are you?"

"Eleven."

"Do you know James?"

The little girl replied she knew James Woollum.

"How much do you weigh?" asked the caller.

The little girl was growing suspicious. She did not answer.

"Do you like money?"

"Yes."

"How much?"

Alarmed at last, the little girl shouted for her mother and the man hung up.

Was Alpha a well-meaning soul—or was Alpha the killer? How about the demented gunman, the suspicious telephone caller, and all the others who were scrambling to enter the act? Nuts? Or was there a killer there somewhere? It all had to be checked out. McCracken and I farmed out most of these leads to other detectives. By now, we were beginning to concentrate on the only logical suspect to have emerged so far.

Roscoe Eskelund's reported encounter with the young Texas hitchhiker continued to puzzle us. After all, his description of the hitchhiker seemed to bear too many striking resemblances to James Woollum's description to be mere coincidence. To begin with, both boys were of the same age and size with the same bangs and red hair. On top of this, Eskelund's hitchhiker carried an orange rattail comb in his back pocket and complained of his right foot hurting. James Woollum, relatives said, had found an orange rattail comb in an abandoned house several days before he disappeared. He also had a painful plantar's wart on the ball of his right foot, which was still bandaged when his body was found.

Other similarities piled up. The hitchhiker had a nervous habit of rubbing his left knee; James Woollum suffered from Osgood Slattery disease, an ailment of the knee which caused him to rub it. The hitchhiker carried a white plastic trash can liner containing unknown items; James had left home with such a white plastic bag in which to carry soft drink bottles. Eskelund's hitchhiker talked of airplanes and his desire to join the Air Force; James dreamed of joining the Air Force and had constructed a cardboard airplane in his back yard to "fly."

There were only a few things that did not add up. Eskelund described his hitchhiker as wearing an old Army fatigue jacket and chain-smoking cigarettes. By all reports, James did not sneak around to smoke, and, of course, he had been clad in a black-and-white windbreaker when last seen.

"Still," McCracken summed up, "there are just too many coincidences."

We were speeding toward Eufaula to question Eskelund in depth.

"If Eskelund did kidnap James Woollum, why would he call police about it?" I pondered. "He could have just kept his mouth shut and no one would ever have suspected."

"Paranoia," Bill suggested. "He gave himself an alibi in Texas the night Woollum turned up missing."

"But he put himself with the boy."

Bill thought about that. "No," he said, "he put himself with a boy who *looked* like James. That gave him a reason for calling police about it in the first place. But chances are he'll claim it wasn't actually James he was with after all."

McCracken was right. After studying a group of James Woollum's photographs, Eskelund decided his hitchhiker and the missing boy were not the same after all. The interrogation went downhill from there.

According to what Eskelund told us, he was a 35-year-old helicopter pilot for an oil company based in Lafayette, Louisiana. After landing at the base at 5:00 p.m. on the same Thursday afternoon James Woollum vanished, Eskelund set out for home in Eufaula in his blue Ford. At 3:00 a.m. on March 22, he picked up the mysterious hitchhiker in Jefferson and let him out 40 minutes later in Dangerfield, Texas. He arrived home near dawn. This last fact was supported by his wife.

Coincidences or not, Roscoe Eskelund could not be our killer. For one thing, records from the Lafayette oil company proved that he was present on the job sight until at least five in the afternoon. Even if James Woollum had managed to travel to Jefferson in time to be picked up hitchhiking, Eskelund could not possibly have killed him, driven his body to Tulsa, and then returned to Eufaula by dawn.

Of course, there was always the possibility that his wife was lying in order to protect him. Maybe he hadn't arrived home until noon. Bill and I had both known wives to protect their husbands, no matter what happened. Still . . .

"I don't think they're lying," was McCracken's studied opinion.

Neither did I. We had to go with that.

We were back where we started. The only thing left to do was to begin running down known child molesters. We questioned contacts in the gay community for the names of homosexuals with a proclivity for both young boys and violence.

250

"I know this one dude with a hangup," confided a well-placed gay. "He not only likes little boys, but the dude's got this crazy thing of looking at pictures showing naked kids posed like they've been murdered."

"Who is he?"

"You'll know him. He's a famous politician. He might even run for president some day."

"You have no right to approach me this way!" the politician threatened after I finally cornered him alone at the state capital.

"Look," I reasoned, "I don't want to destroy you, but you either talk to me or you talk to the press about why you wouldn't."

He decided to talk. He had an alibi, though. The night James Woollum vanished he was in Oklahoma City delivering a speech on the problems of crime control. I paused at his office door before leaving.

"You'll never get my vote," I assured him. "I sincerely hope you never run for the presidency."

It seemed every cop in the state had a suspect or two he thought might be capable of slaying a child. The tips kept pouring in. Nothing rallies police to a case faster than one involving death or injury of children.

Officer Leroy Hughes of Kiefer, Oklahoma, reported a 40-year-old Sapulpa resident who had been tried and acquitted in the strangling death of a youngster 12 years previously. Tulsa Detective Curtis Hanks apprehended a known child molester having sexual intercourse with a mule. Police in Norman called in details of a man who hid in

251

bushes and tried to entice juveniles to him with offers of candy and toys.

On the afternoon of April 9th, Tulsa burglary detective Dennit Morris surprised Tom Dale Corey sitting in his car drinking beer at the dead-end road where James Woollum's body was found. He would have thought little of it, except for the fact that Corey had a long police record for indecent exposure, child molestation, and other sex crimes. Besides, Corey had been as nervous as "a skunk in a dog pen."

He became even more jangled when McCracken and I showed up to question him why he might be loitering near a murder site.

"I go there to drink beer," he explained. "Nobody ever comes to bother me there."

"You go there often?" Bill asked.

"You know, just sometimes."

I glanced at Bill. He nodded slightly. We were going to try a bluff.

"You were seen there on a Thursday afternoon and night, three weeks ago," I began abruptly. "That was on March twenty-first."

"Then I guess I was there," he said after a short pause.

"Tell me about it," I encouraged.

"Not much to tell," he replied. "I left home to go to work about three in the afternoon. I didn't feel like working, so I bought a six-pack and drove up to the dead-end and drank it. I still didn't feel like working, but, you know, I couldn't go home and tell my wife that. So what I did was I took a rock and put my finger on the pavement and smashed it with the rock . . ."

"*What?*"

"I hit my finger and broke it. Then I went to work and stayed there a half-hour and complained to the foreman that I hurt my finger. He sent me home. I got another quart of beer and went back to the dead-end. I stayed till after dark."

I watched his face closely as I sprang the last part of our bluff on him.

"Tom Dale, you were there alone, or supposedly alone, at the very time that little Woollum boy was being killed and his body dumped not a hundred feet away from you."

Corey went limp. "Boy, I'm in a heap of trouble now," he blurted out. Then he seemed to regain control. "No, I'm not," he added, "because I didn't do it."

Sometimes a detecitve has nothing to guide him when it comes to a suspect except his own intuition and his judgment of human character. After two hours of interrogating Corey, McCracken and I reached the same conclusion: While Corey certainly might be capable of a crime like this, he probably hadn't done this one. Just to be sure, we tried to run down an alibi for him. It was a futile effort. On the night our little boy disappeared, Corey had been neither at home nor at work and he couldn't recall where else he might have been. At any rate, that hadn't been the same night he broke his finger; that had happened a week after James was reported missing.

"Mr. Sasser, I swear I couldn't do nothing like that to a little kid," he whined.

253

"You're a suspect until this case is closed," I assured him. "Just think of me as your conscience."

A week later, on April 16th, Bill and I just knew we were on the right track to solving the baffling case when FBI Agent Mickey Harrington telephoned.

"I might have your killer for you," he began.

"Great, Mick. Give me a name."

"Joe Desmond. He's twenty-nine years old, 360 pounds. Has a long record for molesting kids, plus a woman named Marie Gray just reported him for kidnaping and sexually molesting her five-year-old son."

The agent had done his homework. At one point three years earlier, Harrington said, Desmond had been tried in Portland, Oregon, for seven counts of sodomy and sexual abuse of male children. Since then, police in Wichita, Kansas, had confiscated polaroid photographs showing the fat man involved in extremely incriminating poses with very young boys. Apparently, he was out on parole from Oregon and back to his old habits.

"Listen to this," Harrington said. "Desmond owns a small red station wagon. He's a big, bearded man. Does that sound familiar? He lives not far from the Woollum residence."

"Does he have any record of violence against his victims?" I wanted to know.

"No, but you know how that goes. Molesters are unstable. If a victim resisted or threatened to expose him . . . Well, anything could happen."

254

It was the hottest lead we had had so far. At this point, however, neither my partner nor I had any idea that this Joe Desmond might be leading us on a two-year chase, the end of which still might not resolve anything when it came to James Woollum. We found Marie Gray at home with her 5-year-old victim son named Claude.

"Joe had been a friend of the family for about three months," Mrs. Gray told McCracken and me. "Joe's a house painter. He was going to Kansas to appraise a house, so we let Claude go with him."

That was on April 2nd. Desmond was supposed to return the child on April 13th. On April 15th, the Grays contacted the FBI and reported their son kidnaped. That same evening Desmond drove up without being seen and let Claude out.

Little Claude forthrightly explained how "Uncle Joe" took him to an abandoned house in Tulsa where Desmond committed fellatio on the child. After that, they drove various places for the next two weeks while the fat man repeatedly molested his 5-year-old charge.

"Lady, you're a fool," I admonished Claude's mother. "No mom in her right mind would consent to her little son going off with a virtual stranger for nine days."

"You ain't got no right to talk to me like that," she whimpered. "It ain't my fault . . ."

Tulsa County District Attorney S.M. "Buddy" Fallis issued a felony warrant for Desmond's arrest on the molestation case. Included in the pickup description was the advice that the fugitive was also wanted for questioning in the murder of 10-year-old James Riley Woollum. A nationwide UFAP (Unlawful Flight to Avoid Prosecution) warrant soon followed when McCracken and I discovered that the accused molester had apparently fled the state.

His wife live on North Oswego not far from the Woollums. She admitted somewhat ashamedly that she hadn't seen her husband since he left with young Claude Gray on April 2nd. At that time he had been driving a white Ford, leaving her with a red 1963 Chevrolet station wagon which matched the description of the vehicle we had obtained from James's classmate.

"I have no idea where he is now," said Mrs. Desmond, "but I think he knows the police will be after him for what he did to the little Gray boy. Look, I know Joe has problems, but he wouldn't kill one of those kids. He loves all little children."

"Yeah," McCracken remarked with sarcasm. "But he loves them the wrong way."

"Joe never seemed bothered by it," the wife continued. "The little Woollum boy, I mean. He did get a little upset when the newspapers said something about a red station wagon. He said he hoped the police would not come looking for him just because he was on probation for child molestation and owned a red station wagon."

After calling for crime-scene search experts, McCracken and I went through the station wagon for evidence. All we found were a few soft drink bottles to remind us that James was hunting bottles when he vanished. Crime-scene experts photographed the car, dusted it for James Woollum's fingerprints, took paint scrapings to compare with samples McCracken saved from the saplings, and knocked mud from the wheel wells to analyze against soil from the crime scene. The evidence was not particularly encouraging.

Armed with a spread of photo mug shots, including one of our suspect, my partner and I went around to all our witnesses to see if anyone could identify Desmond. James' classmate could not. One of the missing boy's relatives thought Desmond had been at a convenience store on North Cincinnati Avenue around the corner from the Woollum house on the afternoon of James' disappearance. However, the store manager and an employee quickly shot down that hope.

"No, no," they said. "We know who she's talking about. He's a big man like this and he has a beard, but he drives a pickup and is a regular customer. He was in here that same afternoon with another guy he works with."

Our morale plummeted. Moreover, nothing from Desmond's car corresponded scientifically with the few scraps of evidence we had managed to accumulate in the murder case. Not the fingerprints, the paint samples, or the mud from the wheel wells. We were left with virtually nothing except our suspicions and Desmond's modus operandi to connect the suspected molester with the James' killing. Our only hope lay in a quick apprehension of the fugitive. Perhaps if he were caught soon enough, his conscience might still be working and he would confess.

Even that was not to be. The weeks, the months, and eventually the years passed, and Joe Desmond remained at large. We charged him with molesting two additional children, but charging a man with a crime is not the same as catching him and convicting him. The case remains unsolved. Hopeless as it looked, McCracken and I continued to investigate other leads and to interrogate other suspects. A murder case is never solved until a suspect is apprehended and convicted.

On the last day of July that year, our attention was captured and diverted from Joe Desmond by a homely 19-year-old named Suzie Ekberg who was apparently nursing a guilty conscience of her own. Police were summoned when she went to her minister in West Tulsa with an incredible tale of having witnessed the slaying of a young boy. Sergeant Roy Hunt and Detective John Hickey arrested her as a material witness to homicide and held her in the county jail for further investigation.

My other partner, Detective Austin Roberts, has an unusual theory about witnesses which he calls "the fat-girl complex." It is his contention that certain females—notably those who are obese and homely—will do almost anything to place themselves in the center of attention. I thought of Roberts' theory the moment I confronted Suzie Ekberg in the police interrogation cubicle on the morning of August 1st. She fit Roberts' stereotype right down to her rat-colored hair and the 80 extra pounds she carried.

However, she could be extremely persuasive. She

gave a recorded statement that her ex-lover, a married older man named Clovis Blanchard, had strangled young James Woollum to death. She said her lover and she had picked up the youth while he was gathering soft drink bottles for sale in north Tulsa.

"We took him to the store to sell the bottles," she said. "Then, instead of taking the boy home, Clovis took another street."

They kept the boy until after nightfall, she said, before Blanchard drove to a remote area and parked.

"I didn't see any houses around. The road we went on was a deadend . . . There was a fence on down a little ways. . . ."

She hesitated as though pained by the memory.

"Go on," McCracken urged.

"We just got out and sat down by the outside of the car and I went to sleep . . . I guess Clovis and the boy were sitting there talking and drinking beer. I didn't hear anything until the door slammed and woke me up . . . I woke up and looked at Clovis and he had a rope in his hand. The boy was sitting down and looked like he was scared. When I seen Clovis with the rope, I got up and tried to get it from him. I didn't succeed because he hit me in the stomach a couple of times. I landed on the ground and I heard a scream that wasn't very loud. I looked over at them and the boy was laying on the ground and Clovis was on his knees over the boy and crying. He said, 'I've really done it now, Suzie. I've really done it now.' "

They left the body where it fell, Suzie said. Blanchard assured her he would come back later and take care of it.

"I was afraid to go to the police," she concluded. "I told him I would and he told me he would rather see me dead, too, than see himself in jail."

Was she telling the truth? We had been disappointed too many times during our investigation of this case to dare hope now. For another hour we shot trick questions at the girl, trying to get her rattled, trying to confuse her if she was lying and thus squeeze the truth from her. She held up under the onslaught. Afterwards, she even took us to where she claimed they had kidnaped the boy, which was only two blocks from his house, and to the death site itself. If she was lying, she was doing it skillfully and had completed her homework in order to know all the major locations involved in the crime. There was only one thing left to do.

"Arrest and question Clovis Blanchard," Mc-Cracken said.

For a murder suspect, the 46-year-old man wasn't difficult to find. He worked at a machine shop on South Sheridan. Surprise at seeing our shields replaced the drudgery of a lifetime of hard work etched deeply into his homely face.

"You're making a bad mistake!" he cried after I informed him he was under arrest for the murder of James Woollum. His protests continued vigorously even after we confronted him with Suzie Ekberg's statement.

"That girl's crazy," he insisted. "I took her out twice, that's all. We slept together, and then I wanted nothing to do with her. She'd call me, but

I'd put her off. If she told you I killed anybody, she's just trying to get even with me for not taking her out and paying her attention anymore."

That was Blanchard's position and he held onto it before every accusation. Ekberg also retained her position that Blanchard was a murderer. What it finally came down to was her word against his. There was insufficient evidence to prove either Blanchard's guilt or his innocence. The outcome largely depended, again, upon a detective's own intuition and judgment of human character.

I was inclined to go along with Blanchard. I thought him innocent. This, I felt, was another of many cases involving the "fat-girl complex." McCracken went along with me and again we released a suspect in the Woollum murder.

We were right back, again, where we started, only more discouraged than ever of finding a solution to the trying puzzle. But we could not give up.

Winter came. Then a new year. Then another year. Our prime suspect, Joe Desmond, remained at large. Time and again, we followed out tips to his whereabouts, only to be thwarted on each one. We kept hoping that when we found Desmond, he would be our killer and confess to it.

"Sasser, are you certain about Roscoe Eskelund, Tom Dale Corey, Joe Desmond, and Clovis Blanchard?" Sergeant Larry Johnson demanded. "Are you so certain one of them is not our murderer?"

"There's not enough evidence to prove or disprove it," I replied. "All we have to go on is my judgment and Bill's."

Johnson looked at me a moment. "That's always

been good enough for me before," he said.

The Woollum case became a millstone around our necks. I went on to other homicides — and solved most of them. Still, Woollum haunted me. I couldn't drop it and let it collect dust in the bottom drawer of my desk. Every time I learned of an incident involving a child being kidnaped, abused, molested, tortured, or even frightened, I was one of the first cops to begin probing. I scanned the newspapers nationwide for similar crimes, knowing murderers — maybe even Joe Desmond — traveled from place to place to keep from being found out.

Atlanta, Georgia: a man was apprehended for the torture murder of three kidnaped children.

Portland, Oregon: the body of a 3-year-old was found stuffed under an abandoned house.

San Diego, California: a man carried around a dead 11-year-old in his car trunk until the odor brought complaints from neighbors.

Fairfax, Virginia: a 23-year-old was arrested for luring young boys into parks where he molested them, murdered them, and cut off their genitals.

"Do you know if your suspect was in Tulsa, Oklahoma, during 1974?" I asked detectives wherever such a murder occurred. Occasionally, I even traveled to other cities to question likely suspects. My discouragement became outright despair.

Two years after the Woollum homicide and after Joe Desmond was charged in Tulsa with three separate charges of child molestation, Desmond was finally apprehended in Texas and extradited back to Oklahoma. McCracken and I were at the Tulsa County jail to greet him. We were optimistic of at last solving the Woollum case. Desmond *had* to be our killer.

He wasn't. At least I don't think he was. There are detectives to this day who believe I let a cold-blooded murderer go free.

"I can't help myself," the enormous fat man blubbered like a child himself. "I admit everything about what I did to those three little boys, and about what I did in Oregon and in Kansas. But I love children. I just love them too much. I'd never *really* harm one. I'd *never* kill. You have to believe me."

Joe Desmond passed a polygraph exam. He withstood interrogation. Although he was subsequently convicted of child molestation and sentenced to a short prison term, Desmond was not our murderer. I believed it then, and I believe it now.

During the years between then and now, no solid suspect has surfaced in the mysterious killing of Tulsa's little Huck Finn, although McCracken and I have literally questioned hundreds of people about it. Today, had young James lived, had not some unknown pervert decided to satiate his abnormal lusts with a helpless child, this All-American red-headed boy would have been 18 years old with the rest of his young life ahead of him.

There is no statute of limitations on murder. The law has not given up on apprehending James' killer, and neither have I. Sometimes, somewhere, someone will read of James Riley Woollum, or someone will hear of him, and that someone will recognize young James' killer for who he is. When that happens, the killer will at last be brought to the justice he has managed to elude for these ten long years.

EDITOR'S NOTE:
Roscoe Eskelund, Tom Dale Corey, Joe Desmond, Marie Gray, Claude, Suzie Ekberg and Clovis Blanchard are not the real names of the persons so named in the foregoing story. Fictitious names have been used because there is no reason for public interest in the identities of these persons.

"WHO MURDERED CATHY DAWES?"

by Gary C. King

During the Christmas season of 1981, pretty Catherine Grace Dawes, 28, devoted wife and mother of three children, ages 5, 3, and 1, was happy that she could buy her family presents to put under the tree, made possible by a job she obtained a couple of months earlier as a clerk at an East Vancouver, Washington store. She usually worked the evening shift, from 6:00 p.m. to 1:00 a.m., when she closed up. Things went well with the new job, and as a result, she was able to give her family the Christmas presents she wanted to that year.

Cathy Dawes planned to quit the job shortly after Christmas and go back to the demanding, but rewarding, job of full-time mother. However, she decided to continue with the clerk's job for a while longer, perhaps only two or three months more, to help her husband pay off some of the bills they had accumulated. Unknown to her, the decision to stay on the job was a dark twist of fate that would ultimately cost Cathy Dawes her life when she became Clark County's first homicide victim of 1982.

Cathy reported for work, as usual, punctually at

6:00 p.m. on Sunday, January 17, 1982. She parked her car in one of the slots near the door of the store, located in the 10000 block of East Mill Plain Boulevard in Vancouver, entered the store and relieved the clerk on duty. After the cash till had been counted and exchanged for a new one Cathy was officially on duty, all alone except for the coming and going of the store's customers.

Described as an outspoken, self-assured person with a good sense of humor, Cathy handled her customers well. Warm and friendly with most, she nonetheless knew how to deal with the occasional belligerent customer with tact instead of aggression. Her methods worked with most; only with one did they fail.

As the evening wore on, there were fewer customers coming and going, which was true for any evening, for that matter, making the job at times actually quite dull. But it was business as usual just the same, as nothing out of the ordinary occurred until closing time.

At a few minutes before 1:00 a.m., there were three men inside the store with Cathy, and all had been playing the video games located just inside the front door. At the time Cathy announced that she was closing the store at 1:00 a.m., the usual closing time. Two of the men, who were friends, left the store together. The third remained behind, apparently to finish his game, and may have been the last person to see Cathy Dawes alive. Cathy most likely locked the door when the first two men left to prevent any additional customers from entering the store, and probably left the keys dangling from the lock to avoid the hassle of searching for the key each time she needed to unlock and lock the door. As the young man continued playing the video game, Cathy returned to her place behind the checkout counter, where she is known to have made a telephone call as she prepared to close out her cash register till.

Only minutes later, at approximately 1:10 a.m., a male hitchhiker was dropped off in front of the store. Because the hitchhiker was a regular customer, he had become acquainted with Cathy Dawes, he would later tell detectives, and as a result he came to know which car belonged to her. Knowing that Cathy was still inside because of the presence of her car in the parking lot, the hitchhiker tried to open the door to the store only to find that it was locked. Needing change to call a taxi, necessary because his ride was going no further than the street just past the store, the hitchhiker knocked on the glass door of the market. When no one answered, he walked a half block down the street to another store opposite the one where Cathy worked. There he obtained coins, after which he walked back to where Cathy worked to use the pay telephone in front of the store to summon a taxi. However, before the taxi arrived, the hitchhiker was given a ride home by the manager of the store where he'd obtained the coins he needed to call the taxi.

When the taxi arrived, at approximately 1:25 a.m., the driver noted the presence of Cathy's car in the store parking lot, but there didn't appear to be a customer waiting for his taxi. He then circled the store, after which he pulled his car back into the parking lot near the store's front door. He got out of his car, entered through the *unlocked* door, but found no one. Noting that the store appeared to be unattended, the taxi driver went back outside and dialed 9-1-1 to report the suspicious circumstances; then waited in his car for the arrival of sheriff's deputies.

Deputy Rod Townsend was the first to arrive. He'd been patrolling only a few blocks away when he received the dispatcher's call of suspicious circumstances, and he pulled into the store's parking lot at 1:30 a.m. The taxi driver gave Townsend his account of what had occurred, after which the deputy entered the store to investigate.

Not seeing anyone in the main area, Deputy Townsend cautiously entered the rear stockroom where, moments later, he found the body of a young woman lying in a pool of her own blood. Townsend quickly checked for vital signs but discovered, much to his horror and dismay, that the young woman was quite dead, the apparent victim of a shooting and possible sexual assault. He radioed his grim findings back to his dispatcher, who quickly passed on the report to the homicide investigations unit.

Sergeant Mike Davidson was assigned to lead the investigation, assisted by Detectives Pat St. John and Tim McVicker. Since the crime had occurred just outside the city limits of Vancouver, it came under the jurisdiction of the Clark County Sheriff's Department and would be investigated by that department with some assistance from the

Vancouver police.

Telephone calls went out immediately to detectives and other law-enforcement officials, waking most of them from a sound sleep. In spite of the hour, however, Davidson, St. John and McVicker arrived at the East Vancouver location within a relatively short time, as did Prosecutor Art Curtis, Deputy Prosecutor Roger Bennett and Coroner Arch Hamilton. Officers from the Vancouver Police Department arrived also, and cordoned off the store, parking lot and the buildings on both sides of the store by posting signs which read: "POLICE INVESTIGATION AREA. DO NOT ENTER."

It should be pointed out that until the summer of 1980, Clark County had a criminalist of its own who could be at the scene of a crime within 10 minutes or so. But, unfortunately, he resigned, and the county commissioners decided that Vancouver law-enforcement agencies could get by with using their own personnel to collect evidence or, if necessary, they could call in a new branch of the Washington State Patrol Crime Lab in Kelso, some 40 miles to the north, scheduled to open in 1981. However, that branch was not opened as scheduled due to lack of funds, and the police had to wait for the arrival of a crime-lab specialist from Seattle, a trip which might take four or five hours. In the meantime, Vancouver lawmen had to hope that no clues would be lost because of the delay, and they exercised extreme caution at the crime scene to avoid possible contamination of potential evidence.

"We've got a real mess in there," said Sergeant Dale Conn of the homicide division, who was also called in to assist in the case. Conn told curious members of the local press that the investigation would likely be "slow and arduous," and indicated that this crime was similar in terms of the resulting "mess" to the murder of Beverly J. Nelson, also 27, the manager of a nearby fast-food hamburger restaurant. Mrs. Nelson, also a housewife and mother, was brutally murdered while telephoning the 9-1-1 emergency number by two youths who beat and shot her to death during the course of a robbery. That crime scene was extremely messy due to the large amount of blood in the restaurant's office (the Nelson case appeared in the February 1982 issue of our sister publication *True Detective*) and, although the case was eventually solved, law-enforcement officials had been faced with the same situation of waiting for a crime-lab specialist to arrive from Seattle to comb the restaurant for clues.

During their initial inspection of the premises of the store where Cathy Dawes worked, the homicide investigators observed that there were no apparent signs of forced entry into the building, a strong indication that the killer was already inside the store with Mrs. Dawes or perhaps had talked her into opening the door for some reason. Of course it was possible that Cathy had opened the door to someone she knew and trusted, perhaps even a regular customer, but there was no way to substantiate this possibility.

When Clark County Coroner Arch Hamilton visually examined the crime site, which he later described as "bloody," he was careful not to move the victim's body before the state criminalists arrived from Seattle. Although the victim had been tentatively identified as Cathy Dawes, Hamilton said positive identification would likely be accomplished by examination of the victim's personal effects, but that would not be done until the criminalists arrived. Hamilton said there was evidence which indicated that the victim had been sexually assaulted.

"I've been in the business a long time," he said, "and this is among the most sadistic crimes I've ever seen. It was a horrible thing."

Investigators said that the woman's pants had apparently been cut open, her hands were tied behind her back, a piece of cloth was stuffed inside her mouth as a gag and she was blindfolded with a towel. She was shot in the forehead as she lay on her back in the storeroom.

"It looked like she was raped," said Hamilton, who added that the Washington State Patrol Crime Lab in Seattle would make the final determination on that point. Cotton swabs would be used to obtain samples from the victim's vagina, rectum and throat to check for the possible presence of male semen. The swabs would then be saturated with acid phosphatase and, if semen were present, the swabs would turn to a bright pinkish-purple color. Additional efforts would be made to type the perpetrator's blood through the analysis of semen, if any were present.

"I can truly say I've seen some bad ones," said Hamilton, "but not many worse than this . . . Not many things in life affect me, but something like this is hard to get over . . . it was truly an execution."

But what was the motive in this case? Was it robbery? Chuck Brink, chief criminal deputy for the Clark County sheriff's office at the time, now retired, said that the store's safe was open.

"I could see coins in it," said Roger Bennett, Clark County's chief criminal deputy prosecutor. "But I didn't see any bills." Sheriff Frank Kanekoa confirmed that the store's safe had been opened and still contained money, and said his investigators leaned to robbery, but were reluctant, at this point, to officially label the motive in the case.

A short time after the victim's body was found, police officers and sheriff's deputies formed a 10-block dragnet around the store. The cops also brought in "Bronson," a tracking dog from the Vancouver Police Department, to search within the boundaries of the dragnet. Bronson, named after actor Charles Bronson "because he had a Charles Bronson personality—a little rough around the edges, crusty if you will," searched for hours in an attempt to pick up a scent, all to no avail.

During the early-morning phase of the investigation, detectives interviewed the taxi driver who reported the suspicious circumstances to the 9-1-1 emergency dispatcher. The driver told the detectives how he came to the store to pick up a customer who, when the driver arrived, was not there. He told the officers that he circled the store once, parked his car and went inside to purchase a candy bar and to make inquiries regarding his fare. But when he went inside, he said, he noticed that the store appeared to be unattended. In response to questions posed by detectives, the driver said that

272

he did not go into the back room, and he did not see anyone as he circled the store prior to going inside. He said he did not go back inside after notifying police of the suspicious circumstances.

Shortly before 4:00 a.m., detectives contacted the manager of the other store in the area, half a block west of the crime scene, and asked that it be opened so they could conduct a search of the premises. They found nothing significant, but during the course of their contact with the manager they learned of the hitchhiker who came by at closing time to request change so he could call a taxi. The manager, having given the hitchhiker a ride home after seeing him waiting for the taxi in front of the store where the victim was found, was able to provide detectives with the address where he had dropped off the hitchhiker.

The investigators immediately contacted the hitchhiker, who told them how he had obtained a ride as far as the store where Cathy Dawes worked. He said he was dropped off in front at 1:10 a.m., at which time he found the door locked when he tried to enter to obtain change to call a taxi from a pay telephone. The hitchhiker said he thought that Cathy Dawes was still inside at that time because he had seen her car, which he said he recognized because he had been a regular customer for some time.

Needing the change to make the call, though, he told the investigators that he walked half a block up the street to the other store, changed a dollar, walked back to the pay telephone in front of the store where Cathy Dawes worked and telephoned for a taxi. He told the detectives that while waiting for the taxi the manager of the store where he had obtained the change drove by, saw him and offered him a ride home, which he gladly accepted. He was unable to provide any further details.

In the meantime, law-enforcement officers continued their investigations by conducting door-to-door interviews with residents of the area, but their efforts failed to turn up any sound leads. Despite the fact that no one reported hearing any gunshots during the early morning hours, sheriff's deputies did, however, learn that two individuals, both male, had been in the store where Cathy worked at closing time. As it turned out, news of the shocking murder had spread quickly throughout the community and had brought forth the two individuals who told the detectives they had left when Mrs. Dawes told them she was closing but that a third male remained inside, playing video games.

According to the description given to detectives by the two individuals who came forward, the subject who remained inside the store was a white male, 24-25 years of age, 6 feet 1 inch in height, 165-170 pounds, with shoulder-length dark, perhaps black, straight hair. One of the individuals described the subject's clothing as dark green long-sleeve coveralls, or similar apparel, and the other described the subject as wearing a green V-neck rain jacket, similar to a poncho with sleeves, and baggy pants. Aside from that; detectives reported that they had no suspect leads and no firm motive. The man who remained in the store at closing time was being sought as a potential witness, detectives said.

"We believe he was the last person to see the victim alive," said Chuck Brink, chief criminal deputy. "Let's just say that we'd like to talk to him." A description of the male subject was sent out over police wires throughout the northwest, and cops from Washington, Oregon, Idaho and Northern California began hauling in anyone who fit the aforementioned description. However, their efforts would ultimately end in frustrating failure.

Meanwhile, by mid-morning, crime-lab specialists arrived from Seattle in a van filled with the tools of their trade, which also serves as a portable lab. The specialists were experts in dealing with homicides, as was evident from those witnessing their arduous and often tedious work.

"I'd rather take my time, no matter what," said one law-enforcement official, referring to the four-hour wait for the crime lab specialists to arrive from Seattle. "I have seen how they (criminalists) can prove your case. It is not so much that the evidence the experts pick up can lead to a suspect, but most often it is the evidence that later ties a suspect to the crime and leads to a conviction," said the official. It should also be pointed out that such evidence can also clear a suspect of the crime in which he has been accused, that the efforts of the criminalist works for both the guilty and the innocent.

After conferring briefly with detectives and deputies, the specialists began unloading cameras, tripods, lights, crime scene kits and other equipment they would need to complete their job. They began

275

by photographing the scene, inside and out, using various angles and lenses to provide as much detail of the site as possible. Satisfied that they had photographed everything relevant to the case, they then sprayed and dusted for latent fingerprints, of which there were many. They concentrated their efforts, though, in the most likely places, such as doors, the counter top, cash register, safe and surrounding areas and, of course, the video games. They paid particular attention, however, to the back room area where the victim's body had been found. When they finished, the criminalists had many latent prints to deal with, many of which would have to be eliminated through a long and tedious process of matching non-relevant prints to officers, store employees and others.

The criminalists, during the course of their examination of the crime scene, set up bright lights above the back room of the store so they could closely examine the pools of the victim's blood for signs of footprints. They also inched along the floor with tweezers in hand, searching for trace evidence such as hair and fiber samples and depositing anything that had potential into appropriate containers for later study. They took blood samples from the victim as well as from the floor, and searched for signs of semen. However, they declined to reveal whether any semen was present, and they would not comment on what trace evidence was found. After they packed up their gear and left, a police artist was brought in to attempt to draw a composite of the man who had been playing video games shortly before Cathy

Dawes was killed.

"They don't do that in Clark County (bring in an artist)," said Roger Bennett, chief criminal deputy prosecutor, who referred to the use of a police artist in Clark County as "pretty unusual." Normally, police attempt to put together a composite of a suspect, by using an I-denti-Kit, a series of cards that depict varying facial characteristics. But when more detail is needed an artist draws the composite based on descriptions from witnesses.

When the artist completed the composite, the drawing was distributed throughout the region. It appeared in newspapers and television news programs, and was placed inside public buildings, resulting in the sheriff's department receiving numerous tips. However, none of the tips panned out, and the cops were left with merely a face with no name.

A reward offer of more than $5,000 was announced a few days after the tragic, utterly senseless execution-style murder of Cathy Dawes which brought dozens of possible leads to the detectives of the Clark County Sheriff's Department. Chuck Brink, chief criminal deputy at the time, said two teams of detectives on the day shift and two teams on the swing shift followed up on all calls, many of which were from people who said they believed they had seen the man whose description had been circulated by the department. But, Brink said, there was "nothing good" to report in spite of their efforts.

As detectives continued their search for the elusive killer, whose style in this case closely resembled

277

the crimes attributed to the so-called "I-5 Killer" who, by this time, had already been apprehended, they couldn't help but wonder if they had a copy-cat killer on their hands. At this point, however, they could only treat the death of Cathy Dawes as a single, isolated case of brutal, sadistic murder.

As with any crime of this type, people naturally become upset and angry, even afraid, and the community of Clark County was no exception as was evident from comments by area residents following the grisly murder.

"They shouldn't let women work alone there at night," said one woman who lived nearby.

"It's very, very sad that this sort of thing has to happen," said the manager of another nearby store, who added that customers had expressed their anger at what had happened when they learned of the tragedy.

"It's crazy," said a man who works in an office near the crime scene. "People around here are going to start getting nervous."

"It's too close," said another area resident. "It scares me. They just had the hamburger thing (restaurant murder of 1981) nearby, and now this."

Meanwhile, investigators went over the crime scene again and again, questioned and re-questioned potential witnesses, all to no avail. More than 250 telephone tips were checked out by detectives, but ultimately led nowhere. It was frustrating, to say the least, and each of the detectives knew that with the passage of time their chances of apprehending the killer decreased. But they persevered just the same, none of them willing to give

278

up on the case until Cathy Dawes' brutal killer was brought to justice.

What was the motive for the gruesome killing? Robbery? Rape? Perhaps both? It is a question that has been gnawing at Sergeant Mike Davidson's gut since the outset of the case. According to Davidson, robbery seems to be the most likely motive because cash, less than $250, was missing when store officials and detectives counted what was left in the cash register and safe. Although there was evidence that the victim had been raped, the detectives could not say for certain that she had been, because of inconclusive lab tests.

Now, in 1985, more than three years since the murder of Cathy Dawes, Sergeant Davidson and other Clark County officials admit they are not any closer to apprehending a suspect in the case. But they haven't given up. Several of the detectives, including Davidson and Pat St. John, periodically open the multi-volume case file in an attempt to develop new angles or leads. But so far, in spite of the fact that Detective St. John has personally spent nearly 250 hours working on the case, the case remains unsolved with no new leads.

Almost each week a close relative of the victim calls detectives from her out-of-state home to inquire about any possible new leads. Although each time she calls and is informed there are no new leads, the relative has stated that she is impressed by the determination of the detectives at the Clark County Sheriff's Department.

"I ask them (detectives) if they remember (Cathy's) murder," said the relative. "I'm impressed

279

that they do remember . . . There is hardly a night that I don't thank God for the detectives working on the case. They are compassionate. When I have felt really low, I have called them. They have been like counselors . . . I want to know who killed her. I pray I won't die without finding out. I know it won't change anything. I just need to know."

Why was Cathy Dawes killed with such unleashed savagery? No one knows at this point, and perhaps never will. One thing is certain, though. The fact that the killer blindfolded, gagged and bound his victim's hands prior to shooting her in the head is inconsistent. Normally, when the perpetrator of a crime goes to all that trouble he does not kill the victim. The fact that the victim was killed in this case, after being brutalized and bound, is what makes this case such a sadistic one.

"I have never understood that," said Davidson. "I have seen more bizarre crime scenes in terms of panic and terror, but this one was unexplained. Considering the amount of time the crook or crooks went through to bind her and blindfold her, why didn't they just kill her (at the outset) if they were going to? Usually, when someone is bound and blindfolded, the intent isn't to kill them," said Davidson. Making the case even more "coldblooded and calculating," said Davidson, was the fact that the victim was not beaten and there was no signs of a struggle.

"We discuss this case a great deal," said Davidson in a recent interview. "This is a crime I can personally associate with. She, the victim, was a mother—a decent human being. Many people who become homicide victims do so because of their lifestyle, but that's not so in this case. She was a totally innocent victim.

"In this case," Davidson continued, "the killer was extremely lucky, or skilled, or both. Either way, I don't like to lose. If in ten years this isn't solved, my attitude will still be the same. I want to arrest the person who killed her."

The killer who murdered Cathy Dawes in cold blood is still at large, and his identity is unknown to police. It is possible he will kill again, if he hasn't already done so.

"SLAIN SOCIALITE IN THE TOWNHOUSE"

by Bud Ampolsk

There is an ancient Middle Eastern legend that purports to prove the futility of attempting to escape one's fate.

The irony-tinged tale goes like this: A traveler was making his way through a twisting alley in Jerusalem when he saw the hooded form of Death approaching him. The panic-stricken traveler immediately fled the area and journeyed to the town of Samara. When informed of the traveler's action, Death expressed great surprise. Said Death, "But my appointment with the traveler is set for Samara."

The story of the ill-advised and ill-fated traveler could well have been that of a remarkably beautiful and fabulously wealthy divorcee who had traveled four decades and thousands of miles from the horror, corruption, and slaughter of World War II, only to have death single her out on one of Manhattan's most opulent and privileged byways.

The ill-fated woman's saga had its origins in

the rubble of post-World War II Germany. Its tragic climax would be written in blood on East 73rd Street just a block or so away from the glories that are Fifth Avenue and Central Park.

The epilogue is as yet unwritten, although there is a great deal of background material awaiting the fashioning of a denouement. That material resides in the files of the New York Police Department's 19th Precinct headquarters on East 94th Street and those of the department's homicide bureau at One Police Plaza in Manhattan.

The story of Anny Janssen begins in the immediate post-World War II era in Allied-occupied Germany. At that time, Anny Janssen was a sad-eyed little girl of six or so years. Like millions upon millions of other European children, she was probably classified as a displaced person.

It is believed that little Anny was born in Czechoslovakia and that she had been orphaned in the war. Somehow she managed to survive her anguished infancy. Undoubtedly, she must have been physically and emotionally strong. Neither malnutrition nor the endemic diseases of the displaced (such as typhus and tuberculosis) could destroy Anny's beauty, which even under the worst of conditions was readily observable.

Anny made it through her childhood and teen years. With each passing day, she became more lovely. The bone structure in her face was magnificent. Her large eyes were nicely framed by the straightness of her nose and by her high cheekbones. Her hair was dark, silken and lustrous. In every sense, Anny could have been described as a "world-class beauty."

In time, Anny was able to put the horrifying past behind her and concentrate on a better life to come. Strikingly attractive to men, she discovered romance. She married and built the kind of life that most young women only fantasize about. She was determined that her children would never experience the type of deprivations their parents had faced.

To make these dreams come true would take an outpouring of raw courage and tireless energy. If intelligence and industry were what was required to turn fantasy into glowing reality, no effort would be spared.

In the 1960s, Anny and her husband made their big move. They gambled that America was all they had heard it would be. They would meet it on its own terms and make sure that they were not denied the opportunities offered.

Friends would later say the couple turned their backs on the Old World at a point in their lives when they "didn't have a penny." However, that obstacle was just one of many to be overcome. And overcome it they would.

Arriving in New York, the couple began making small and prudent investments in real estate. The American real estate industry was at that time just about to take off. There were other enterprises as well.

In time, Anny Janssen would count her personal wealth in the millions. She would be the half-owner of a successful refrigeration business. Her holdings would include a half-interest in a townhouse on East 73rd Street that had an estimated value of $3 million. There was also a jointly owned townhouse on East 74th Street with a similar estimated valuation.

In her own right, Anny Janssen held the deeds to other parcels in Germany and France. She now spent her summers at a luxurious villa she owned on the French Riviera.

The woman who had once been a war-displaced orphan now was able to send her own two children to the best private schools available. In every way she impressed neighbors with her ongoing devotion to her youngsters.

However, life in the United States had not been without anguish and strife for the beautiful brunette. In 1983, she had begun divorce proceedings. The decree (which resulted in an apportionment of wealth and property between the two contestants) had been hammered out in a series of court appearances best described as "confrontational."

Now an unmarried woman, Anny Janssen had begun to date once more. Because of her classic and seemingly ageless beauty, she had no trouble attracting men.

All in all, Anny Janssen was now not unlike any number of privileged middle-aged women who had opted to go it alone. She suffered no economic stress. She lived in the lap of luxury. Most of all, she was able to maintain the aura of privacy that she valued so highly.

The 48-year-old woman's townhouse was a place of splendor. It was nestled cheek by jowl among similar multi-million dollar structures that lined immaculate, tree-lined 73rd Street between Madison and Park Avenues.

Anny Janssen occupied the top two floors of the building, which had been turned into a sumptuous duplex apartment. The lower three floors were leased out to three other tenants at rents worthy of the Big Apple's most expensive neighborhood.

The building itself was fabulously furnished with marble hallways. It featured handsome bay windows overlooking the street. From a security standpoint, it provided the most modern and sophisticated devices, including a self-service elevator that could be operated only by use of special keys. Thus, any unauthorized person would find it virtually impossible to gain entry to the townhouse's upper floors—even if the person should gain entry to the lobby.

In addition, an electronically controlled surveillance camera was positioned over the townhouse's heavy iron front door. The unit was designed to photograph anybody entering or leaving the premises.

Given the nature of the block and the emphasis on security shown by its residents, it came as something of a surprise, to detectives at the 19th Precinct when a call concerning Anny Janssen sent them racing to the townhouse she owned. Their experience told them that homicides rarely, if ever, occur in such posh surroundings. One might expect burglaries or armed robbery, but the type of violence that had been described to the emergency 911 operator by a breathless caller didn't go with the turf that included the East Side address.

But even as the first crime scene units arrived at East 73rd Street, they became aware that the caller had not exaggerated. The caller, a tenant in the Anny Janssen-owned townhouse, had placed the report at approximately noon on Monday, November 30, 1987. The grisly discovery had been made at the foot of the basement steps that led from the ground floor to the building's laundry room.

What responding officers found was a scene of wanton violence. The bullets and knife thrusts that had claimed Anny Janssen's life made almost impossible any appraisal of her living beauty by those now faced with the sight of her bloody corpse lying face up on the basement floor.

Assistant Chief Aaron Rosenthal, who was heading the probe into the apparent murder of the 48-year-old divorcee, described the fury that had left her dead. He said the killer had apparently opened fire on Anny in the first-floor hallway. Janssen had been struck four times: once each in her neck, in the center of her chest, in her right breast, and in her right armpit. The universally respected police chief surmised that the wound in Anny's right armpit had been suffered as the victim instinctively raised her hand to ward off the fusillade that was to cost her her life.

There were indications that the killer's frenzy had caused his aim to waver. According to investigating officers, a number of holes apparently caused by bullets had been discovered in the hallway walls.

Police were puzzled by the location of Anny Janssen's body in the basement. It could not be said positively whether she had been propelled backward down the staircase by the force of the bullets, or whether her murderer had vented a portion of his rage against her by tossing her down the steps himself. What was readily apparent was that the slayer had made every effort to ensure that the victim would die. This was attested to by the five knife wounds discovered in Anny Janssen's abdomen. It was believed that the killer had slashed the divorcee after she had already succumbed to the gunshots, which had been fired at almost point-blank range.

There seemed little likelihood that the murderer had been sexually motivated. Anny Janssen's body was not only fully clothed, she had been bundled for the outdoors. At the moment of her death, she had been wearing a sweater, a skirt, a scarf, and a coat.

The police theorized that Anny had been intercepted by the deadly intruder as she was either leaving or entering her home. A preliminary estimate of time of death indicated that Anny Janssen had been killed approximately 20 hours before the discovery of her body by the building tenant. Based on this assumption, it was felt that the victim had been shot and stabbed to death sometime over the latter part of Thanksgiving weekend.

Giving weight to this theory was the fact that the woman's 13-year-old son had been returned to the 73rd Street house on Saturday evening after a visit with his father. When there was no response to the buzzer in Anny Janssen's duplex apartment, the youngster was taken back to his father's home.

What about the possibility that the killer had been somebody bent on burglary or robbery?

This hypothesis seemed unlikely, because detectives felt they were dealing with a "locked-door" mystery. Not only had there been no signs of tampering with the sophisticated locks on the iron front door, but the proximity of the dead woman's pocketbook to her body indicated that her killer had not been a panic-stricken burglar.

This information came from Chief Rosenthal, who said there were no signs of forced entry into the townhouse and that robbery didn't appear to be the motive. The first check of the victim's handbag caused police to believe that nothing of value was taken from it.

As detectives, forensic experts, and ballistics personnel went about their grim business, the mirrors that paneled the walls reflected the ugly scene of crime scene technicians coaxing the remains of a once-beautiful woman into a medical examiner's body bag for the trip to the mortuary at Bellevue.

Outside the townhouse, the officers were watched by a crowd of residents of the posh neighborhood, many of whom had never before witnessed the workings of real police personnel actually searching for homicide scene clues.

The crowd viewed the scene with something akin to awe as a graying and bespectacled detective dusted the townhouse's front door for possible latent prints. They noted the uniformed patrolman who had been stationed in front of the building to keep the idly curious away. Absent were the usual attempts at gallows humor that are so often the gawker's show of bravado. These onlookers were very much aware of the dire seriousness of what had occurred on their block. The brutal murder of one of their neighbors left them with a sense of their own vulnerability.

For their part, the investigators, led by Chief Rosenthal, hoped that among the stunned onlookers might be someone who could provide information to help them generate logical theories about what had happened to Anny Janssen and the reasons behind her murder. With this in mind, detectives set up a command post at the 19th Precinct's 94th Street station house where potential witnesses would be interviewed. There, too, would come the reports of canvassers who were even then moving among passersby traversing East 73rd Street and the surrounding blocks in the hopes that somebody might be able to come forward with meaningful observations.

Probers learned from neighbors that Anny Janssen indeed had been a fabulously wealthy woman in her own right. Many of the properties that were now in her name had been provided as part of the divorce decree, which had been handed down on January 26, 1984. But the dead woman's finances were only part of the story as far as detectives were concerned. They wanted to know everything that might be determined about her personality and her personal life.

At the back of their minds was the hunch that Anny Janssen might have known her slayer.

A number of those from the so-called "poodle-walking set" of East 73rd Street described the victim as an aloof woman who, perhaps because of her traumatic childhood, kept to herself and didn't share any polite chitchat with those she met on the street. However, according to their version, the dead woman had not tried to avoid attracting attention. As a matter of fact, it was thought that the opposite had been true. Anny Janssen had approached life in the manner of a woman who recognized that her physical beauty was something that set her apart from others. Even in her most routine comings and goings she had been meticulous in her attire.

Several people described Anny as "an attention-getter." They told of how the divorcee had favored a beehive style for her lush black hair, how she had worn spiked heels and long black fake eyelashes as she traveled through the area. For the middle-aged mother of two, there had been none of the casualness that marked the fashions of the 1980s.

One woman compared Anny Janssen's manner of dress to that which had been the rage of the 1960s. The neighbor said, "She [Anny Janssen] looked a lot like Jackie Kennedy used to look."

A male neighbor added, "She looked like a *Vogue* [magazine] model from the '60s — always impeccably dressed, with perfect makeup, hair, everything."

But others who had watched and spoken to the brunette over the course of time left the impression that there was another side to Anny that was far more serious. They told of her tremendous devotion to her son, who had a neurological condition.

According to friends and acquaintances, almost every day Anny Janssen would pick the boy up from the private school he attended. When the weather permitted, she would take him to Conservatory Lake (near Fifth Avenue and just north of 72nd Street) in Central Park. There, in the lovely setting, she would sit and chat with other mothers and nannies as the boy rode his bicycle around the miniature pond, enjoying the sight of a fleet of radio-controlled model sailboats going through their intricate maneuvers in the clear water.

Park regulars described Anny Janssen as friendly and elegantly dressed, "a stunningly beautiful middle-aged woman."

Although the divorcee had been friendly with the other bench-sitters and had chatted with them at length, they said she had never taken her eyes off her son for so much as a second.

To those who remembered her visits to the model boat basin, Anny Janssen would always be remembered as a woman who recognized that there were things in life far more important than

292

the items money could buy.

Said one acquaintance, "She certainly had the money to hire somebody to go out with him — but she went. She'd sit there for hours every day."

Another woman told of Anny Janssen's equanimity in the face of her marriage's breakup. The woman described Anny as "very composed. She had the ability to adjust."

Meanwhile, detectives were conducting conversations at 19th Precincy headquarters with a number of people who had known the dead woman.

It was learned from sources that in recent months Anny Janssen had been dating. Unlike many women in situations similar to hers, the divorcee seemed to be attracted to men of nearly her own age rather than those who might be considerably younger than she was.

One of the men had been involved in radio work. Although police expressed a desire to talk to him, Chief Rosenthal emphasized that he was not a suspect in the case. As a matter of fact, Rosenthal noted that there were no suspects and that the slaying remained just as baffling as it had been in the first moments after the divorcee's body had been discovered in her basement.

In the hopes that the offer of a substantial reward would hasten a break in the case, family members of the slain brunette posted a reward notice for $10,000 to anyone providing information that would lead to the arrest and conviction of the killer.

Of the person who had been dating Anny,

Chief Rosenthal said, "I understand he is waiting for counsel. He can be helpful. I would like to speak to him, but I have to respect his constitutional rights."

While this phase of the probe was going on, Rosenthal turned his attention back to the facts provided by his department as well as by the medical examiner's office.

The police felt that the murderer had definitely not been a professional hitman.

On this point Rosenthal said, "Usually, they [professional killers] are better shots than that."

Supporting the detective chief's argument was the final tally of bullets fired in the townhouse. It was now said that four of the eight slugs that had been fired at point-blank range had missed their mark.

The medical examiner's office confirmed that the first bullet that crashed into Anny Janssen's brain had killed her. The five savage knife thrusts to her abdomen bespoke an uncontrollable rage rather than a coolly applied coup de grace.

Since no subsequent evidence disproved the original theory that there had been no forced entry into the victim's building, police were leaning toward the possibility that the dead woman had known her slayer.

However, giving pause to the investigators was the nagging question of why no money was found in the purse that lay beside the victim's body. Police had recovered some jewelry, but no cash.

Detectives could not totally discount the possibility that the murderer had been bent on robbing Anny Janssen and was maddened by the vigor of her self-defense. Police wondered if the killer had been a street person who had followed his victim into the building, gaining entrance before she had time to secure the door behind her. Were this hypothetical robber high on crack, it could easily have seduced him into an orgy of overkill. This would be especially true if the victim had shown the ability and spunk to try to protect herself, as the bullet wound in Anny Janssen's armpit suggested she had. The amateurish viciousness of the attack — as evidenced by the stray bullet holes in the walls, the repeated, unnecessary knife thrusts into the victim's abdomen, and the possibility that she had been hurled down the stairs — seemed to corroborate this line of reasoning.

Particularly puzzling to police was the 20-hour estimated time lapse between the moment Anny Janssen died and the moment the tenant spotted her corpse at the bottom of the staircase. Was it indeed more than 20 hours? A telling aspect of the victim's character has led some investigators familiar with the case to think so.

Here was a woman who would not allow anybody other than herself to pick her son up from school each day. She would be the one to take him to Conservatory Lake and watch over him as he rode his bicycle around the elliptical path surrounding the lake. Taking all this into consideration, does it seem likely that, if alive, she was absent from the building at the appointed time for the youngster's return home on Saturday evening, November 28th? Or is it more likely that Anny was already in the house, dead in the laundry room?

All that can be said for sure is that almost three years have elapsed since that Thanksgiving weekend of 1987 when a vicious fate caught up with Anny Janssen. In that time, the search has continued.

Chief Rosenthal has now retired as chief of Manhattan detectives. Other detectives involved in the case have reached retirement age as well.

But this does not mean that the Anny Janssen murder case has been forgotten. It remains under intensive investigation. There is always the hope that some vital clue will suddenly emerge and all the frustrating questions will be answered.

As of now, that hasn't happened.

The situation as of this writing is that there are no suspects. There have been no arrests. If you happen to walk along East 73rd Street between Park and Madison Avenues, you will see nothing that sets the townhouse murder site off from its neighbors. It stands much as it did on Monday, November 30, 1987. Its second-floor bay windows are an architectural delight. In the summer, the branches of the shade trees that line 73rd Street reach out to cast a cooling shadow over the house's front door.

People walk easily back and forth, sensing the wealth it would take to purchase such a property. Not too many of them recall or are even aware of what occurred here.

But the detectives who work on the case remember in agonizing detail. The people who mourn Anny Janssen—the spirited woman who, as a child, beat insurmountable odds, only to have fate reach out over 3,000 miles of trackless ocean and across four decades to claim her—cannot forget her.

"STRANGEST HOLLYWOOD MURDER MYSTERY EVER!"

by Sheila Barnes

One wag called it a "shot that was heard around the world"—the single .38-caliber bullet that ended the life of a dashing, debonair movie director.

The year was 1922, a time when Harold Lloyd was able to climb tall buildings, handsome Rudolph Valentino was the love object of thousands, and Mary Pickford and Douglas Fairbanks were the reigning monarchs in Hollywood. Warren G. Harding was in the White House, there was to be a New York subway series later that year between the Yankees and the old New York Giants, and in California, Aimee Semple McPherson, heralding later televangelists, begged for a silent collection—no coins, please! The first sound-on-film motion picture, called Phonofilm, was still a year away. Meanwhile it was the heyday of the silents.

William Desmond Taylor, 45-year-old English-born, top-flight movie director, was the victim. He was found on his living room floor, shot in the back. The ensuing investigation ruined the careers of one established star and of another who was being groomed as Mary Pickford's rival, and it roiled up Hollywood at a time when the industry was doing its best to present a pristine image to the nation. Worse, it threw a spotlight on the drug scene that Tinseltown would have preferred to leave in the shadows, ironically, the beam flicked on because of Taylor himself. An arch-foe of drug traffickers, he had worked with authorities to uncover them.

Handsome and suave, Taylor could have been a screen star—in fact, he appeared in a number of movies—but he made his mark in directing. He was the consummate man-about-town, wearing elegant clothes, driving fast cars, squiring beautiful women. He was also a man of mystery.

On the evening of February 1, 1922, Taylor phoned the apartment of Mabel Normand, Hollywood's premiere comedienne. Her maid told him Miss Normand was out shopping. He asked that she be told he had a couple of books for her. Perhaps she could drop by for them or he could drop them off at her home. Soon after, when Miss Normand called, she was also given the message and also told that she had an early studio call. Dropping her original plan to see a movie (a Harold Lloyd comedy), she decided to stop off at Taylor's cottage.

When she arrived at Taylor's, he was on the phone. She waited for him to finish, then entered the house. The host and his guest were served cocktails by Taylor's new butler, Henry Peavey.

As they sipped their drinks, Taylor complained bitterly about his former butler-valet, an Englishman named Edward Sands. He displayed a sheaf of checks forged so cleverly that Taylor himself wasn't sure who'd signed them—Sands or Taylor himself. Too, he accused the servant of running up charges on various accounts, stealing clothes, pawning jewelry and smashing both of his cars. And—Sands had disappeared.

Peavey finished a few chores, then left for the night, and, shortly before eight o'clock, so did Mabel Normand, a book under her arm. She was escorted by Taylor to her car parked at the curb.

A half-hour later, some neighbors, Mr. and Mrs. James Mitchell and their maid, heard a sudden noise, something like an automobile backfiring or a firecracker. Mrs. Mitchell looked outside and saw a man—or a woman dressed like a man—descend the Taylor front steps, then walk away. The person was described as being on the short, stocky side, and wearing a heavy jacket, a cap pulled low, and a muffler. The neighbor paid no more attention to the incident.

When Henry Peavey arrived for work the following morning, he found Taylor's body stretched out face up on the living room floor. Except for the dried blood around his mouth, the movie director looked perfectly—and unnaturally—composed, his clothing neatly arranged, his arms at his side, his feet together.

The frantic Peavey rushed outside for help. He encountered a doctor passing by. The doctor came in, checked the body, and pronounced Taylor dead of a gastric hemorrhage. But when the police arrived shortly after, they discovered that Taylor had been shot, a .38 bullet having entered near the left shoulder blade.

Meanwhile, another neighbor, film star Edna Purviance (she was Charlie Chaplin's leading lady at the time), was attracted by the commotion. Once she'd found out what had happened, she went immediately to the phone and relayed the bad news to Mabel Normand and Mary Miles Minter. The petite, blonde Minter, still in adolescence, was a star in her own right and she was being groomed as a rival to Mary Pickford.

Who was William Desmond Taylor and where had he come from? As police launched a probe into his past, a number of interesting facts emerged.

To begin with, he was born William Cunningham Deane-Tanner, the son of a British officer, in Ireland. The father pointed him toward a military career, but poor eyesight was a handicap not to be overcome, it was found.

Although young William had shown some interest in a theatrical career and had worked as a secretary for an acting company at the age of 18, the father shipped the young man and his brother off to an American ranch, presumably to make real men of them. A couple of years in the Kansas prairie convinced William that he was not cut out to be a cowboy.

The next stop was New York. There, as with many aspiring to a career in the theatre, William Deane-Tanner found another job. Working in an antique shop, he rose to become its vice president and manager. Moreover, he married, moved to the suburbs, and became the father of a child.

But on October 23, 1908, William Deane-Tanner walked out of the fashionable antique shop for lunch—and never returned, neither to his home nor to his business. The following day, he arranged to receive $600 delivered by messenger to his hotel. Then he dropped completely out of sight. It seemed to be a family trait: in 1912, his brother, Dennis Deane-Tanner, also disappeared.

Although William Deane-Tanner *may* have seemed a conformist, he was anything but. In the years between his vanishing act and his highly successful movie career, he lived a life of adventure, prospecting in the goldfields of Colorado, Montana and the Klondike. He also put in a year of service with the Canadian Army in 1918.

Earlier, however, while he'd been in Alaska, his theatrical hopes had reignited when he joined a theatrical company. Then it was on to Hollywood with a new name—William Desmond Taylor—and a background which he only partially revealed. His skills won him acting roles and a chance at directing and, as time passed, it was as a film director that he became famous. His charm and openhandedness soon made him a leading Hollywood playboy. Women adored him.

The wife he'd abandoned in 1908 had divorced him and remarried. Attending a movie in 1912 with their daughter, she suddenly stood up and pointed at the screen, shouting, "That's your father!"

Taylor's success as a director led to the presidency of the Motion Picture Directors Association. He was powerful enough in Hollywood to take on drug traffickers, vowing to rid the screen capital of narcotics. And he was effective in bringing about federal arrests throughout the country. It was a campaign that drew even more attention after his murder. Had Taylor become the target of a drug revenge slaying?

Another baffling question arose. Edward Sands, the rascally butler, had lived with Taylor during 1921. It was while Taylor was abroad that Sands' depredations took place. Some thought Sands may have been blackmailing Taylor.

Strangely, pawn tickets for stolen articles were returned to Taylor and they bore the name, *Deane-Tanner!* Was Sands the long-lost brother of Taylor?

When Edna Purviance phoned Mary Miles Minter with the news of Taylor's slaying, she unleashed a flood of emotion that was to drown the young actress. Despite the best efforts of a relative to restrain her, Minter rushed to the scene, now crowded with police and reporters. The relative, it developed, was violently opposed to Minter's attachment to Taylor. Furthermore, that relative possessed a .38.

The young star was hysterical. She pulled at her blonde curls, beat her little fists against the chest of detectives, and generally comported herself in a manner that called maximum attention to herself — and her relative.

In a search of the dead man's possessions, the authorities found various pieces of lingerie, including pink silk nightgowns monogrammed "MMM" — and letters written by Mary Miles Minter to her beloved. In fact, said the star, she and the director were secretly engaged, waiting only until she reached the age of 18 to marry.

Taylor's death was only the beginning of Miss Minter's tragedy. She and her relative quarreled bitterly, not only about their difference on the Taylor question, but about the fortune the actress earned in motion pictures. Although she and her relative were cleared after questioning, the scandals pursued her and effectively ended her career. She never married.

Mabel Normand, the leading comedienne, also felt an unwelcome spotlight on her. Normand considered Taylor a mentor, and perhaps something more. Police found a letter from her to him that began "Dearest Daddy" and ended with "Beloved Baby."

Miss Normand herself came in for questioning. She never quite recovered from the thought that she might have been considered a suspect, though she was quickly absolved of any connection with the crime.

During the investigation, her apartment was crashed by cops, curious neighbors, and the throng of reporters bent on squeezing the last bit of newsprint out of the Taylor murder. Questions were shot at her until she broke down and cried. It took longer, but her career also came to an end as a result of the case. A defeated woman, she succumbed eight years later to tuberculosis.

Then who killed William Desmond Taylor?

The neighbor who spotted a person leaving Taylor's house right after the shooting said it *could* have been Edward Sands that she saw. Or it could have been a woman dressed as a man. Or maybe, police considered, someone who'd been fingered by Taylor's war on drugs.

There was no evidence linking Mary Miles Minter, her relative, or Mabel Normand to the crime; just the same, they suffered mightily.

Now, almost 70 years later, the secret of Taylor's death has been buried with the murderer. Still lingering is a mystery stranger than any ever devised for the silver screen.

EDITOR'S NOTE:
Mr. and Mrs. James Mitchell are not the real names of the persons so named in the foregoing story. Fictitious names have been used because there is no reason for public interest in the identities of these persons.

"REIGN OF TERROR OF THE GREEN RIVER KILLER!"

by Gary C. King

On Thursday, July 15, 1982, two young boys were entertaining themselves by bicycling along a path which runs along the banks of the Green River in an area just north of the Meeker Street Bridge in Kent, Washington, located in south King County near Seattle.

The summer of 1982 would be a summer they would never forget, no matter how hard they tried, because what started out as a day of brightness and high spirits for the two boys quickly turned into a haunting nightmare when they looked down the banks toward the river from the path above. What they saw was the dead body of a teenage girl partially submerged and snagged in pilings near the bank of the Green River.

When the King County authorities arrived at the crime scene, located near a popular lovers lane, they treated the obvious homicide routinely by following proper police procedure, just as they would treat any other such case. What the cops didn't realize as they fished the young lady's body out of the river, and wouldn't realize for some time yet, was that the macabre discovery they were dealing with was only a sample of what was yet to come. It would ultimately tie in with the murders of at least 25 additional females whose bodies or remains would be found over the following two years in or near the vicinity of the Green River near the Seattle-Tacoma International Airport. The case at the time of this writing would become the biggest active murder investigation in the United States.

The young victim of July 15, 1982, the first victim of what was to be called the Green River Killer, was a cute, 5-foot-4-inch blue-eyed blonde, somewhat chunky at 140 pounds. Although her body was bruised and bloated, the cops guessed that the girl was a teenager and, because of several tattoos on her body, the investigators reasoned that positive identification would not be too difficult to attain.

They entered the victim's physical description into their notebooks and described the tattoo of a Harley-Davidson motorcycle emblem on her back, the tattoo of a cross entwined with vines on her left shoulder, two butterflies just above her left breast, a unicorn on the left side of her lower abdomen and a tattoo of a heart entangled with additional vines on her left forearm. Suspected cause of death was listed as strangulation, which was confirmed following a thorough autopsy by the King County coroner's office.

The victim of July 15, 1982 was soon identified as 16-year-old Wendy Lee Coffield, who had been reported missing from a foster care home seven days earlier. The identity was confirmed visually by a close relative, who also told the investigators that Wendy disappeared after she left the foster care home to spend the night with her grandfather.

Background investigation of the victim revealed that Wendy was a persistent, incessant runaway who dropped out of high school and took to the streets, eventually selling her body as a prostitute to help support a drug habit and to otherwise help sustain her troubled life. In addition to prostitution, Wendy managed to build a criminal record for herself by stealing lunch tickets at her high school prior to dropping out, and was sent to a juvenile detention facility for the theft. When she returned home in May, 1982, she stole $140 worth of food stamps from a neighbor and was convicted, resulting in her being returned to the juvenile detention facility. After a short period of incarceration, she was released to the custody of the foster care home and was subsequently murdered, leaving investigators with no solid leads to point them in the direction of a prime suspect.

Time slipped forward to August as detectives made little or no progress with the Wendy Coffield case. King County authorities also had several other unsolved murders involving young females linked to prostitution on their books, but were treating them as separate cases due to the lack of similarities regarding the killer's method of operation. It wasn't until August 12, 1982, when the body of 23-year-old Deborah Lynn Bonner of nearby Tacoma was found a half mile upstream from where Wendy Coffield's body had been found in the Green River, that the police were able to make a connection linking any of the cases together.

The sleuths still had a string of unsolved murders of young women, some of which were linked to prostitution and some of which were not, that they had to deal with as separate cases. But there were striking similarities regarding the murders of Wendy Coffield and Deborah Bonner, which prompted the detectives to theorize that their deaths were the work of the same man, thus allowing them to combine the two into one case.

After checking the latest victim's background, the detectives learned that Bonner had been involved in prostitution activities in Portland, Oregon, for which she had been arrested several times. They also learned that she had made numerous collect telephone calls from Portland to Seattle, which established a link to King County where her body was discovered.

As King County authorities worked around the clock attempting to make even a little headway with the Coffield-Bonner case, a Seattle-area self-described psychic volunteered to help by attempting to pick up psychic images of victim Wendy

Coffield, ultimately achieving some startling, if not useful, results.

Laura Thompson, the psychic, and a friend went to the area of the Meeker Street Bridge in Kent on a pleasant weekend evening in August, the area where Wendy Coffield's body was found floating in the Green River, in hopeful anticipation of picking up psychic images. Shortly after parking in an area near the bridge, Thompson later reported that she began picking up the name Opal and, as a result, thought she should be looking for a car by that name, but spelled O-p-e-l. However, no such car was spotted.

At approximately 2:00 a.m., Thompson and her friend heard a scream coming from the river that made their blood run cold. Wasting no time, they followed the stream and caught a brief look of a tall, slender man taking long, giant steps, but not quite running, across a clearing near the river. He got into a car, at which time Thompson was able to glimpse the man's profile. Thompson and her friend followed in their own car in hot pursuit, but were unable to catch up with the man because he was driving a car "that was all souped up. I was driving sixty miles an hour but he knew how to drive. He took the curves like an expert," she said. Although Thompson was unable to catch up with the car to get a license number, she was at least able to give detectives a sketchy description of the man driving the speeding vehicle.

"He's white," said Thompson, "has brown hair,

thin legs and I'm not sure of his age, but he walks with a long stride with long, slow-swinging arms." Admittedly, it wasn't much to go on, but, according to one detective, police from agencies around the country have used psychics and have at times achieved positive, desired results. The key, however, of being able to use psychic results effectively is dependent on the investigators' ability to find and gather hard evidence which will stand up in court.

Thompson, who fears for her own safety because of media attention surrounding this case and for which reason a fictitious name has been used here, says that a good deal of her psychic ability is related to rapes and murders of younger age girls and women and claims 90 percent accuracy. "In the beginning," she said of her psychic experiences, which began at age 17 (she's now in her forties), "I thought it was depressing, because I would see people I care about die and accidents happen to them." Now she uses the voice of her subconscious to help authorities whenever possible, but says that she is not able to recognize the "location, identity or meaning" of most of her psychic experiences.

One thing is certain, though: On the weekend night in August, 1982, when Thompson and her friend were parked by the Meeker Street Bridge trying to pick up psychic signals, they were indeed having a high degree of success for, on Sunday, August 15th, King County authorities discovered the nude and decomposed bodies of

311

three young black women floating in the Green River near the area where Thompson was parked. The victims were later identified as Cynthia Jean Hinds, 17; Marcia Faye Chapman, 31, and Opal Charmaine Mills, 16.

"I was parked there (near the bridge) the night Opal Charmaine Mills was killed," said Thompson. "I had been picking up the name, Opal."

The day after the three latest victims' bodies were found, August 16th, the King County authorities had no doubts that they had a serious problem on their hands—a problem that frighteningly resembled the area's numerous "Ted" killings, eight years earlier. In that reign of terror, several young women were brutally slain in serial-type killings attributed to Ted Bundy. As a result of the discovery of the three latest victims, a 25-member unit known as the King County Task Force (later to be called the Green River Task Force) was formed to investigate the homicides.

Background information revealed that one of the latest victims, Marcia Faye Chapman, had been arrested by King County authorities for prostitution along "the strip" near Seattle-Tacoma International Airport (Sea-Tac), a busy avenue where there are many cheap, sleazy motels frequented by prostitutes, pimps and their customers. Chapman lived near the airport, police said, which is not far from the Green River where the bodies were found. Police said that victims Cynthia Hinds and Opal Mills, however, had not been convicted of prostitution, but had been associated or linked to "the strip" area and that some of the victims knew each other.

Although it was revealed early in the investigation that Wendy Coffield had been strangled, police refused to reveal the causes of death of the other victims at this point. But, according to King County Police Major Richard Kraske, task force investigators were theorizing that the five victims, two whites and three blacks, were killed by the same person who disposed of their bodies by tossing them into the Green River on separate occasions. Police also said that because of this series of obviously connected murders, additional unsolved homicides would be looked at again and compared with the Green River killings.

One such killing that was looked at again by the investigators was of 15-year-old Patrisa Jo Crossman, whose blood-soaked body was found on June 13, 1982, lying in shrubs outside an apartment house near Sea-Tac International Airport. According to King County Homicide Detective Larry Peterson, the slender young girl had been raped and repeatedly stabbed. Peterson said that Crossman, linked to prostitution activities in Seattle and Portland, had been "a chronic runaway for over a year," and was well-known on several Portland street corners.

"It's very tragic," Peterson remarked. "They don't believe there are risks. They believe that it always happens to the other person, that they won't get into a car with a bad guy," he said, predicting that young prostitutes would continue to be murdered.

Another death looked at by investigators in the wake of the so-called Green River killings was that of Leann Virginia Wilcox, 16, also known as Renee Virginia Ramirez, of Tacoma. Wilcox's body was found lying in a field in nearby Federal Way, Washington, on January 22, 1982, and autopsy results revealed that she had been strangled. She, too, had been linked to prostitution and, like Crossman and Bonner, Wilcox's activities had been traced to Portland. However, investigators linked Wilcox to a specific pimp and believed that she may have been killed to prevent her from testifying against the pimp in a Seattle prostitution trial.

Still other deaths were scrutinized again by King County authorities to determine whether or not any links exist between those deaths and the Green River killings. Among those cases looked at again:

Angelita Bell Axelson, 25, whose decomposed body was found June 18, 1981—she had been strangled;

25-year-old Desiree Hawkins, a convicted prostitute who had been beaten to death with a crescent wrench in Kent, Washington, on July 4, 1981 (James Patrick Laherty, 33-year-old taxicab driver, was charged and convicted in Hawkins' death and was sentenced to 20 years in prison);

19-year-old Virginia Kay Taylor, a nude dancer, whose corpse was found, strangled on January

29, 1982, in a vacant lot near South Seattle Community College;

16-year-old Joan Lucinda Reed Conner, who was found strangled the following month after leaving her home to sell Campfire Girl mints;

Theresa Kline, 27, who was found strangled after having been seen hitchhiking on Aurora Avenue in Seattle on April 27, 1982.

Of the 12 known victims being looked at here, six were found to have been linked to prostitution—Wendy Coffield, Deborah Bonner, Marcia Chapman, Patrisa Crossman, Leann Wilcox and Desiree Hawkins. Two of the known victims, Cynthia Hinds and Opal Mills, had no convictions for prostitution but had been linked to "the strip" area near Sea-Tac International Airport, which is frequented by pimps and prostitutes. Four of the known victims—Theresa Kline, Joan Conner, Virginia Taylor and Angelita Axelson—had no links to prostitution or to "the strip."

In order to avoid "copycat" killings and to provide detectives with a way in which to verify that they had the right man in the event an arrest were made, certain key elements of the case, such as causes of death, were kept secret, particularly after it had been established that several of the killings, namely the deaths of Coffield, Bonner, Chapman, Hinds and Mills, could be linked to a single killer. Before such a link had been established, though, it had been revealed that Coffield was strangled and, according to a

315

source close to the investigation who did not want to be identified, several of the killings were carried out in precisely the same manner.

By August 19th, King County investigators had compiled association charts on the victims to determine if any common friends and acquaintances existed between them, and special attention was given to the five victims whose bodies were found in or near the Green River. As the 25-member task force worked around the clock to piece together bits of evidence they had gathered, King County police spokesman Pat Ferguson reiterated the importance behind the reason investigators remained tight-lipped as to how the women were killed.

"That is one of the few things we have in common with the killer right now," said Ferguson. "The killer knows how he or she killed them and so do we, so that will help when we focus in on a suspect." Ferguson would not disclose whether or not police believed that the killer was male or female, but said that the FBI was putting together a psychological profile of the killer for the task force. "We've got a lot of work to do. It's progressing, but slowly," he said.

By the end of August, 1982, prostitutes working the Tacoma-Seattle area became frightened because of the prostitute slayings there. As a result of their growing fear, several hookers fled to Portland because they felt it was safer to work there, among other reasons.

"I'm afraid to work up there (in Seattle)," said

one prostitute who fled to Portland shortly after prostitutes began getting murdered in Seattle. "There are a lot of girls from Seattle here because of that. Besides, it's so hot in Seattle the police don't let the girls work."

By September, 1982, investigators reported that they had more than two dozen people under investigation and felt more optimistic about the case in spite of the fact that the 25-member task force had so far been unable to turn up enough evidence to point them towards one suspect. Also by this point in the investigation, police sources had been quoted as having said that all the Green River victims had been strangled. Some of them had been strangled with items of their own clothing.

Three weeks passed without any additional bodies turning up, and the special task force members worked energetically as they attempted to put the pieces of their horrible puzzle together. But in spite of their efforts to find the killer and their emphatic warnings to the numerous street-walkers in the area, the bodies continued to pile up, serving only to keep the investigators stymied despite the numerous profiles of possible suspects they looked at.

On Saturday, September 25, 1982, the discovery of the nude body of a young woman found tangled in heavy underbrush in a wooded area just south of a Sea-Tac International Airport runway was added to the growing list of slayings attributed to the Green River Killer, dead proof

317

that he was still committing his hideous acts of violence in the Seattle area, even though he had dumped the latest victim's body six miles from the location where five of his victims had been dumped in or near the Green River.

"We feel there is a connection with the other (five) homicides (found in or near the Green River)," said police spokesman Frank Kinney.

The latest victim was identified as 17-year-old Gisele Lovvorn who, like some of the other victims, had worked as a prostitute along "the strip." However, unlike some of the others who chose the life of being a hooker, background information on Ms. Lovvorn revealed that she'd been a drifter looking for thrills and was known to mix her "work" with pleasure, an unsavory lifestyle that ultimately ended with her violent demise before she saw the age of 18.

By the end of September, 1982, investigators with the Green River Task Force felt reasonably certain they could narrow the scope of their investigation to include only those six victims found in the vicinity of the Green River between July 15, 1982, and September 28, 1982. Even though several of the Seattle slayings had gone unsolved, in which several of the victims were strangled, task force investigators cited notable differences between those slayings and the slayings they were now attributing exclusively to the Green River killer. They would not elaborate on just what those differences were out of fear of jeopardizing their case, but did say they believe all of the so-called Green River victims died at the hands of a single man whom the investigators theorized was likely a deranged customer.

Meanwhile, as speculation surrounding the Green River case began to circulate and grow, two teenagers from south King County were reported missing, last seen in late August. According to police spokesman Kinney, Terri Rene Milligan and Kase Ann Lee, both 16, "fit the general profile of the Green River homicide victims," a fact which prompted police to theorize that the two missing teenagers may be the crazed killer's latest victims.

"There is no evidence to indicate that they also are victims," said Kinney, "but the possibility cannot be discounted," particularly since the two girls fit the profile of the other six victims. An appeal was made to the public to help find the two girls, and their names were added to a list of possible victims.

In an unusual move on Monday, October 4th, a middle-aged Seattle ex-cab driver named Tom Davis contacted news media from the local area and announced that police considered him a prime suspect in the Green River killings because he came to them and offered to help in the investigation. Davis told reporters that he suggested to detectives that they check out two other cabbies in the area, but they instead focused their attention on him.

"I feel like I've got absolutely nothing to hide because I haven't done anything," said Davis, who admitted that he knew five of the six victims and said that he flunked a lie-detector test when he denied to detectives that he killed the women. The ex-cab driver, who had two convictions related to car thefts, said he flunked the tests because he had a nervous disorder which prevented him from passing such tests. He added that he got to know five of the victims because he associated with "street kids."

When asked about Davis, King County police acknowledged that they had questioned him extensively but denied that the investigation had been narrowed to the point where the task force was focusing on a single suspect. The task force, it was reported, had in fact looked at the profiles of more than 2400 possible suspects in a tedious process of elimination. "I'm sure this guy is under some suspicion . . . but somebody is reading a lot into something that is very questionable," said Sergeant Don Rutherford.

Meanwhile, an FBI profile of the Green River killer indicates that the perpetrator responsible for the strangling deaths of the six women found since mid-July had a deep hatred of women, might be a married man who probably came from a broken home and quite possibly hates his mother. The profile states, or suggests, that the killer is probably between 20 and 40 years old and white, a heavy smoker who likes to drink but is fairly intelligent and likes the outdoors, possibly a fisherman or a hunter. The killer may have a background of sexual crimes and/or assault.

The profile suggests that the killer likes to drive and craves publicity, with a strong compulsion to return to the scenes of his crimes. The killer probably has knowledge of where the bodies have so far been discovered, and has possibly posed as a police officer to gain his victim's trust. The profile suggests that the killer chooses prostitutes to prey upon because their lifestyles make them the most accessible or approachable, or he may pick prostitutes because he simply hates loose women.

Unlike mass murderers, who usually know at least some of their victims (as in the case of Seattle's Chinatown massacre, in which 13 victims were killed) and kill them all at the same time, the serial killer stalks strangers and kills them one by one over an extended period of time and quite often involves different locales where the killer travels from city to city or state to state. A Justice Department report suggests there are at least 35 serial killers operating in the United States, including the Green River Killer.

According to Robert D. Keppel, chief criminal investigator for the Washington attorney general's office and a consultant to the King County Police Green River Task Force, serial murder is one of the rarest forms of homicide in spite of the number of victims who die at the hands of a single killer and is probably one of the most, if not the most, frustrating types of homicides for an investigator to deal with. One of the reasons that serial murder is so frustrating and different to deal with is that the killing has usually gone on for quite some time before lawmen recognize the connections between the victims and can link them to one killer.

"Most of the time you're right in the middle of the serial by the time you recognize it," said Keppel, who has investigated or consulted on 10 serial murder cases ranging from the Ted Bundy killings to the Atlanta child murders and now the Green River case. "If you're right in the middle, and here we are with sixteen deaths, imagine how many he's done beforehand!" Keppel believes the Green River case began prior to the finding of the first bodies in or near the Green River in the summer of 1982, citing that the killer may be the most, or at least among the most, prolific serial killers in the history of the United States.

"The obvious difference (in this case) is that the volume of calls in the Green River case is a lot less," said Keppel, "to the extent of thousands of calls less than we received in the 'Ted' case," citing the fact they had witnesses who could describe the suspect in the "Ted" case. Witnesses could also describe his car, how he approached some of his victims, the way he walked and even certain mannerisms. Unfortunately, detectives are getting no such calls in the Green River case.

"You have to understand," said Keppel, "there is a difference in victims. In the 'Ted' case, the type of girls that were missing were just what everybody fears: Someone like their own daughter is the victim. In the 'Ted' case you had a little bathing beauty on a beach in front of 20,000 people. All of a sudden she'd disappear and be found dead a month and a half later. You had people who were taken from their basement bedroom and beaten to death in the middle of the night. You had people that were in a tavern and taken away. You had people who were on a college campus and feeling depressed and just needing somebody to talk to and just happened to be talking to the potential killer."

According to task force investigators, public silence has greatly hampered the lawmen's efforts in the Green River probe. So far, investigators have been unable to determine the type of car the killer drives, and in most of the cases the cops have been unable to determine when a victim first disappeared. Even worse is their inability due to lack of witnesses to develop a description of the killer himself. According to Keppel, a good deal of the phone calls the task force receives are simply about "crazies" running loose, but Keppel points out that serial killers, particularly the Green River Killer, are more intelligent and clever than that.

"They appear to be bright people," said Keppel, "clearly literate . . . streetwise . . . What they do, other than kidnap and kill, they look like the normal public when they're doing it.

They're not standing out in the middle of Pacific Highway South with a bloody knife in their mouth chasing prostitutes.

"Right now," said Keppel, "he's stuck mainly to prostitutes, but his M.O. could change," as did that of Hillside Strangler Kenneth Bianchi, who started out murdering prostitutes but later changed his M.O. to include other females. "You also have to remember that serial murderers generally are cruisers and travelers," said Keppel. "They put a lot of mileage on their cars. He (the killer) could very easily have gone to Portland or to Vancouver, British Columbia for some reason. It's a rather well-known fact that the natural path of prostitutes is from Portland to Tacoma to Seattle. If for some reason the killer felt the heat was on here (in Seattle), he may well look to other areas."

It is precisely for that reason that investigators studying the death of 17-year-old Trina Deanne Hunter, a North Portland black girl with a record for prostitution, are looking at the Green River killer as a possible suspect. Her body, nude from the waist down, was found in a swampy area near Battle Ground, Washington, on December 29, 1982, her head submerged in a shallow pond. An autopsy revealed that she drowned. A background check revealed that Miss Hunter, several months before she had been killed, told a judge that she was forced to work as a prostitute by a man she knew. Other than the fact that she was last heard from on December 7th, few other details were known.

The winter of 1982 passed gently into the spring of 1983 without the discovery of any new bodies that could be attributed to the Green River Killer. If there were additional bodies, they had not yet been found. However, the task force was aware of and looking into a couple of missing-person cases: Mary Bridgit Meehan, 19, of Seattle, was last seen on September 15, 1982. She had no history of prostitution arrests. Shawndra Lee Summers, 17, of Bellevue, was last seen on October 7, 1982. Still missing were Kase Ann Lee and Terri Rene Milligan, both 17.

Because the Green River killer seemingly took a break from his heinous activities beginning the fall of 1982, many people felt that perhaps he had stopped killing or had moved on to another area of the country that was not as "hot" for him. Captain Frank Adamson, who heads the Green River Task Force, did not share that view.

"Some people may have made the assumption in 1982 that the person was gone," said Adamson. "Clearly, he wasn't." The body of Carol Ann Christensen, a 21-year-old from Seattle, was discovered on May 8, 1983, in the vicinity of Maple Valley, Washington. Like several of the other victims she had been strangled, but she had no record of prostitution arrests.

"I still don't think he's gone. I don't think he's dead," said Adamson. "I think he'll be back. More bodies are going to be found—there's no doubt in my mind about that."

Meanwhile, additional missing persons were reported. Kimi Kai Pitsor, a 16-year-old from Seattle was last seen on April 28, 1983, and police suspect that she was abducted from a downtown Seattle street. If, in fact, she turned out to be a Green River victim, the scope of the investigation would be widened to include the area of downtown Seattle. In addition to Pitsor, the task force learned that Yvonne S. Antosh, 19, from Vancouver, British Columbia, was last seen on May 30, 1983. However, it should be pointed out that at this juncture in the investigation there was no conclusive evidence that Pitsor and Antosh were in fact victims of the Green River Killer, merely cautious speculation.

In the meantime, it was learned that convicted killer John Norris Hanks of San Francisco was being looked at by King County authorities as a possible suspect in the Green River killings because of his presence in the Seattle area when several of the murders occurred and because, according to one investigator, "women start coming up dead" in locations where Hanks goes. Hanks served 5½ years in prison for second-degree murder in the 1966 stabbing death of his sister-in-law, said police.

Furthermore, court records show that Hanks has been charged with twice assaulting his wife in Seattle in September, 1982, by choking her until she became unconscious and, according to police, he was arrested on March 3, 1977, in San Francisco and charged with the murder of Patricia Ann Crawford. However, those charges were dropped due to lack of evidence when his former wife refused to testify against him. More recently, though, Hanks has been charged with the June 21, 1980 strangling of 30-year-old Arnetta Oakes, an East Palo Alto, California woman whose body was found beside a creek bed in San Jose.

According to Lieutenant Robert Moir of the San Jose Police Department, Hanks was focused on as a suspect after a tedious investigation during which police learned that Hanks was a friend of Oakes. Charges were not filed until nearly three and a half years after Oakes' body was found.

"It was through scientific analysis of evidence, through criminalistics and crime lab analyses similar to that used in the Atlanta murders that we were able to focus on him . . . as a prime suspect (in the Oakes case)," said Moir, 14 months before Hanks was charged with the strangling.

According to police reports, Hanks allegedly told one of his former wives that he felt powerful when he choked women, and the wife told investigators that Hanks assaulted her seven times, and during two of such assaults he allegedly choked her into unconsciousness. Furthermore, according to court documents, Hanks allegedly told a San Francisco police investigator in 1982 that if he were convicted in a San Francisco homicide case "he would confess to numerous other murders." At that time he was being viewed by police as a possible suspect in eight San Francisco homicides.

"We are looking at Hanks as a suspect because he's been involved in similar types of assault in the past," said Sergeant David Maehren, King County Police Department. Aside from the Oakes case in San Francisco, however, Hanks has not been charged in any other homicides and Captain Adamson of the Green River Task Force said that Hanks has been ruled out of some "but not all" of the unsolved homicides being investigated in the Seattle area.

On Monday, June 13, 1983, the Green River Task Force had another body to consider as a possible victim in the growing chain of killings occurring in the northern Washington area. This time, however, the body was found some 50 miles southeast from the location where many of the other victims attributed to the Green River killer have been found. According to Detective Walt Stout of the Pierce County Sheriff's Department, the nude body of a young woman was found floating in the Nisqually River near the entrance to Mount Rainier National Park at Ashford.

Stout described the victim as a white female in her mid-20s with red hair, approximately 5 feet 5 to 6 inches tall weighing 125 pounds. She had visible scars from old injuries on her right lower arm, and her left wrist and thumb. Stout said that the only items on her body were a pair of small pierced gold earrings with tiny green stones in their centers. Stout said an autopsy surgeon tentatively listed the cause of death as strangulation.

The victim was eventually identified as 27-year-old Kimberly Ann Reames of Vancouver, Washington, and, although Reames did not have any known involvement or activities relating to prostitution, there were some striking similarities with the earlier Green River victims.

For example, Reames was a young woman who had been strangled, and her nude body had been dumped into a river, though not the Green River. Although she had not been involved in prostitution, the subsequent follow-up investigation revealed that she had last been seen the evening of June 12th at a motel along "the strip" just south of Tacoma, where she had been staying with a female friend who, along with Reames, had planned to leave for the Midwest the next morning via Sea-Tac International Airport.

"There is, in all probability, no connection between the case of Kim Reames and the Green River murders," said Detective Stout. "My gut feeling is that it is not connected. You always look for common factors," he said in obvious reference to the striking similarities between the way Kim Reames died and the way the Green River victims were killed.

"Now," he continued, "I believe that what happened to Kim was the same type of thing that happened to a lot of those girls in King County.

But there's just no way you can say they are all connected. I don't necessarily happen to think that the ones they're all calling 'Green River victims' are precisely that. There's no way to tell."

Although Kim Reames was not initially added to the list of victims officially attributed to the Green River Killer, task force investigators could not rule out the possibility that she was a victim, particularly if the killer had mistaken her for a prostitute on "the strip" on the night of June 12, 1983, where she had last been seen alive. For that reason, she was added to the list of possible victims which included Leann Virginia Wilcox and Trina Deanne Hunter.

The summer of 1983 brought forth still additional victims and more missing women police believed were possible victims, evidence that the killer was indeed still in the area or had returned from an absence at another location. The task force added the following women to their growing list of missing females, whom they feared to be victims whose remains would later be found or, worse yet, never located at all:

Constance Elizabeth Naon, 21, of nearby Burien, was last heard from on June 8, 1983. Background investigation revealed that she had a history of prostitution arrests. Others added to the list were: Denise Darcel Bush, 24; Shirley Marie Sherrill, 19, last seen alive in Portland; Sandra K. Gabbert, 17; Marie M. Malvar, 18, from Des Moines, Washington; Kell K. McGuinness, 18; Debbie May Abernathy, 26; Tina Lee

Tomson, 26, and Tracy Winston, 20, also known as Tracy Gordon.

Among those victims whose remains were discovered and identified the summer and early part of fall 1983 were those of Shawndra Lee Summers, a 17-year-old who was last seen on October 7, 1982. The task force investigators revealed that her remains were identified on August 11, 1983, and also revealed that bone fragments found in a wooded area south of North Bend, which is east of Seattle near Issaquah, were identified on October 18, 1983, as those of Yvonne S. Antosh, 19, from Vancouver, British Columbia.

On October 27, 1983, bones identified as the remains of Constance Elizabeth Naon, 21, of Burien, were found about a block from "the strip," along with the bones of another woman who remains unidentified. Naon had last been heard from on June 8, 1983.

On Thursday, November 3, 1983, Leann Virginia Wilcox, whose body was found January 21, 1982, in a south King County parking lot, was taken off the task force's list of possible victims and added to the official list of Green River victims and, 10 days later, the remains of Mary Briget Meehan were discovered lying in a shallow grave less than a mile south of the airport, barely a block off "the strip" and just across the road from where Constance Naon's remains were found less than a month before. Because of the condition of her remains, the county medical examiner could only say that Meehan died "of homicidal violence of undetermined origin."

As the bodies continued to pile up and the list of possible victims grew it seemed, by the fall of 1983, that the Green River Task Force was not any closer to cracking the case than they had been from the very beginning. Naturally, everyone, police and the general public alike, wanted to know why.

"Usually, in a homicide, the suspect can be found somewhere in the victim's background," said King County Police Captain Michael Nault. "In this case that hasn't proven true. This crime is not personally oriented . . . but is someone who wants to kill prostitutes.

"We've been in contact with every major city in the United States and also with Interpol," Nault continued. "We've been able to determine certain suspects and to determine that there are no similar crimes anywhere in the country or anywhere in the free world.

"It is possible some victims may be the victims of a copycat killer," said Nault, "but the probability is that there is one killer."

At one point in the investigation, detectives considered the possibility that their elusive killer might have held a seasonal job in 1982, particularly since the killing seemed to stop from autumn, 1982 until April of 1983. If that were in fact the case, it seemed possible that the perpetrator of these heinous crimes may have been, and perhaps still is, employed in the tourist industry, an industry which provides an abundance of seasonal jobs in the Northwest each year from May through October.

Each year there are numerous jobs available in national parks, ferry operations, restaurants, hotels, motels and resorts as tour guides, cooks, waiters, waitresses, bartenders, desk clerks, maids and janitors. It was just such employment possibilities, as well as many others too numerous to mention here, that the task force investigators were, and still are, looking into, particularly since their killer seems to take a vacation from his dirty deeds from fall until spring. However, it should be pointed out that this is just one of many theories investigators are considering regarding the apparent seasonal slayings, and should not be construed as implying that its the task force's only avenue of investigation and, more importantly, additional body discoveries could render that hypothesis obsolete.

As the investigation into the Green River killings continues, the task force occasionally receives helpful leads from unusual and unlikely sources. For example, recently the task force received a letter from a woman in Chicago who, after reading about the Green River killer in a Chicago newspaper, felt that task force investigators should be aware of an unpleasant and frightening experience she had at a motel on "the strip" in 1983.

According to Bob Keppel, task force consul-

333

tant, the woman told investigators in her letter that she was apparently mistaken as a prostitute by a man who boldly confronted her and followed her for quite some distance until she managed to eventually shake him off and escape. She told the task force what she could about the man who assailed her, details investigators felt hopeful about involved one of the women on the task force's missing list, 26-year-old Tina Tomson, also known as Linda Lee Barkay. According to investigators the day Tomson disappeared, Halloween Day, a girlfriend had left her at a bus stop on Pacific Highway South at 11:00 a.m., and the girlfriend later told another friend that she hadn't seen Tomson since.

After the police had been alerted, detectives learned that Tomson had been arrested several times for prostitution and, as a result, her name was added to their list of potential victims, the first name placed on the list since June, 1983. Two of the missing women from that list were later confirmed as victims of the killer when their bodies or remains were eventually found, a fact which prompted detectives to consider the possibility that Tomson's disappearance might indicate that the killer was still at work on the last day of October, 1983 which would, of course, cast considerable doubt on the previous hypothesis that the killer stopped killing from fall until spring.

Knowing it was important to track Tina Tomson's last known activities, which could, ultimately bring the cops closer to their elusive killer, detectives checked court records to learn her last known address. The court records indicated that she resided at a North Seattle apartment complex; when the cops arrived at the complex and talked with the manager, they learned that no one by the name Tomson or Barkey had been a tenant there. Knowing that prostitutes often provide false addresses when arrested, the cops felt that they'd hit another dead end. However, betting on a longshot, they showed the missing woman's mug shot to the manager, who told them she looked familiar.

Admittedly, it didn't seem like much help. But by backgrounding Tomson, the investigators learned some contrasting information which, if she turned out to be a victim, would show that the killer was still operating in the fall of the year, had picked a victim whose prostitution activities took place on Aurora Avenue North instead of the usual Sea-Tac airport strip in the south end of King County, and that the killer had chosen a victim who, at 5 feet 10 inches and 140 to 150 pounds, was larger than any of the others on the missing or the dead list. It was enough to make the cops wonder if their killer had changed his M.O. If he had, only time and the discovery of new bodies would tell.

During the course of this intensive, continuing investigation, the Green River Task Force has been expanded to 45 investigators due to the possibility of a larger group of victims, some of which have not been involved in prostitution and may indicate for the first time in the investigation that the killer is selecting women other than prostitutes. As a result Kimberly Ann Reames, 27, whose nude body was found in the Nisqually River in June, 1983, and previously thought not to be connected to the Green River case, was added to the victim list because, perhaps, of the killer's "signature" being left behind at many of the sites where his victim's bodies have been found. Police would not elaborate on the killer's "signature," and would only say that it links the known victims.

In spite of a $25,000 reward fund for information "resulting in the arrest and prosecution of the person or persons responsible for the Green River murders," not to mention the stepped-up efforts of the increased task force, bodies attributed to the killer continued to turn up in late 1983 and early 1984, and new names of missing women were added to the missing list of potential victims.

Laura Thompson, the self-described psychic who said she received images of victim Opal Mills in August, 1982, found part of a skull near an Auburn, Washington cemetery in December, 1983 after being led to the location by psychic images. The skull was later identified as Kimi-Kai Pitsor, 16, of Bellevue, who had last been seen in downtown Seattle in April, 1983.

336

In the spring of 1984, Thompson returned to the location where she found part of Pitsor's skull, located about 25 miles east of Seattle near Interstate 90 and state Highway 18. Thompson said she was led to the location by an intuitive "voice" or "vision" of Kimi-Kai Pitsor, to search for another body.

Kimi's vision told me to go back, that I missed (the body in December), to check a little bit farther," said Thompson. As a result of the vision, Thompson walked approximately 70 feet from a service road into an alder grove where she found a skeleton lying on a clear sheet of plastic, covered by a dark sheet of plastic. When she uncovered the skeleton, she said, some of the bones adhered to the dark cover sheet. She said the skeleton had long, dark hair, but refused to reveal any additional details out of fear that a copycat killer might crop up or that the killer might change his M.O.

As the investigation continued, new names were added to the missing list. Among those were: Carrie Rois, 16; Patricia Lee Osborn, 19, last seen January 24, 1984; Martina T. Authorlee, 18, who was last seen in downtown Seattle on May 15, 1983; Mary Bellow, no age or details available; Debra Lorraine Estes, 16, also known as Debra Lorraine Jones, reported as a runaway in July, 1982, and was last seen on "the strip" on September 14, 1982, and had prior "contacts"

337

with police for prostitution and theft; Becky Marrero, 20, also known as Rebecca Murrero, Vicky Johnson and Rebecca Fashaw, was last seen on December 2, 1982, when she left home after receiving a phone call, and was a friend of Debra Estes; Joanne Michelle Hovland, 16, also known as Joanne Michelle Harbard, reported missing on March 16, 1983, and was last seen May 8, 1983, when released from an Everett, Washington detention center, had prior "contacts" with police for prostitution; April Dawn Buttram, 17, also known as April Manuel, last seen leaving home on August 4, 1983, and Mary Exzetta West, 16, also known as Alisa Annette West, last seen on February 6, 1984.

Several victims whose bodies were found and added to the dead list appeared previously on original and updated missing lists. Among those were: Debbie May Abernathy, 26; Terri Rene Milligan, 16, and Sandra K. Gabbert, 17. Although the remains of Joanne Michelle Hovland were found in a wooded Snohomish County site she was not immediately added to the official task force list of 26 dead victims, some of which have not yet been identified. Among those remains found and identified and added to the list of 26 dead are: Cheryl Lee Wyms, 18, who police say did not fit the mold as do most of the other victims; Alma Ann Smith, 19; Colleen Renee Brockman, 15; the remaining victims on the list of dead have been previously mentioned, with the exception of those remains that are still unidenti-

338

fied. It should be pointed out that investigators are also looking into the death of Amina Agisheff, 36, who was reported missing on July 7, 1982, and whose skeletal remains were found on April 20, 1984. Agisheff had no links to prostitution, and has not as yet been added to the official list of victims.

Has the killer struck in 1984? Captain Adamson, head of the task force, thinks not. Will he strike again?

"I'm not optimistic that there won't be any more (victims) if we don't catch him sometime soon," said Adamson, whose task force has expanded its investigation into three counties. "Bodies have been found north and south of the airport and in the Green River," he said. Bodies have also been found off of Interstate 90 east of North Bend, about 35 miles from Seattle, and the killer has a tendency to "cluster dump" his victims, as many as five bodies found in close proximity to each other.

"The proximity of the last two skeletons to both Interstate 90 and Highway 18 was just the final link I'd needed to connect the North Bend ones with Green River," said Adamson. "But there are quite a few similarities in the various scenes, enough commonalities for us to investigate . . . from the very beginning."

The Green River Task Force has looked at similar deaths in various cities as part of its ongoing investigation, including Portland, Oregon. Between March 23, 1983 and April 23, 1984, the bodies of four female victims between 16 and 24 years old were found dumped at North Portland locations. All of the women were black; three died as a result of strangulation and one was stabbed.

According to Portland Police Detective David Simpson, the nude body of Essie Jackson, 24, was found on an embankment near Overlook Park and had been strangled. Simpson said Jackson had been arrested for prostitution, and that all four Portland victims had "similar backgrounds."

Tonja Harry, 20, was found dead of asphyxiation in the Columbia River Slough on July 9, 1983. The strangled body of Angela Anderson, 16, was found December 22, 1983 inside a vacant house, and the body of 19-year-old Vickie L. Williams was found tangled in some bushes near Lloyd Center Mall on April 23, 1984. She had been stabbed to death.

"We're extremely interested in the circumstances surrounding those cases," said Bob Keppel, task force consultant, "as we would be in Vancouver, as we would be in almost any city that we find out those prostitutes migrate to." But so far no firm links have been established between the Portland cases and the Green River case, leaving the Portland cases unsolved at this point.

When they are not studying aerial photographs in preparation for extensive searches in the wooded areas of King, Pierce and Snohomish Counties, task force investigators are busy studying profiles on their list of suspects numbering 500-600, sometimes narrowing their focus down to two or three names, but never narrowing their ever-fluctuating list to focus on one single suspect. Although they sometimes narrow their view to focus more on a given suspect at a given time, new leads and developments direct their attention in many different directions.

For example, at one point the task force's attention was drawn to a man who had been jailed on statutory rape and indecent liberties charges stemming from the complaints of two 13-year-old girls who lived in the apartment complex the suspect managed. The man had also driven a taxi in the Sea-Tac International Airport area and had purportedly witnessed another taxi driver kidnap a young girl from "the strip," but so far nothing has developed on either of those lines and task force investigators said they did not have anything that would link the man to any of the victims.

On another occasion, more recently, an "associate" of victim Alma Anne Smith, whose body was found April 2, 1984, near Star Lake Road south of Seattle, told task force investigators that Smith was picked up at 9:00 p.m. on March 3, 1983, by a man on "the strip," and was never seen alive again. Later that same evening Smith's "associate" was approached for a "date" by the same man. However, she refused the offer.

Smith's associate described the man who picked up Smith as white, 6 feet tall, 27 to 30

341

years old, weighing 160 pounds, with greasy-brown shoulder-length hair and light blue eyes. The man was driving a mid-1970s Ford pickup, dark in color, possibly blue, with large mirrors on either side. According to Green River Task Force spokeswoman Fae Brooks, the man is not considered a suspect in the case, but police do want to question him to discuss the activities of the victim. A composite drawing was released by Green River Police.

A short time later, former cab driver Tom Davis, who was earlier considered a suspect in the case, came back into the picture by reporting to task force investigators that he saw the man pictured in the sketch at a south Seattle convenience store.

Although Davis said he didn't know the man's name he said, "I know where he drinks," and added that if he could get the man's license-plate number he would turn it over to the task force. "That's as close as I'll come," he said. "He could have a gun."

In another development, at one point in the investigation the task force seized a list of 5,000 names of customers during a raid on a Seattle escort service by Seattle police. King County prosecutors alleged that the escort service was used as a front, and served to provide introductions to prostitutes. Of use to task force investigators was the customer index files, which included customers' addresses, business and employment information, telephone numbers, credit card numbers, dates the service was used, amounts paid and personal background information including the customers' behavior. The task force checked the files in an attempt to identify customers who were considered potentially dangerous, but investigators did not say whether or not they obtained nay significant leads from the information.

There are other efforts being made and other avenues of investigation being pursued by task force members in their never-ending attempt to generate new leads, among those efforts being the reconstruction of the unidentified victims' faces from their skulls. For this somewhat macabre job the task force commissioned Betty Gatliff, 53, of Norman, Oklahoma, who worked as a consultant during the filming of the motion picture "Gorky Park," in which a detective used reconstructed heads to identify the mutilated and defaced bodies discovered in the frozen depths of the Moscow Park.

Gatliff reconstructed two of the oldest unidentified skeletons found in the latter part of 1983, which added to her vast experience of 87 prior reconstructions. Once the reconstructions were complete, pictures were made of the faces and released to the public with the hopes they would trigger recognition in someone who could aid investigators in identifying the victims. Although officials admit there is only a 50-50 chance the reconstructions would trigger someone's memory, they said if any new leads were generated as a result of the reconstructions they would commission Gatliff to reconstruct the faces of six additional unidentified victims.

With a 45-member task force actively working on the case and the recent approval to purchase a $200,000 computer system to help track down the killer, not to mention the help of outside consultants like Bob Keppel, Pierce Brooks and Betty Gatliff, many are wondering why the killer hasn't been caught yet. Some say he's too clever, always outsmarting the cops. Others, like the co-founder of a support group called Families and Friends of Missing Persons and Violent Crime Victims, say the killer hasn't been caught yet because the public's attitude has been too lax and apathetic, perhaps because most of the victims have been prostitutes and the general public is less sympathetic toward that group of human beings, which makes one wonder what the public's attitude would be if it were Mr. and Mr. Joe America's daughters who were being killed instead of prostitutes. Would they still be apathetic? Probably not, and most of those associated with the investigation of the Green River killings agree that the public would be less apathetic and more willing to help if they simply took a few moments to remember that the prostitutes killed by the Green River killer have families, too, who must survive and re-live the horrible ordeal again and again.

Does the Green River Task Force presently have any good suspects and, if so, what are the chances of an arrest in the near future?

"We have a lot of interesting information we're working on," said Captain Adamson, "but that's different from saying any particular person is a good suspect.

"I wish I could say we're closer to an arrest, but I don't think I can say that."

"THE SKULKING SEX MONSTER WHO PREYS ON YOUNG LOVERS!"

by Jon McInnes

For the last 17 years, a sexual maniac has been terrorizing the picturesque Italian city of Florence. His victims have been young lovers parked on dark, lonely roads on the outskirts of the city. He has killed 16 people to date—all young lovers and foreign tourists parked in the countryside between the olive trees and grapevines.

He has always used the same weapon—a .22-caliber Beretta with the same series of bullets—Winchester, Series H—bought in the 1950s. And he has consistently mutilated the bodies of the female victims with a knife—a mutilation spree that has escalated in its atrocity over the years. This is the up-to-date story on "The Monster of Florence"—the most wanted man in Italy.

The most recent murder was committed on Saturday, September 8, 1985. Nadine Mauriot and Jean-Michel Kravechivilli, both French, were wrapping up a 10-day vacation in Italy. Not much time for a summer vacation, but that was all they could afford; money was limited. Nadine, 36 years old, had two children, ages 10 and 14. She had left them with her husband in France. They were waiting for her to return.

Separated from her husband, Nadine had been going out with Jean-Michel, a drummer in a no-name rock and roll band, for the past six months. On their way back to France, coming from Rome, they made all the tourist stops. After the Tower of Pisa, they headed east toward Florence.

They were running late. One last stop and then a final, long drive home. They had their tent and camping equipment packed in the trunk. It was a perfect night for sleeping under the stars. They were driving along the old highway, originally built by the Romans, when they saw a road on the right. The road cut through a thick forest. There were no houses and very little traffic.

They followed the road for a mile when they saw an opening on the right — a dusty, well-beaten fire lane that led into the woods. Carefully, they drove their Volkswagen Golf onto the side road. The lane ran parallel to the paved road for about 50 yards before coming to a dead end.

It was a perfect campsite — a beautiful spot, so typically Florentine, situated on a hill overlooking deep valleys, covered with vineyards, well-manicured cool, green woods and a magnificent red sunset. They found a clear, flat piece of ground under a huge maritime pine where they stretched their tent.

Nadine and Jean-Michel had no idea where they were. It was somewhere in the country outside of Florence. They didn't know they were on a lover's lane. They didn't know that just up the road, another 100 yards, there was an inexpensive country restaurant, named the Barrachinia. They didn't know that just 300 yards up the road there was a Hare Krishna villa where hundreds of devotees were living, working and worshipping their Indian God. Nor did they know that 400 meters up the road was the house where Machiavelli, the famous political scientist of the 1400s, wrote *The Prince*. For Nadine and Jean-Michel, they were just somewhere outside of Florence, in the middle of nowhere.

After the sun set, the couple crawled into their tent to go to sleep. But music was coming from the Krishna village—sounds of cymbals, tambourines and chanting. The tavern under Machiavelli's old house and the Barrachinia restaurant were full. It was Saturday night. People were eating, drinking and enjoying life.

In the woods, the French couple stretched out, naked atop their sleeping bags. It is such a nice warm, moonless night. They touch, kiss, and begin making love.

A man is stalking around outside the tent. They don't see or hear him. He has been watching them for quite a while. As he listens to their lovemaking in the darkness, a strange rapture seizes him. He reaches into his pocket, pulls out a knife and cuts a vertical slit in the back of the tent. The couple stop their lovemaking. Too late, they realize that their tent has become a lethal trap.

The man sticks a gun through the slit in the tent wall and starts firing. The woman falls silent; the man escapes. Naked, he runs blindly through the woods, straight into a briar patch. The thorns cut him, but he pushes through. He comes out of the brambles and starts running again, not realizing that he is now going in the direction he came from.

Suddenly, he comes face to face with his assailant. Escape is impossible.

Desperately, Jean-Michel grabs the man and tries to fight him. The young Frenchman is strong, but his opponent has no intention of wrestling tonight. He slashes out with a knife. Jean-Michel falls dead to the ground, his throat cut. The assailant shoots him in the heart as a coup de grace.

The assassin returns to the tent, crawls inside and begins a well-practiced ritual with the knife. Quickly and adeptly he cuts off the woman's sex organ and carefully places it into a jar he has brought with him. Then he cuts off her left breast, puts it into the jar and closes the lid. He will take home these trophies.

It's a dark night. No traffic passes on the road below. He has all the time in the world to cover up his evil deed. He zips up the tent and goes over to Jean-Michel's body. He carries the corpse over to the car and then drops it under the bushes. Collecting garbage strewn around the area, he tosses it on top of the corpse. Then he disappears into the dead of the night.

It will be late Monday morning before anyone

349

comes along. A 19-year-old boy who lives in the local village of San Casciano is out hunting mushrooms. He is walking across the clearing when he notices an unpleasant odor in the air. He hears the hum of hundreds of flies in the bushes. Glancing over where the sounds are coming from, he sees two bare feet sticking out from under the bushes. He races back to the village, tells of his discovery, and escorts the carabinieri (Italian police) back to the dusty lovers' lane.

Two hours later, this quiet, sleepy hillside looks like a circus. The police from Florence arrive. After a preliminary investigation, they make their first deduction: the Monster of Florence has struck again. The alarm goes off in the afternoon. Orders go out to the other police officers: don't touch anything. The instructions are to wait for Francesco De Fazio, the criminologist in charge of the case. His standing orders are: The next time it happens, don't touch anything till I get there.

And that's the way it will be. De Fazio is rated as the best criminologist in Italy. Trouble is, he works out of Modena, which is a three-hour drive from Florence.

Police and carabinieri from all over Florence are called in. They are angry and impatient. They'll stay away from the scene of the crime, but the woods are open territory. A manhunt gets under way. Bloodhounds go baying through the woods.

Word gets out about the monster's latest attack. Reporters and television crews start to arrive. It's front-page, special-edition time. The notice goes out on the radio and TV. The curious, the mystery buffs and the village kids all show up. The police rope off a three-square-mile area around the scene of the crime—and they have one hell of a time trying to keep everyone out.

At around 8:00 p.m., De Fazio arrives. He is a short, stocky man, about 50 years old, with black hair, graying at the sides. He's wearing a black suit and a white shirt without a tie.

He crawls into the tent where the corpse of Nadine is still lying. He kneels down and examines her wounds. She had been shot five times. The assassin has carefully cut and extracted her sex organ, an operation duplicating the mutilation of his last four female victims. He has also cut her throat and amputated her left breast. De Fazio notices that she is lying with her arms folded across her chest. Her long, manicured fingernails are buried into the palms of her hands.

Was she still alive when the assassin returned to the tent to carry out his sexual ritual? De Fazio tends to believe the latter. After 10 minutes, he comes out of the tent and walks over to the body of Jean-Michel.

He examines the victim's wounds. The detectives show De Fazio the skin scraped under the man's fingernails. Perhaps he had fought with the assassin and the scratched skin belongs to the killer? Stuff for the lab. They point to the deep footprints near the corpse—size 10 shoe. The footprints belong to a heavy man—or a man carrying a corpse. The probers show De Fazio nu-

351

merous bloodstains in and around the briar patch. They show him empty cartridges on the ground—these look like the same old bullets used in the last attacks. De Fazio tells the sleuths to take everything to the lab.

What did the dogs turn up? A couple of yards outside of the tent, nothing. They just go in circles. The assassin must have taken the amputated parts home with him again. De Fazio strolls through the bushes and surveys the scene.

The journalists are finally allowed into the area. Like the dogs, they go crazy at the crime scene. While taking photos, they try to find someone to interview.

Only one man—Mario Spezi, a 50-year-old journalist for *La Nazione,* the daily paper of Florence—lingers at the outskirts, chain-smoking cigarettes. He knows as much as anyone about the assassin, if not more. He has covered the murders since 1968. Four years earlier he wrote a book on the subject entitled—what else?—*The Monster of Florence.*

De Fazio orders the corpses taken away. Spezi catches him as he is making a bee-line for his car. He stops the criminologist and pulls out a pad and paper.

"How long ago were they killed?"

De Fazio stops, looks at Spezi and scratches his head. "It's hard to say. The temperature of the tent is hotter than the external temperature. Could be anywhere between twelve and sixty hours."

The journalist wants solid answers, the criminologist has none. He sees that the only way to get to his dinner is to throw a usable quote to the press. "I just want to say that it's disappointing to have to investigate the murders of this man. He's so careful about carrying out each one of his criminal acts. He's capable of programming even the smallest details of his crimes. It's as if he were trying to perfect his executions. Obviously he loves to gamble. He loves big stakes. But he's not insane. If he were, it would be easier to catch him.

"He thinks he's unbeatable. It isn't going to be easy to catch him. But this time we have something to take to the lab. I'm sure a clue will come out of it all."

Did a clue turn up? Well, they got his blood type and some information on his skin composition. And in the next couple of weeks, the monster amused himself by giving them a slew of clues to play with.

Late on Monday night, Mario Spezi returned to his computer terminal at the newsroom and wrote Tuesday's front-page story on the monster's latest attack. He wrote: "The author of horror has written another chapter in this macabre tale of murder . . . His big advantage in this case is that he has had 17 years to perfect his crime." The developments on the monster story would be a continuing front-page story for the next 30 days. Mario also wrote: "There's one thing we can say about the assassin—at least he's not an exhibitionist. He doesn't send messages to the newspapers and police." But Mario soon had to eat those words.

353

The next day, a letter from the assassin was received by Silvia Della Monica, a judge, the only female authority assigned to investigate the case. Inside was a folded piece of typing paper containing two inch-wide strips of skin. The letter was sent the night of the murder from a village northeast of Florence. The lab immediately confirmed that the skin strips were peeled from the amputated breast of Nadine.

De Fazio ordered the newspapers to hold that story, hoping the assassin, not seeing his story in the paper or on TV, would be disappointed and try to relay another message. It worked.

Two weeks later, a bullet—a .22-caliber Winchester—was found in the parking lot of a hospital south of Florence, a parking lot reserved for doctors and hospital management. That same week, another message was sent to the three judges leading the investigation. Each judge was sent one of the unmistakable bullets wrapped inside the finger cut from a surgical glove with a note typed on a common Olivetti typewriter, a note with an Italian grammar error which read: "One bullet is all you need for yourself."

The communications were rushed to the lab; the bullets were confirmed as being from the same set of bullets used in all of the other murders—bullets fabricated in the late 1950s. The police ordered the press to hold that story, too. But they didn't, and no more communications from the assassin followed.

The Monster of Florence is the most wanted man in Italy. The mystery of his executions are

the favorite subject of parlor talk in Florence—
much more interesting than the latest terrorist attacks. Youths casually joke about him in the
discos; people pray for him in the churches.
When you talk about monsters in Florence, the
children don't imagine King Kong, the Werewolf
or Dracula. They imagine a faceless sex-maniac
prowling the countryside.

Who is the author of these executions? What
kind of man is he? How can he be caught? Let's
trace his first seven crimes to see if we can come
up with some answers.

The first "Monster of Florence" murder occurred on Saturday, August 21, 1963. Barbara
Locci and her lover, Antonio Lo Biano, were the
first two victims. Antonio was 32 years old, Barbara was 20. Both were married, but not to each
other. Both had children. One of hers, a 6-year-
old boy, sat in the back seat of Antonio's Alfa
Romero . . .

It is late at night. The boy is asleep. Antonio
and Barbara have parked the car in the countryside behind an abandoned cemetery so no one
can see them. As they are making love, someone
approaches the car. A series of shots ring out.
The child in the back seat is awakened by the
shots. Has the murderer seen the child? Has the
presence of the child stopped him from mutilating
the woman's body? The boy has not seen anyone.
Awakened by the shots, he sits up motionless, silent, trembling with fear. Then he throws himself
on his mother's body, trying to wake her up.
"Mommy, Mommy!" he cries, shaking his mother,

getting himself wet with the woman's blood.

But the mother doesn't wake up. The boy leaves the car and runs up the road. It is 2:00 a.m. as he walks up to a house and rings the doorbell. The owner of the house cautiously opens the door to find a little boy on his doorstep, crying.

For the police, the first murder was an open-and-shut case. The man killed in the car with Barbara Locci wasn't the boy's "uncle" at all. The boy called all of his mother's boyfriends uncle. Who was this woman who would take her son along with her on her amorous encounters?

She was a woman from the island of Sadegna. She had emigrated to Florence in the 1950s. Her husband was a shepherd. They were tough, determined people. Barbara Locci had a habit of sleeping around. Her infidelity to her husband wasn't a secret. The police had a suspect. They arrested the husband.

For the police it was just another simple crime of passion. Woman runs around on her husband once too often. He loses his patience, catches her with her lover and shoots them both dead. In southern Italy, the law of honor justifies such passion crimes. The judge will let you off with a light prison sentence for temporary insanity, and when you come out, your honor is intact. Perfectly acceptable social behavior.

So when the police asked the suspect if he did it, he said yes. But the next day, he thought about it some more and said no. He was noted for being a little bit crazy, a little dense, or both.

356

Ballistics put out a report that the couple was killed with a Beretta .22-caliber pistol.

"Where's the gun?" they asked the suspect. He didn't know. Sometimes he would say he gave the gun away; other times he would say that he threw it away. But they didn't have the weapon. The husband went to Cagliari Prison while the search for the gun continued.

The second murder took place on Saturday, September 14, 1974. All had been quiet for six years. Then, on a Saturday night Giovanni Foggi and Carmela De Nuccio were parked in Giovanni's Fiat in the fields of Scandicci, a suburb outside of Florence. Giovanni was 30 years old; Carmela was 21. They had known each other for only a few weeks, but in that short time they had announced their engagement.

After a night out on the town, Giovanni and Carmela parked on a tractor path that plowed into the fields. The couple were embracing when a man approached the car, firing two shots through the window on the driver's side. The shots hit and killed Giovanni immediately, but only grazed Carmela's wrist. She leaped for the door on the passenger side, flung it open and started running across the field with the murderer hot on her heels. It was too dark for Carmela and she ran smack into an irrigation ditch. She fell, got up and was climbing out when her assailant jumped in the ditch with her. He shoved the barrel of the gun into her neck and pulled the trigger. Three times. But it didn't end there. The man pulled out a knife and cut off her sex organs—a horrendous act that would become the mark of the Monster of Florence.

The bodies were discovered by an off-duty policeman and his son who were walking their dog through the fields on Sunday morning. The police didn't know what to make of this murder. There was no motive, no suspects, no clues. The murder weapon was a .22-caliber pistol. But the police didn't connect it to the 1968 murder of Barbara Locci and Antonio Lo Bianco. That case was closed.

The third murder was on Saturday, June 6, 1981. More than seven years had passed. Pasquale Gentilone and Stefani Pettini, both 19 years old, parked in the countryside late one night. Pasquale had borrowed his father's car. There was a tape-player in it, the seats were rolled back, and he was on a date with his girlfriend.

The next morning, a farmer saw a car parked in his field near a row of trees. As he approached, he saw a young man sitting in the driver's seat with his head down as if he was sleeping. The farmer cautiously came nearer. He didn't want to wake the man, but then he saw that the car window on the driver's side had been smashed. An accident?

He noticed that the man was naked and had a lot of little black dots on his neck and chest. He looked in the back seat and saw a girl lying with her arms and legs spread-eagled. There were more than 300 artistically placed knifepoint punctures on her lower body and a severed grapevine had been planted in one of the abdominal incisions.

As in the murders of 1968 and 1974, a .22-caliber pistol had been used. The girl's body was mutilated. But this time the sex organ wasn't cut off, and the police hesitated to connect this murder with the murder of 1974.

The fourth murder went down on Saturday, October 23, 1981. Just four months after the last murder, the killer struck again. Susanna Cambi and Stefano Rossi, both 24 years old, were sitting in their car, a black Volkswagen Golf, parked between the rows of vineyards, listening to the radio. They were less than one kilometer from the house where the girl lived with her parents. The monster murdered the couple, shooting them in the head with a .22-caliber pistol and repeating his bloody ritual of cutting way the girl's sex organ. This time there were no doubts. The police made a public announcement. A sexual maniac was at large in the city of Florence. He may have struck a total of four times to date, killing eight people in all. The newspapers gave him a name— "The Monster of Florence." But who was—who is this person? The monster could be anyone.

Pressure was put on the suspect now in jail. The police confirmed that the same gun that killed the first two people killed the next six people; the Beretta .22 has a distorted barrel that leaves two deep scratches on the bullet visible to the naked eye. What did the suspect do with the gun after killing his wife and her lover?

The police asked him again. This time he said he passed it on to Francesco Vinci, his wife's most jealous lover. He was set free. The police arrested Vinci and locked him up while the investigations were under way.

The fifth murder cropped up on Saturday, June 19, 1982. The maniac strikes again outside the village of Montespertoli, near Florence. The victims are Paolo Mainardi, 22, and Antonella Migliorini, 19. But this time, things don't go so smoothly for him. Paolo sees that someone is sneaking up on his parked car. He starts the engine. A shot rings out, passes through the window, hitting him in the car. He throws it into reverse and steps on it. The car flies out of the field and across the paved road. But the back wheels end up in the ditch on the other side. He tries to drive out but the wheels spin.

The murderer approaches the car. He shoots out the car's headlights. Then he aims at the windshield, shooting first the driver and then the passenger. Since the car is in the middle of the road, he doesn't have time to leave his mark. He leaves the car sitting in the ditch.

The police are divided on the case. The "Guidici Instrutore" Franco Rotella, the magistrate responsible for charging and arresting people for a crime, believes in the "Sardegna Trail." The Sardegna Trail is the theory of a connection between the murder of the first woman, Barbara Locci, from Sardegna, and the other murders committed with the .22-caliber. Possibility: The first suspect killed his wife and lover and then passed the gun on to one or more of his friends who committed the other 14 murders. This explains the numerous arrests, to date, of his friends, all of whom, with the exception of one, Francesco Vinci (who is still in prison today charged with the murder of his wife), were released following successive attacks.

But if the "Guidice Instrutore" doesn't have an open-and-shut case, they pass the case on to the "Procura della Repubblica" another branch of the judicial department, in charge of carrying out the investigations in felony cases. This department is run by Magistrate Francesco Fluery, one of the judges in charge of the monster case. His department has never accepted the Sardegna Trail Theory. They believe that the first suspect is mentally unstable and didn't even have anything to do with the first case. Their department is looking for a single sex-maniac responsible for all 16 murders.

The sixth murder—Saturday, September 9, 1983. It was the following summer, another Saturday night. The monster killed two more people. But again, things don't turn out as planned. Two young Germans from Munster, Horst Wilhelm Meyer and Uwe Rusch Sens, both 24, were asleep in their van near Scandicci. One of them had long blond hair and could have passed for a girl at a distance. They hadn't been asleep long before someone shot them through the window of the camper. The assassin entered the van, but upon discovering his mistake, quickly left.

A general identi-kit image of the monster was released. It was a compiled description of the men seen driving around the scene of the crime before the fact. Sure enough, 1,000 people called in, saying they knew who the monster is. The police started investigating the calls. Meanwhile, a restaurant owner, believed to be the Monster of Florence, committed suicide.

The seventh murder—Saturday, July 30, 1984. Claudio Stefanacci, a 22-year-old salesman and Pia Rontini, an 18-year-old bar waitress in the train station, were parked in the countryside. Their bodies were found outside the car. They were both shot with the .22-caliber pistol. The monster, besides cutting away the woman's sex organ, also cut off her left breast.

Including the French couple killed in 1984, the total number of victims has now risen to 16. The monster hasn't struck in the last two years, but this spring he has made several threats that he is ready to strike again. Over the last 19 years, the police have made a series of investigations. But only in the last six years did they realize that they were dealing with a sex-maniac. Since then, one of the most extensive manhunts in Italian history has been mounted. The top criminologists have been called in, the police have organized a special anti-monster squad, called S.A.M., to work on the case full time, and the city of Florence has launched a very expensive publicity campaign warning young couples and tourists about the ever-present danger of the monster.

Magistrate Fluery's department organized the massive manhunt with the code name S.A.M. The number of policemen working on S.A.M. has varied over the years, but 10 men have been working on the case full-time. A lot of information concerning their investigation is top secret. But it is known that they have special patrol units. They have set up roadblocks, stopping all the single men driving alone in the countryside at night, taken the names and license numbers of the cars and put them on the computer.

The computer work this department has done is phenomenal. They have collected the names of all the single men in the region of Tuscany and entered them in the computer. Eliminating all of the men who would have been too young to commit the first murders, they tried to match the names with the statistics of the men who had been in mental institutions or in jail between 1968 and 1981, six-year periods when the assassin did not strike (perhaps he was locked up in an institution). Thousands of hours of computer work—installation, research, checks and cross-checks—but nothing has come of it all, yet.

One of the policemen on the S.A.M. squad says he is sure that their work will pay off. Maybe the assassin will be foolish enough to use his own car and someone will remember the model of the car or part of the license number. If that happens, the computer will kick out some very useful information.

Why not trace the Beretta .22 which the assassin used to shoot off a total of 56 bullets in the last eight attacks? The S.A.M. squad tried that. The Beretta is not a deadly gun like the .38 or magnum .44, but it is easy to use, quiet and easy to conceal. But in this case it's impossible to trace. Since the gun was first made in the 1950s, 14,000 had been sold in Tuscany. Problem: Most of the pre-1966 gun registrations were destroyed in the disastrous Florence flood in 1966.

Exasperated, they called in criminologist De Fazio. Together with his squad of 24 specialists, he has been working on the case for the last two years. They have written hundreds of reports, thousands of pages. Their objective is to develop the assassin's personality, to trace the intimate compulsions that push him to kill and to lure him out in the open.

De Fazio knows that this is a once-in-a-lifetime challenge on his hands. The failure to catch this internationally known assassin will be his failure, but if the maniac is caught, the success will be his. The journalists say De Fazio's collaboration is overrated. He's only given a social-psychological interpretation of the assassin. But for De Fazio, understanding the man is the key to catching him.

Sitting in his office in the old historical center of Modena, De Fazio elaborated on the case. "Who is the assassin? Who knows? It could be anyone. It won't surprise me if it turns out to be somebody completely different than what we expect. Hell, it might even be a woman.

"Our man is rather indifferent to society. He doesn't love people but he doesn't avoid them, either. During his adolescence he was probably an aggressive, picky kid. He had a lot of problems in the family, with the authorities and with his friends. He's excited by violence and cruelty in films, books and real life.

"Our individual is battling four different, somewhat opposing urges—he has to act, to kill, because his impulses push him in that direction; he has the urge not to kill because he has vague social remorse; and he has the fear of being surprised at the scene of the crime. This is a fear that has been growing in him over the years. Society is alarmed. The individual is being hunted and he is very aware of it. I think this is causing a fourth urge in him—the urge to challenge capture.

"He will strike again when the balance between his urges and his need for security is acceptable. We mustn't forget that he has always attacked when he was sure that he could get away with it. He has struck eight times, but he may have tried to kill eight hundred times, never finding the suitable situation. If he had the chance, his crimes would have been many, many more.

"Remember, he is pushed by a sexual stimulation—stimulations that can manifest themselves dozens of times in one month. If he doesn't strike it's because he doesn't feel secure and not because he's satisfied."

De Fazio has consulted with a number of criminologists in Europe and America. One of them, Professor George Abraham, top psychiatrist in sexology in Europe, is inviting the monster to come out of the closet and write his memoirs. He says, "This man isn't psychotic. If he were, he would be schizophrenic and we would have caught him by now. No, this man has big sexual problems.

"In the beginning, he may have been a Peeping Tom. Then, something happened to him—maybe he was caught, and he became aggressive. After killing for the first time, he saw how easy it was and killed again and again. He became the city's Public Enemy Number One and now he lives in function of the character he created.

"Like Jack the Ripper (who killed seven prostitutes in 1880, dissected their bodies and was never caught) he has become a prisoner of his public character. He must strike again and again until he's captured or dies.

"But I would like to say to him that it doesn't have to end like this. There are many different endings to choose from. The police are trying to capture him with their conventional methods. But we psychiatrists must try to establish a dialogue with this person.

"Listen—You must realize that all of your predecessors were caught in the end. Murderers, caught by the police, are eventually forgotten by the public. But you can change this by coming out in public. You can surrender and explain everything to us, maybe even write your memoirs. Now that the police and the public are convinced of your uncapturability, you can retire from the ring, like a champion boxer, unbeaten. At this point, to kill again is senseless. All that remains is to explain to us why you acted in this way."

While the police department is on the hunt, the city of Florence is on the defensive. Last summer an ambitious public information campaign against the monster began. Nothing like it was ever carried out in Italy before.

This summer, 20,000 posters and 2,000,000 postcards are being circulated in the city once again. In addition, road signs in four languages, warning of the danger, were dug in next to the expressways entering and exiting Florence. Video clips are also being run in the discos, video bars and on national and European television. The spot begins with the image of the Tuscan countryside illuminated in a bright sunlight gradually fading into darkness; a menacing eye appears on the screen while a voice-over in three languages says: "Danger—Aggression."

What are the hopes that the monster will be caught? There are only three things that can pin him to the crimes: (1) They catch him during one of his executions. (2) They find him in possession of the .22-caliber Beretta with the distorted barrel. (3) They find him in possession of his macabre trophies.

The tourists are returning to Florence. The campsites are full. Many travelers drive out of town to camp in the countryside. The Florentine couples drive into the hills and park on the lovers' lanes with their windows fogged. For some, parking in the countryside is the sexual novelty of the year. They are young. They all think: "It will never happen to me." People forget. The monster lives somewhere in Florence. He has been silent for two years. They don't want to think about it.

How long will this lethal cat-and-mouse game with the authorities continue? Can a 20th-century

Jack the Ripper successfully terrorize a city for decades and never be caught? This isn't Europe in 1880. Today, the authorities have access to the most up-to-date techniques. How much longer can the Monster of Florence continue to outrun them all?

"WHO MURDERED EVELYN MARIE SMITH?"

by Gary C. King

Sunday, April 26, 1981 seemed like a good day for Eleos Blaine to catch up on his work. Blaine was an employee of the Medford, Oregon School District, and he had reasoned that since there would be no students to get in his way, what with this being a Sunday and all, he could clean up the locker rooms of the Medford Mid-High School stadium. The locker rooms were normally used by the football players and other sports-participating jocks. But this particular weekend the stadium hadn't been used, which meant, naturally, that the locker rooms hadn't been used, either. The only activity that he'd been aware of this weekend was the annual March of Dimes Super Walk which had begun Saturday morning at the high school. This meant that the locker rooms should be reasonably clean, and would need only the routine cleaning that allowed him to stay a little bit ahead with his work.

It was 3:10 p.m. as Blaine made his way through the tunnel directly beneath the west side seating sections of the stadium, his footsteps, movements and occasional whistling echoing as he went along. With any luck, he could be out of the locker rooms by 4 p.m., finish his work in the main school building, and still be home by 5 p.m. That is, he could have been home by 5 until he saw something that made him stop dead in his tracks.

As Blaine stared straight ahead he saw something white near the end of the dark tunnel. It was lying on the concrete floor, directly beneath and in front of several stacked benches that were being stored in the tunnel, safely out of the way of busy feet of hurrying athletes at half-time. As Blaine walked toward the form on the floor, it suddenly became familiar, frighteningly familiar.

"Hey! What the hell is going on down here?" he yelled at the person lying on the floor. But there was no reply, and no movement. As he neared the body he could see quite clearly that it was a young female, totally nude. Thinking that she had been out partying with friends, perhaps had a little too much to drink, had passed out and had been taken advantage of, the school employee continued to attempt to arouse the young girl. But there was no response, and she would not move. Afraid to touch her, Eleos Blaine ran as fast as his feet could carry him, let himself into the main school building, and called the Medford Police Department.

When the first police units arrived, Blaine led the officers to the location of the body near the stadium locker rooms. As they walked toward the body through the damp corridor, a gentle April breeze could be felt blowing into the tunnel

370

through the open end, creating an eerie feeling. As they approached the girl's body, the outline of her figure was slightly defined by the dim light.

When they reached the body, which was lying face down on the cold cement floor, they checked for signs of life. However, she was cold to the touch and they quickly determined that she was quite dead. The officers noted that her eyes were wild, peculiar and remote, and had lost most of their luster as they stared unseeing into the depths of the tunnel. The expression of her eyes and the look of her hideous leering face that was once very pretty left a permanent scar on the minds and hearts of the officers. She was so young, they reflected as they took notes, only a teenager.

As they made their initial observations the cops noted to themselves that she'd had a beautiful complexion before her death, with skin the color of honey. But now her lips and face had turned to an ugly color, and her cheeks were now hollow, their luster and resilience gone forever. Her hands looked white and bloodless, and her fingers had gone dead white, leaving the lawmen with a feeling of emptiness as cold as ice.

With his face screwed up in an effort to understand what had happened here, the senior officer informed his partner to stay with the girl's body while he notified headquarters of the situation. The dispatcher relayed the message to the homicide division, and assured the officer that detectives would be there soon. The officer reluctantly returned to the tunnel, where he began securing the area, identifying it as a crime scene with printed warnings to the public to keep out.

Minutes later, Medford Deputy Police Chief Glen Johnston arrived at the scene, accompanied by Detectives Tom McCleary and Chuck Millard. They conferred briefly with the officers who had arrived first, then sent directly into the locker room tunnel to examine the nude female body.

Johnston, McCleary and Millard noted that the girl appeared to be in her upper teens, maybe 17 or 18 at most. The cops noted the presence of a homemade tattoo of a heart on her left shoulder, and she was wearing a cheap chain necklace that supported a key with the numerals 451 scratched onto it. She was wearing three rings on her left hand and one on her right hand. During their initial observations, the investigators noted that the girl had sustained several cuts, scrapes and abrasions, which indicated to them that she "appeared to have been beaten."

While examining the key on the necklace, one of the investigators noted discolorations and abrasions in the area of the girl's throat, raising the possibility that she had been strangled after having been beaten. The fact that the girl had no clothes on her body also indicated that she may have been raped or that her killer had taken her clothing with him as an effort to hinder identification of the body, or both. Chemical tests would have to be performed before detectives could determine whether or not the victim had been sexually assaulted.

Strangulation victims are not a pretty sight. As the detectives continued their observations, they

372

noted many of the typical, tell-tale signs of a horrible death by asphyxia, such as tightly clenched hands (which naturally forces most of the blood out of the hands and fingers, leaving them "dead" white), and a grotesquely protruding tongue that had been forced out of the girl's mouth. Other signs that she'd been strangled were the presence of bluish or purple colored lips, the hue of which extended upward and discolored the face and ears as well. Changes in the color of the victim's finger and toenails were also noted, and there was dried froth or foam mixed with a small amount of blood about the mouth and nose. The discolorations and abrasions in the area of the throat had caused the neck to swell the unnatural markings upward, indicating that she had been strangled by someone who exerted a tremendous amount of force. It was not immediately determined what had been used to strangle her.

It is pertinent to note that death by asphyxia, particularly strangulation, is the result of a rupture or an obstruction of the blood vessels in the brain caused, naturally, by the pressure exerted on the blood vessels in the neck forcing the blood upward into the brain; or, death can result because of the obstruction of the trachea or windpipe, ultimately cutting off all sources of getting oxygen into the body. Or, in some cases, both of the aforementioned causes of death by asphyxia may apply.

Other signs of strangulation were apparent during this initial stage of the investigation, but the detectives could not say with one hundred percent certainty that the teenage girl had in fact been strangled. They would simply have to wait and see what turned up during the autopsy, such as a fractured hyoid bone or thyroid cartilage, or evidence of hemorrhaging or bruising of the epiglottis and internal glands of the neck.

It's common knowledge, at least among detectives and medical examining personnel, that a strangulation victim puts up a tremendous fight with his or her attacker, as their adrenal glands release additional energy or strength they never even knew they had. It is known that the victim will struggle frenziedly with the strangler in an attempt to wrench, twist or force his hands away from the throat, violent acts which almost always leave signs such as scratches or abrasions in the area of the neck. It was possible that such actions on the part of the victim in this case resulted in some of the injuries to herself, but the bruises and abrasions on other parts of her body left no doubt to the detectives that she had sustained a serious beating sometime prior to her death, a beating most likely inflicted by her killer.

Reflecting on the likelihood that the victim left some markings of her own on her killer, such as scratches on his face and hands, Deputy Chief Johnston made a note to himself to request that fingernail scrapings be taken from the victim for lab analysis. If she had been able to scratch her assailant, Johnston noted, the act would likely have left traces of her killer's flesh underneath the victim's fingernails, evidence which would not be overlooked in a case such as this.

"The details of what happened to this girl are certainly grotesque," said a source close to the investigation who pointed out that the last time anything so violent had occurred in the area was in December, 1979 in nearby Ashland, 11 miles south of Medford, when a sexual sadist by the name of Manuel Cortez tortured, raped and murdered two 11-year-old girls. Cases similar to this have occurred in other parts of the state, but homicides of such a violent, senseless nature are rare to Medford. "It is unique (to Medford), and is a frightening case," a spokesman said.

A preliminary search of the tunnel and the locker rooms failed to turn up any articles of clothing that might have belonged to the dead girl. Likewise, there were no discarded pieces of identification.

"There were no pants, shirt or blouse, undergarments, socks or shoes," said one of the investigators. "So far, we've been unable to find a purse or wallet, or any pieces of identification. For the moment, she's being treated as a Jane Doe."

Meanwhile, detectives requested the assistance of the Oregon State Police crime labs, and notified Jackson County Medical Examiner Dr. Albert Kearns. They also informed Jackson County District Attorney Justin Smith of the discovery of the murdered girl's body. Smith and Dr. Kearns arrived a short time later, followed by the OSP crime labs unit.

Before Dr. Kearns examined the girl's body, a police photographer was allowed behind the crime scene barriers, and he photographed the body from many different angles. He took closeups and longshots, and concentrated on the victim's visible wounds. When he was finished, he had taken nearly 100 photographs in color and in black and white. A police artist also drew sketches of the body and the surrounding area.

When Dr. Kearns examined the girl's body, he confirmed that she had been beaten and had likely died as a result of strangulation, though he would not commit himself one hundred percent pending the outcome of the autopsy, to be performed by a pathologist from the State Medical Examiner's Office. Dr. Kearns conceded that he could not confirm that the girl had been raped, but stated that he couldn't rule out the possibility, either. He told the detectives that she likely had died within 24 hours prior to the discovery of her body, but he was unable to immediately pinpoint her exact time of death.

A short time later, a van from the OSP crime lab's Medford office arrived at the scene, carrying several evidence technicians and their equipment. The crime lab investigators were briefed by the detectives upon their arrival, and they immediately determined the initial areas they would process.

A covered gurney was brought into the stadium tunnel. Using extreme caution, the crime lab investigators picked the girl's body off the cement floor and placed it on the gurney, where it would be subjected to an additional examination by a crime lab expert before being removed to the morgue. It should be noted that the body was placed *on top* of the covering, so that any minute or trace evidence that might be present would be safely retained if it fell from her body during the examination and/or subsequent movement.

During the additional examination, the crime lab technician brushed or combed the victim's hair for any clues that might be there, and removed strands of her head hair for purposes of comparison if an unlike type were found on her body or at other locations within the designated crime scene. The same was done with her pubic hair. Although such procedure may seem mundane and unnecessary to the layman, a good cop knows that more times than not such evidence and procedures prove to be an invaluable aid in clearing a case.

As part of the examination, cotton swabs were used by the technician to obtain samples from the victim's vagina, rectum and throat to check for the possible presence of the male ejaculatory fluid, semen. The swabs would later be saturated with acid phosphatase and, if semen were indeed present, the swabs would turn a bright pinkish-purple color. If it turned out that the acid phosphatase test was positive, additional tests could be run in an attempt to type the perpetrator's blood through the analysis of semen.

Knowing that seminal stains are sometimes found on floors and other areas that would be difficult to remove for extensive laboratory analysis the investigators, aided by bright lights, crawled on their hands and knees looking for the telltale fluid while they at the same time looked for other minute clues which might be present. With razor blades in hand, used for dislodging crusty or solid items with evidentiary value, the investigators crawled over the hard, rough-textured cement floor for what seemed like an eternity, placing potentially positive evidence inside pill boxes, small envelopes and on filter paper, each sealed and marked with proper identification information. They didn't know at this point what significance any of the items they found had, if any, but they would have them just the same in case they were needed when the case finally broke.

In the meantime the girl's body was placed in the custody of Dr. Kearns, the medical examiner, and was removed to the Jackson County Morgue, where a definitive autopsy would be performed by Deputy State Medical Examiner Dr. Ronald O'Halloran upon his arrival from Portland.

As the hours continued to slip by with little progress achieved in the case, the investigators knew from experience that they would have to identify the girl's corpse before their case could advance very far. Without an identification, they really didn't have good, solid starting point in their Jane Doe Strangulation case.

According to a deputy medical examiner in Oregon, female victims can, and often are, the most difficult to identify. If they do not have a criminal record and have not served in one of the branches of the military, it's likely that they don't have their fingerprints on file. In the case at hand, it was possible the victim had a criminal record but, because of her young age, it was doubtful that she had served in the armed forces.

According to the chief deputy medical examiner of Multnomah County, Bob Felton, who also works out of the State Medical Examiner's Office, his office first checks with the missing person departments of all the local police agencies when an unidentified corpse is brought in. "That's standard procedure," he said. "Then we have the body fingerprinted by the appropriate police agency," usually the OSP crime labs. Afterward, the unidentified corpse's fingerprints are then taken to the State Bureau of Identification and are also distributed to the local police agencies concerned.

"From there," said Felton, "they go to the FBI. The process takes a while, but can be expedited, if it's a criminal death. Obviously, if that does not turn anything up, we are somewhat with our backs up against a wall." He said that it's at that point that his office seeks help from the public and the news media, with the hope that someone will come forward who can establish the dead person's identity.

If those methods fail, all that's left for the investigators to use are medical records, particularly x-rays, which might reveal certain bone fractures or other characteristics, dental records, and other distinguishing marks, such as tattoos.

"Once you reach the point you have exhausted fingerprints," said Felton, "you are going to be unsuccessful unless an individual comes forward with information. Dental records don't mean a thing unless there are records to compare." And unless at least a tentative identification is made, or unless investigators are given a list of possibles whose dental and medical records they can compare, as pointed out by Felton, investigators' efforts at identifying a corpse consist mostly of longshots.

Deputy Police Chief Johnston and Detectives Millard and McCleary, aided by their assistants, soon began the tedious task of sorting through the piles and piles of female missing person reports filed from around the area, categorizing the reports first according to locale, then singling out those reports which listed the missing person as having been within close proximity of Medford at the time of their disappearance. But as they drudged on through the piles of reports, none fit the description of their young female homicide victim waiting to be identified in the county morgue. It looked as if Jane Doe would have to be fingerprinted.

Faced with the macabre task of fingerprinting the corpse, an OSP technician removed the sheet covering the dead young girl and soon discovered that rigor mortis was at an advanced stage. It was a frequently encountered problem for the technicians assigned to the task of fingerprinting the dead, and he instantly knew he would have to limber up the corpse before he could fingerprint it. Within minutes a complete set of fingerprints had been obtained from both hands of the vic-

380

tim, and these were sent to the appropriate department where additional attempts would be made to identify the victim by comparing her prints with those of all missing females whose prints were included in their files.

When all else failed, the Medford detectives asked the local media for help in identifying their Jane Doe. As a result, descriptions of the dead girl appeared on television and in all of the local newspapers, urging local residents to come forward if they had any information about the victim or her identity.

According to Sergeant Robert Stedman of the Medford Police Department, the stadium tunnel in which the young girl's body was found is a half-block from the nearest residence which, naturally, would make it difficult for anyone to have heard any screams. It was still necessary, however, that area residents be interviewed by detectives because, though they likely hadn't heard anything, they might have seen something, such as a car or truck, or someone, perhaps the killer himself. According to Stedman, all six of the department's homicide detectives had been assigned to the case, and they would "leave no stone unturned."

Although a chain-link fence surrounds the football stadium and is not normally open to the public except during scheduled events, school officials conceded that the gates are often left open to enable joggers to go inside and use the track. "It is not a real secure area, and people are going to go in there," said Sergeant Stedman.

Because of the thin evidence and the scarcity of significant clues, Deputy Chief Johnston organized a group of investigators from his office, and "borrowed" state troopers and reserve sheriff's deputies, to go over the crime site again, this time expanding their search efforts beyond the original crime scene dimensions. They began a "sector search" of the area, in which individual searchers were assigned lanes of a designated width by Johnston. When an individual had completed a thorough search of his assigned lane, he switched places with another prober and went over the designated area again, in an effort to prevent the loss of any evidence which might have been missed the first time around. Primarily interested at this point in finding the girl's clothing and the murder weapon, if there was one, the southern Oregon investigators combed the stadium and the athletic fields, as well as the adjacent school grounds. Although some articles of clothing were found, none were believed to have belonged to the dead girl.

Had the girl's killer gone into the locker room adjacent to where her body had been found? Had he touched anything in the stadium tunnel and/or the locker room? Of course it was possible, and for this reason a fingerprint technician from the State Bureau of Identification unloaded his kit from the van he was driving and made his way into the stadium tunnels still cordoned off. Among the items he removed from his case was a six-inch long brush that fluffed out at least three inches in diameter, several containers of various colored powders (dark powder for light surfaces and light powder for dark surfaces), an atomizer filled with ninhydrin, adhesive tape and several white cards.

The fingerprint technician then took his brush and powders and began dusting down every likely place a latent print might be, including the stacked benches, the locker room door, smooth surface walls and fixtures inside the locker room, spreading the light gray to black powder with the silky filaments of his dusting brush in an attempt to obtain clear, identifiable prints. He knew it was a long-shot, that the chances were slim that he would obtain the killer's prints, but it was a longshot that had to be taken. After all, if the girl were identified and a suspect apprehended, such prints would be necessary to positively place the suspect at the scene of the crime.

As the fingerprint technician continued with his slow, tedious work, he occasionally switched shades of powder, using a new brush for each shade and from time to time he took out his atomizer filled with ninhydrin and sprayed porous surfaces where he suspected a print might be. If the ninhydrin hit its target, a fingerprint, the porous surfaces would turn purple as it dried, thus exposing the presence of a latent print. Each time he found a good, identifiable specimen, he lifted it with tape and transferred it to one of the white cards. When he had finished he had several good prints but, at this point, he didn't know if any of them belonged to the perpetrator of the heinous crime.

In the meantime, the Medford detectives continued to comb the area for clues, and OSP crime lab technicians removed two sections of the gate that covered the entrance to the stadium tunnel and sent it to the crime labs for analysis. They did not reveal, however, what they were looking for.

Eventually, a female who said she might be a relative of the victim, showed up at the Jackson County Morgue to make an attempt to identify the dead girl. When the young woman, who wished not to be identified, saw the body as it was pulled out of its refrigerated drawer, tears came to her eyes. Struggling to hold back the sobs, she began to whimper softly when she saw the tattoo of the heart on the victim's left shoulder. There was no doubt, she said. The body was that of 17-year-old Evelyn Marie Smith of Medford.

The detectives investigating the case soon learned that Evelyn Smith had been born in Medford and had attended local schools. She was not, however, a student at Medford Mid-High, where her body was found, at the time of her death. Instead, they learned, she had attended the Alternative Learning School at the Medford YWCA for the two years prior to her death. Although not enrolled in classes at the school at the time of her death, she was on the all girls Hot Heads Softball Team in nearby White City.

As the investigation continued, Medford police detectives learned that Evelyn Smith was last seen about 9 p.m. Saturday, April 25th. Likewise, the investigators said they believe she was killed sometime between 9 p.m. Saturday and "several hours" prior to when her body had been found by the school district employee. At this point in the puzzling homicide case, police conceded that they had no significant leads and no firm suspects.

"The clearance rate on these types of crimes is high," said Deputy Police Chief Glen Johnston. "The fact that two days have gone by doesn't mean we have less of a chance of solving it . . . In some investigations it's all right there for you, and in others it takes a little more time to put the pieces together."

After meeting with the other investigators working on the case to exchange information, discuss leads and possible suspects, Johnston said that the only likely break in the case might occur when the final results of tests and analyses of the skimpy physical evidence came back from the Oregon State Police crime lab in Portland, where most of the items were sent. "I am anxious to see the crime lab results," said Johnston. "But I have no idea what they will contain, so whether they will be of value or not is impossible to predict at this point."

Shortly after the body had been identified as Evelyn Smith, Dr. O'Halloran of the State Medical Examiner's Office in Portland traveled to Medford where he performed a definitive autopsy on the teenage girl's body. Before going inside the girl's body, O'Halloran placed a clear plastic "overlay" on top of the corpse. By using various colored marking pens, the medical examiner was able to show the exact size, shape and location of the injuries the victim had sustained. As points of reference, Dr. O'Halloran noted the shape of the girl's body, as well as other anatomical characteristics. It was an effective and inexpensive way for the medical examiner to show the injuries that had been inflicted, and is recognized as an invaluable tool in a court of law, as it allows the prosecution and defense lawyers to illustrate the position of the victim's wounds, often without showing macabre, gory photographs.

The autopsy was completed with few significant results. Dr. O'Halloran had determined that Evelyn Smith died as a result of being strangled, and confirmed that the body had sustained cuts and abrasions apparently caused from a beating she had sustained before her death. There was evidence of petechiae in the lungs, tiny hemorrhagic spots within the membranes. Petechial hemorrhaging in the lungs is common in strangulation victims, and is caused by capillaries that burst when the victim tries frantically to breathe air into the lungs but can't because of an obstructed air passageway. During the autopsy O'Halloran found no evidence of rape. Following the completion of chemical tests, rape was ruled out completely. Toxicology tests were also performed to determine whether or not drugs played any part in the girl's death, the results of which turned out negative.

Drugs and alcohol had not been used by the victim. O'Halloran said it would be difficult, if not impossible, to pinpoint the precise time of death. However, he did say that it appeared that the victim had been dead "more than several hours, but less than a day" when her body had been found. He said the girl had likely been killed "sometime Sunday morning," April 26th.

After learning the victim's identity, all of the homicide detectives assigned to the case (the entire division) initially interviewed 12 of the girl's friends and acquaintances and expected to talk to many more. "She had a lot of friends," said Sergeant Stedman. After piercing together the information gleaned from the interviews, police had a good description of the clothing Evelyn Smith was wearing when last seen.

At approximately 9 p.m. on Saturday, April 25th, the night before her death, Evelyn Smith was believed to have been wearing the following articles of clothing: A black ski jacket with a quilted pattern, white cotton pants, a fuzzy purple or lavender sweater that had a pattern of pink threads which ran horizontally through it, and a pair of worn-out brown jogging shoes with stripes.

In the days that followed, law enforcement officials made public the descriptions of the girl's clothing and asked anyone who had seen any discarded garments matching the descriptions to come forward and report it to police. Also, as an added effort to locate the missing garments, detectives sorted through truckloads of trash at the

Jacksonville dump. Searching through the rubbish became a daily routine as the investigators concentrated their efforts on rubbish brought in from the southwest section of Medford that surrounded the high school where Evelyn Smith's body was found. But as each day passed with no trace of the girl's clothes, the investigators were left with a feeling bordering on despair in their search for useful clues. It had begun to seem hopeless, as if the case might never be solved.

Police are also at a loss as to the murder weapon. Law enforcement officials quickly ruled out a rope, ligature or piece of cloth, primarily because of the autopsy findings, but have speculated that a rigid object of some type had been used to strangle the girl.

"We are speculating that it may have been an arm, or a board, or something of that nature," said District Attorney Smith. "But so far we have not found any implement we can associate with (Ms. Smith's death)." Smith said that police detectives had spent several days during which they interviewed more than 40 friends and acquaintances of the victim in an attempt to determine where she had been the evening prior to her death. But Smith said police had no suspects to focus on in spite of their efforts and countless man-hours, and conceded that the case may not be quickly solved.

"In situations where the assailant is known to the victim," said Smith, "we can usually count on some good leads from talking with friends and acquaintances. But if the assailant and victim are unknown to each other, it can be very difficult to solve. This may be one of those cases."

By the time three weeks had passed since the death of Evelyn Marie Smith, detectives had interviewed more than 100 friends and acquaintances of the murder victim. Sergeant Stedman said that investigators had administered lie detector tests to eight individuals, some of whom were cooperative and some who were not, but the results proved inconclusive and ultimately were not helpful.

"Polygraphs are good tools," said Stedman, "but their findings are not conclusive, nor are they admissible in court."

What about leads in the case?

"In the last three weeks, some leads developed but they all came to a dead end," said Stedman. "Some citizens came forward with information that they had seen the girl the day the body was found, but that information was unfounded."

According to Stedman, detectives initially followed up on a lead in their attempts to identify a suspect in which a female school counselor reported being accosted in the parking lot of the Mid-High School by a man wearing a ski mask. That was on April 14th at 10:45 p.m., 12 days before Evelyn Smith was believed murdered. Police reports indicated that the woman had been inside her car when the man attempted to get her to open her car door. She refused to cooperate with him, and he fled into the night. Although the incident was not tied to the murder of Evelyn Smith, Sergeant Stedman said that it was "just another thing we've got to look into."

Stedman said investigators remain hopeful that a break will eventually come about in which detectives will be able to identify a suspect. He said the break could come as a corroborated confession, discovery of new evidence such as the victim's clothing, or perhaps detectives will uncover enough circumstantial evidence that will show the perpetrator's guilt "beyond a reasonable doubt." First, however, the perpetrator must be identified.

More than four years have passed since the murder of Evelyn Marie Smith, and the question of who killed her remains as much a mystery today as it did four years ago. Police have no suspects, and no new leads. Sergeant Stedman said that although an officer remains assigned to the case, he is not able under those circumstances to actively investigate the girl's death. The investigation is "ongoing," and will continue as new leads come in. "We are continuing to follow leads as they are furnished to us or as we develop them," said Stedman. Unfortunately, however, leads stopped coming in long ago.

EDITOR'S NOTE:
Eleos Blaine is not the real name of the person so named in the foregoing story. A fictitious name has been used because there is no reason for public interest in the identity of this person.

"I'VE BEEN SHOT. SEND HELP!"

by Bud Ampolsk

It's been going on for decades, according to federal and local lawmen. Known as the "Trash War," its battleground has spread over the New York City metropolitan area and branched out into the bedroom communities of Nassau and Suffolk Counties.

Since the trash-disposal problem first surfaced in the mid-1950s, the intense competition for collection contracts has brought terror and dread to small, legitimate trash carting companies and their employees. For many in the industry, the Trash War has caused a sense of helplessness in the face of the strong-arm tactics of a few carting companies with ties to organized crime.

Refuse carters are extremely vulnerable to mob harassment. Many of their garages are in low-rent, scantly populated districts where they make easy targets for those whose activities can't bear police scrutiny. Drivers ply thousands of miles of backroads where they can be waylaid at any time. Law enforcement agencies, with their limited staffs, cannot provide trash-disposal companies a 100-percent effective shield against mob influence.

Why all the violence surrounding trash collection

by private firms? One important reason is that trash collection is a social necessity with a permanently upward-spiraling demand curve. As such, it is easily open to exploitation, particularly from cartels who, by sheer force of numbers, can out-muscle the competition and take control of the entire industry.

An example of how this works was provided by Andrew J. Maloney, the United States Attorney for the Eastern District of New York, during the summer of 1989. It was contained in the paper he filed in a civil suit against 44 individual carters, a trade association representing them, and two major crime families, as well as 64 individuals.

The suit was brought under provision of the Racketeer Influenced, Corrupt Organizations Act, a federal statute commonly known as RICO. The suit charged that the defendants effectively eliminated competition from the sanitation industry on Long Island.

In announcing the suit, Maloney said the industry was run as a cartel "under which individual companies were allocated specific residential and commercial waste collection stops which became the property of the carters."

The Maloney action was by no means the first brought against the alleged cartel. In 1984 and 1985, for example, both the New York State Organized Crime Task Force and the State Attorney General's Office accused the two crime families, a trade group, and several dozen hauling companies of conspiring to control the trash collection industry.

At that time, Ronald Goldstock, director of the State Organized Crime Task Force, said, "The carting industry has been controlled for such a long time that it is very unusual for individuals to speak out against those who are doing the controlling."

Indeed, this evaluation was borne out by reactions of those honest but terrified businessmen and employees who earned their livings collecting the refuse of Nassau and Suffolk Counties.

A typical comment came from one carting company employee who stated, "If you shoot your mouth off, something is bound to happen."

However, in any war, no matter how desperate the odds and dire the potential reprisals, there are those with the courage to fight back. Their sense of right and wrong compels them to put their lives on the line and make a difference.

One such hero was Robert M. Kubecka, the 40-year-old owner of several East Northport, Long Island, carting companies. Kubecka, who had taken over his family's refuse hauling operation, was a legend in both his community and his trade for his intrepid forays against the cartels. He had gained a reputation as a rebel hauler who had the guts to question the way the industry was being run. Friends and neighbors would say of him that his battle with other haulers and his testimony at their trials was much admired in the community.

Obviously, Kubecka's activities made him a number of enemies. Just how many may never be determined. However, he had also earned the gratitude and respect of federal and local lawmen for his ongoing cooperation in trying to bring legitimacy to his trade.

Kubecka was by no means unaware of the peril he faced. It is said that he maintained a direct wire to Suffolk County police in his company headquarters at 41 Brightside Avenue in East Northport. The building was located near the village's main commercial center.

It was over that wire that Suffolk County cops first heard the terrible news, according to Sergeant Edward Fandrey of the Suffolk County police homicide squad.

The call was received in the cool early-morning hours of what was to be another blistering summer day. The exact time was 6:14 a.m. The date was Thursday, August 10, 1989.

There was no question of the urgency of the words. All doubts were dispelled by the way they were gasped out. The caller seemed to be struggling to save his dying breath in order to complete the terse message.

"I've been shot. Two people have been shot. Send help," the caller intoned.

Moments later, county patrol cars, dispatched to the scene, arrived at Brightside Avenue. The first on-site officers to enter the carting company headquarters were greeted by the grim sight of a man lying inert on the floor in front of the main office. Apparently the man had died instantly of gunshot wounds.

Noting that the victim was already beyond all medical aid, the on-site officers made their way into the inner office, where they discovered Robert Kubecka slumped across his desk, still alive, but just barely.

As they knelt beside the gravely wounded man, advance life support medics who had been dispatched by the East Northport Rescue Squad arrived. They employed their state-of-the-art defibrillator and other emergency equipment as they rushed Kubecka to Huntington Hospital, where alerted emergency room personnel waited to receive their mortally stricken patient.

However, there would be no way that medical science, no matter how sophisticated, could reverse the damage that a killer's bullets had caused.

Robert M. Kubecka, the man who for so long had fought the cartel, was pronounced dead soon after his arrival at Huntington Hospital.

Meanwhile, as Suffolk County police homicide squad personnel and other forensic experts began their inch-by-inch investigation of the office building where the double shooting had taken place, a positive ID was made of the second victim. The muscular, athletic body in the hallway proved to be that of Donald Barstow, the 35-year-old brother-in-law of Kubecka.

Barstow had worked alongside Kubecka in the family business. He was described by friends as "a macho type" who had built up his body with extensive weightlifting.

First reports concerning the condition of the two bodies would prove rather sketchy as Sergeant Fandrey and the other Suffolk County officers played it close to the vest. However, it was said that each man had been shot several times. No weapon had been found at the crime scene, and the exact caliber of the bullets that had killed Kubecka and Barstow was not revealed.

Although Sergeant Fandrey noted that Kubecka was conscious upon his arrival at Huntington Hospital, no word was given as to whether or not he had made any kind of deathbed statement or in any way had been able to identify his slayer or slayers.

Nor would the police reveal whether anything of value had been stolen from the Brightside Avenue offices of the murdered carting company executives.

However, two longtime and highly trusted employees of Kubecka's firm were cooperating with the police. They had been called in from their regular routes to make an inspection of the homicide premises. Lawmen were hopeful that the employees might be able to determine whether anything was missing or whether the killer or killers had left anything incriminating in their wake.

The employees would later say that they had seen marks on a refrigerator that could have been left either by shotgun pellets or by an errant bullet. They also noted that police officers had appeared to be interested in a duffel bag that might have been abandoned in the office by the intruder or intruders.

The witnesses reported that Kubecka had not carried a gun on his person and that the only weapon in the building was a pistol, which was kept locked in the office safe.

Both employees told of a special button device on the office telephone, which when pressed would automatically dial the police. It was thought that this accounted for Kubecka's ability to make the call although he had suffered mortal wounds.

One of the witnesses was able to narrow down the time frame of the actual shootings. He said he had last seen Kubecka alive at about 5:15 a.m., when the witness and nine other drivers had left the building to begin the rounds of their daily routes.

He also revealed that Barstow was in the habit of coming into the office to join Kubecka at 5:30 a.m. According to this source, Barstow had been employed by the firm as both a manager and a truck driver.

It became obvious to investigators that Robert Kubecka's and Donald Barstow's regular early-morning habits might have made things more simple for their killers. The witness noted that the two men were always alone at that time of the morning. Good friends as well as in-laws and business associates, the pair had made it a habit over the previous 10 years to remain alone in the office for a few minutes after Barstow's arrival there, then repair to a nearby diner where they breakfasted together.

The victims' regular routine had been in disregard of warnings given to them by professional law enforcement personnel with whom they had been cooperating in ongoing probes of the carting industry.

Investigators who had known Kubecka over the years said that he had been instructed not to follow patterns of routine, never to meet other carters in unusual or remote locations, never to be alone, and always to observe and report strange or suspicious vehicles or persons in his immediate environs.

The feeling was that Kubecka might have become somewhat careless over the passage of time and that this factor had caused him to ignore the advice to exercise prudence.

The concern expressed by federal agents and local police for Kubecka stemmed from his and his family's long-time anti-cartel fight.

It was said the courageous carter's battle had begun in 1982 when he volunteered to have himself wired to make tape recordings of conversations linking numerous industry figures to a price-fixing scheme. The resulting investigation, which had been triggered by Kubecka's taping activities, led to the indictment of 26 persons and 16 corporations accused of being part of a conspiracy to rig cartage prices.

A number of those indicted were later convicted.

For Kubecka, the struggle to bring a semblance of law and order to the troubled carting industry would continue.

In 1987, a report commissioned and published by the prestigious Rand Corporation revealed that Kubecka had provoked the ire of many members of the carting industry both by refusing to go along with the industry's practice of carving up business and by his work with law enforcement officials.

The Rand report noted that the family business that Kubecka headed had been expelled from an industry trade group after Kubecka argued against a price increase that the trade group had supported. Later, the industry and the trade group in question would be the focus of a number of federal, state, and local investigations at both the criminal and civil levels.

Speaking about Kubecka's input, Organized Crime Task Force director Goldstock would say Kubecka's testimony in these cases was "crucial in both developing the evidence and acting it out."

There had been reprisals against Kubecka and his family, according to U.S. Attorney Maloney, who claimed that one crime family and a number of haulers had forced Kubecka during the early 1980s to turn over parts of his business and to refrain from bidding on contracts.

In the racketeering suit that Maloney had filed in Federal Court earlier in the summer of 1989, a spokeswoman for the U.S. Attorney's Office now said that both Kubecka and his brother-in-law Barstow had been expected to testify as government witnesses.

The spokeswoman said, on the day of the double murder of Kubecka and Barstow, that it was still too early to assess what bearing the victims' deaths would have on the prosecution of the pending RICO action.

Still, one of the key allegations of the federal case was that the defendants had threatened Kubecka, ordering him to turn over parts of his business and refrain from competitive bidding or they would harm his family members.

However, as the probe into the slayings continued, law enforcement officials said they did not know whether the murders of Kubecka and Barstow had been a reprisal because of their cooperation with the authorities or whether the deaths were the outgrowth of a dispute over routes with individual carters. These sources said Kubecka had recently been battling with other companies for commercial stops.

Said Goldstock, "If the killings were in any way connected with Kubecka's role as a witness, it is going to prove counterproductive to those behind it. We will apprehend and prosecute those responsible."

Meanwhile, the Federal Bureau of Investigation was standing by, assessing what, if any, role the FBI would take in the ongoing murder probe. Murder is not a federal offense, and the FBI does not become involved in local murder cases unless federal laws are broken in their commission.

Commented Joseph Valiquette, spokesman for the FBI's New York office, the FBI itself was not at that point investigating the shootings. However, he added, "There's an obvious FBI interest, but it's too early to see if there is a federal violation [in the shootings]." Valiquette was referring to the fact that Kubecka and Barstow had been scheduled to be government witnesses in the pending Eastern District Federal Court case.

Meanwhile, the burden of the homicide probe remained under the jurisdiction of the Suffolk County Police and prosecutor's office.

Their personnel were moving through East Northport and canvassing locals who might have had information on the slayings.

Suffolk County Police Department Sergeant Fandrey revealed he had learned that Kubecka had received a threatening telephone call on Wednesday evening, August 9th, the day before the shooting.

There was a particularly grisly twist in the baffling case. That was when a Kubecka employee reported that about a month before the fatal shootings, somebody had deposited the carcass of a dead dog on Kubecka's lawn. This was taken to have been an obvious warning for Kubecka to keep his mouth shut.

There had been other threats to Kubecka and some of his relatives, as well.

For his part, Suffolk County District Attorney Patrick Henry could offer no theories concerning the motive behind the double rubout.

Said Henry, "I won't speculate on the motive for

their murder. He [Kubecka] has been a forthright citizen in the investigation. Kubecka and his brother-in-law have been cooperative witnesses in grand juries and trials, but right now we don't know who is responsible."

There was no question that authorities had taken threats to Robert Kubecka seriously. They had offered him a new identity under the Federal Witness Protection Program. However, Kubecka had turned down the offer. It was said that he had refused the posting of round-the-clock local police protection as well.

An elderly relative of the murdered men commented, "All I know is" that the victims "were very courageous, and so was I. I just hope they get those bastards [who killed them]."

The question of whether the murders had been in reprisal for past testimony by Kubecka and Barstow, as a means of preventing them from testifying in future court action, or the result of a dispute over collection routes, had different meanings for different people.

Particularly upset by the possibility that the route dispute had triggered the shootings, one man said, "I'm worried about my life. The question is: Did someone just want to get them out of the way or are they after all the routes? Are they going to attack the drivers?"

Added another, "We never thought this would happen. It's because they [Kubecka and Barstow] wouldn't let anybody take away their business."

Concerned industry members gravely noted that the slayings of Kubecka and Barstow had occurred almost two months to the day after the rubout of a

Queens, New York, man with ties to a hauling firm. That murder had occurred just hours after the federal lawsuit in which Kubecka and Barstow had been scheduled to testify had been filed.

The victim, 51-year-old John Spensieri, had been discovered in the basement of his Astoria home on Thursday, June 8, 1989. He had been shot several times in the head.

The grisly discovery of his corpse had been made by a relative at 11:00 p.m.

The possible connection between Spensieri and the pending federal trial remained a mystery, since the dead man had not been one of those named in the indictments. However, it was said that he had been employed in a carting company owned by a relative.

Said NYPD Detective Ralph Blasi of the 114th Precinct in Astoria, "We're trying to see if there's a connection [to the federal court papers]." Detective Blasi was investigating Spensieri's slaying.

Police officers who had been called to the Astoria home following the discovery of Spensieri's corpse were overwhelmed by the opulence of his home.

Said one crime scene officer of the home, "It would make some nightclubs in New York look like dumps.

"There was a built-in swimming pool, a bar, and a kitchen in the basement where the body was found," he said.

Detective Blasi revealed that several 9-mm shells had been recovered. They had been spotted near Spensieri's body on the basement floor. However, no weapon was recovered. Nor were there any signs of forced entry.

The John Spensieri slaying would prove just as baffling as the slayings of Robert Kubecka and Donald Barstow. The case is still open and an active investigation continues. Thus far, there have been no suspects or arrests.

The status of the probe is pretty much what it was on the day of the Spensieri killing. At that time NYPD Deputy Inspector Joseph DiPierro told the press, "Right now, everything is being investigated."

It has been almost two years since the morning of Thursday, August 10, 1989, when somebody walked into the Brightside Avenue office of Robert M. Kubecka and shot him and Donald Barstow to death in cold blood.

At this writing, the motives behind the double slaying remain just as puzzling as the identity of the gunman.

Still unanswered is the question of whether the mob-style hits were meant to avenge those who had done prison time because of Kubecka's cooperation with the authorities in earlier cases.

At least one investigator believes they were. The veteran cop recalls that in 1984, Kubecka was the key witness in a New York State criminal probe that exposed organized crime's stranglehold on private carting in Long Island.

He says, "It was definitely a payback. Why did they wait so long to get him? They always wait."

Notes U.S. Attorney Maloney, "This is the kind of violence too long connected with the carting industry."

Another possibility is that Kubecka and Barstow

were killed to prevent their testimony in coming cases from implicating a new set of defendants.

Then there is the possibility that Kubecka and his brother-in-law refused to knuckle under to demands to give up part of their hard-earned business to others or possibly to agree not to bid on new territories.

There appears to be little doubt that Kubecka was the prime target of the hitman. Some go so far as to say that Barstow was just an innocent bystander who happened to be in the wrong place at the wrong time and paid for it with his life.

As of this writing, the search for the hitman and the interests who may have hired him goes on.

On Thursday, January 24, 1991, a spokesperson for Drew Biondo, director of public information for the Suffolk County District Attorney's Office, reported that thus far there have been no suspects and no indictments. But the official expressed the hope that at sometime soon, the dedication and perseverance of those who have worked so hard and long to bring a killer or killers to the bar of justice will prevail.

"WHO KILLED KRISSIE POVOLISH?"

by Richard Siekmann

There are any number of reasons a person might sign on with the United States Postal Service—the opportunity to work in the fresh air, for example, or the adequate pay and benefits package. But for many, the primary attraction is the safe, steady (some would say boring), and relatively unchanging nature of the work.

The carrier assigned to the rural East Carondelet route along Bluffside Road considered himself especially fortunate. Besides the occasional farm dog adding spice to his day, his was a pleasant beat, full of friendly, well-established customers who lived among the lush, seasonal vegetation indigenous to St. Clair County, Illinois, due east of St. Louis, Missouri. Little, as they say, to write home about.

July 28, 1987, had begun as a typical enough day. The weather was hot, 95 degrees and climbing. As the carrier worked his way north along Bluffside toward Imbs Station Road, he was approaching the home stretch and whatever cool drink would satisfy his growing thirst.

A quarter-mile south of Imbs Station Road, there is a slight depression in the roadway that cannot be seen from any of the nearby houses. As the carrier passed this familiar spot, a peculiar odor caught his attention. Normally, the smells of the country—the chemically treated crops and fresh road kills—are no cause for alarm, but this odor was different. There was a curious bite to it that seemed to demand investigation.

The carrier parked his mail car and walked over to the east side of the roadway toward a drainage ditch that seemed to hold the source of the smell. As he reached the edge of the pavement, the carrier saw the form of a female lying face down some 15 feet from the roadway. The carrier's first—and very normal—thought was that he was looking at a mannequin; there was a waxy, inhuman texture to the skin. But the bloated discoloration and foul odor quickly belied that impression. No, what he was looking at was very human . . . and obviously very dead.

The carrier quickly concluded his investigation and drove to the next stop along his route, the home of Greg Bux, a deputy sheriff with the St. Clair Sheriff's Department. From there the sheriff's department was called, and Deputy Janet Bertelsman was the first to arrive at the scene.

At that point, the real investigation began. Sheriff's detectives responded within minutes, and shortly thereafter, the decision was made to activate the Major Case Squad, a cooperative arrangement involving topnotch detectives from virtually every police agency in the bi-state Greater St. Louis metropolitan area and its environs.

As the name implies, the Major Case Squad, by charter, investigates only major felony cases. In actual practice, they restrict their operations to major (as opposed to minor, or misdemeanor) homicides,

406

those that are particularly heinous, and those that are particularly hard to solve. Even so, the task force has a remarkable track record: an 85 percent clearance rate, well above the national average. By Midwest standards, this was a major case.

Sixteen, so the theory goes, is supposed to be a special time for young girls. And summertime, with drive-ins, pools, and parties, should only add to the picture. For Kristina "Krissie" Marie Povolish, things were looking up. Sure, she was having difficulties with her boyfriends, but what pretty teenage girl doesn't? And besides, she had recently beaten a bout of depression (a common teenage woe), and she was finally starting to feel good about herself again. A large party loomed on the horizon. The last one at the same site had had a beer truck parked in the barn—quite a drawing card for a 16-year-old. But that wasn't until Saturday, July 25th. Tragically, Kristina Povolish would never make it.

On Friday, Krissie had wanted to go to a local "dry" nightclub that catered specifically to those too young to drink. It was a safe place to party, away from the local cops, who always seemed to hassle the kids cruising on Main Street. The music there was good, and everyone knew everyone else. But Krissie's boyfriend, Mark Rogers, had other ideas, and the two bickered as he sent her home early in the evening.

Of course, that was not an insurmountable problem. Krissie's other boyfriend, Gary Johnston, would gladly take her where she wanted to go. Johnston picked her up at about 9:30 p.m. By that time she had changed her mind, and they went to a game room instead. At 11:30 p.m., she was home.

Krissie decided then to walk to Mark Rogers'

trailer across town. Regardless of her thinking, it was too far to walk, especially at night, but relatives were unable to dissuade her, so Krissie left home again at 12:05 a.m. A couple of blocks down the road, a neighbor, Ronnie Myer, spotted Krissie and offered her a ride at least part of the way to her destination. At 12:30 a.m., Myer dropped Krissie off at a gas station, still some 30 blocks from the trailer. Krissie elected to continue on foot . . . and she was never seen again.

Mark Rogers entertained friends that evening. They listened to music, drank some beer, and watched the Cardinals baseball game on TV before he kicked everyone out around 12:30 a.m. Rogers had mentioned to his guests that he and Krissie had been fighting lately, but otherwise it had been a pleasant gathering.

After the party, Rogers was given a ride to a friend's house, where he borrowed a motorcycle and rode to still another friend's home. He was home by 2:00 a.m. when Krissie's relatives called to see if she had made it safely.

She had not, however. And when she failed to turn up during the night, and her purse was found several miles away near Imbs Station Road, a missing-person report was filed with the Belleville Police Department.

Although missing person reports are usually resolved, this one was a mystery: What happened to Krissie Povolish?

Part of the answer became apparent on July 28th, on Bluffside Road, when the mail carrier stumbled upon the remains of a dead female. Identification of the remains, despite the advanced state of decomposition, was a foregone conclusion.

Kristina Povolish had died a violent death—she was strangled—at the hands of an unknown assailant. Identifying the remains was the job of the St. Clair County Coroner's Office; identifying the killer was the job of the Major Case Squad.

Homicides, for the most part, are easy to solve; some 60 to 70 percent of all known murders in the country are successfully cleared. (This compared to an overall national clearance rate of roughly 21 percent for all index crimes.) Homicide cops rely heavily on the principles that A) the victim always knows his or her slayer, and B) the motives involved are transparent. If you ask the right people the right questions, an arrest will almost surely follow.

Such was the first, most promising lead in what was filed under Major Case #147, Sheriff's File #87-01-006. Perhaps Mark Rogers had simply gone berserk and killed Krissie in a fit of rage, sleuths theorized. Detectives had no choice but to pursue the possibility. In a case like this, the most obvious solution is usually the right one.

But what about the motive? Did Mark Rogers have a reason to kill Krissie? Task force detectives quickly learned that Mark and Krissie had had a history of sometimes violent conflict. An incident that occurred within a week of Krissie's murder was reported wherein Mark had dragged Krissie from his car while shouting, "I've got to get rid of this bitch; she's crazy; no one can live with her!" Was Rogers subconsciously telegraphing his ultimate, festering desire? It seemed a reasonable hypothesis. Reasonable, that is, to cops who had long ago learned that human motivations are often both petty and bewildering.

Hypotheses, though, need proof—or, in the language of the trade, evidence. Fingerprints, fibers, eyewitnesses, and the like can often substantiate a good working hypothesis. But this case had none of those. There were, however, other more subtle clues that raised the collective antennae of several of the investigators working the case.

First, they realized that the premise under which they had been operating—that Krissie had not made it to Rogers' trailer—was a dubious one at best. In other words, just because Mark Rogers said it was so didn't make it so. If he was the killer, then he had every reason to lie, and none whatsoever to tell the truth. He had to divert suspicion somehow.

With no more than that to go on, Rogers was brought in for questioning. Of course, he denied any involvement in Krissie's murder. (Rare indeed is the suspect who doesn't initially proclaim his innocence.) Although he continued to express profound concern for Krissie, his denials, to some members of the task force, sounded contrived. Nevertheless, they were unable to shake him.

As a matter of procedure, the investigators sought and obtained written permission to search Rogers' trailer for any evidence relevant to the case. This search yielded another subtle clue pointing to Rogers: a pair of tennis shoes.

When Krissie left home that fateful night, she was described as wearing a silk blouse, Jordache jeans, and white tennis shoes. Several pairs of shoes were seized pursuant to the search, and among them was a pair of white tennis shoes. The shoes were shown to Krissie's relatives, and one positively identified the white tennis shoes as the pair she was wearing as she walked out the door. So, if the relative could be believed, Krissie had indeed made it to Rogers' trailer.

The silk blouse and Jordache jeans, along with Krissie's purse, were found on Imbs Station Road; the shoes, however, were not.

Did Rogers overlook a crucial piece of evidence linking him to the crime? It appeared so. Mark Rogers was offered a polygraph examination, and he accepted. When the test was over, it was the qualified opinion of the examiner that Rogers was telling the truth. He was not involved in the death of Kristina Povolish.

With this news, the steadily progressing investigation was immediately knocked off track. The shoes were just not enough to go on. And there was no other evidence to implicate Mark Rogers. Moreover, his alibis were confirmed. He was where he said he had been throughout the night, detectives found out. There were, however, two other eminently logical suspects for detectives yet to consider: Ronnie Myer and Gary Johnston.

Myer was an intriguing suspect, because he was, for all practical purposes, the last one to have seen Krissie Povolish alive. And the same principle of investigation that applied to Mark Rogers—that the correct solution is usually the most glaring one— applied equally well to Myer. Was Myer's alleged act of kindness, the ride, merely a fictitious ruse to point investigators in the wrong direction? Did he take her somewhere other than the gas station as he had claimed? Legwork, the gumshoe's secret weapon, was required here, and a team of detectives was assigned the lead.

Almost immediately, a witness came forward who had overheard Ronnie Myer remark, "I can't believe I was the last one to see her alive." This comment was made the day after Krissie's disappearance, still

411

days before the discovery of her body. And it implied, in not-so-subtle fashion, a knowledge of the death before it was an established fact. Unlikely as it appeared, it was at that point still a possibility that Krissie Povolish had simply run away from home. No one could say for sure that Krissie was dead until the body was found. Had Myer slipped?

Again, the investigation began to snowball. In an amazing display of investigative prowess, the detectives managed to locate several of the customers who had been at the gas station when Myer claimed to have dropped off his passenger. While at least one remembered Myer and his truck, no one had seen Krissie Povolish. And there were among the customers some who knew her well. Some, that is, whom she would have felt comfortable speaking with or accepting a ride from. But no rides were given, and no conversation ever took place.

Was Krissie by then an unwilling captive of Myer? If so, why would he even have stopped? To do so would have invited discovery. The detectives were perplexed but nevertheless continued to press on.

Myer was questioned thoroughly. He stated that he had picked up Krissie near her home, driven her to the gas station, and returned home within 15 minutes. He had only dropped her off because he had not wanted to take the time to drive all the way to Rogers' trailer.

Myer was also given a polygraph, and like Mark Rogers, he passed. Myer's wife confirmed the timing of his account. The timing would not have allowed Myer to drive all the way out to Imbs Station Road to dispose of his prey, had he had any prey to dispose of.

So the Major Case Squad was again thwarted. In

what amounted to a last-ditch effort to solve the case, the task force now zeroed in on Gary Johnston.

The suspicion was not without merit. Johnston was with Krissie on the night she was murdered. Had there been a conflict between the two? Something so severe that Johnston later returned to stalk his victim and ultimately bring her to her death? Krissie's relatives reported nothing unusual about her demeanor after her date with Johnston, but for whatever reason, she did leave the house again. Was she seeking in Rogers a "safe port in a storm"? The lead was tenuous at best, but it received the support of a single anonymous caller who claimed to have been threatened by Johnston: "Do what I said, or I'll do to you what I did to Kris Povolish!" The caller, as might be expected, refused to get involved.

As with Myer, a detailed account of Johnston's activity was obtained. He claimed to have driven to O'Fallon, Illinois, after dropping Krissie off at home. There was no one home in O'Fallon, he said, so to show that he had been there, he left a six-pack cooler on the doorstep. He then drove to a nearby store where he ate a sandwich before going home. Johnston had spoken with no one who could verify his alibi.

The beer cooler on the doorstep raised a nagging question: Why had Johnston bothered to leave it there? It was as if he had wanted—even needed—to establish his whereabouts when Krissie was killed. He seemed to have made a rather big production out of driving to O'Fallon—the exact opposite direction from where Krissie was ultimately found—and leaving some record of his presence there.

Naturally, Johnston was offered a polygraph, and as was somewhat fitting, he passed. In the absence

413

of physical evidence and eyewitnesses, the investigation was damned to languish unsolved.

On August 1, 1987, incarnation #147 of the Major Case Squad was officially disbanded. The task force typically works five days on a given case before turning it back over to the primary investigating agency, unless circumstances warrant an extension. No extension was warranted in this case because it was clear to all that the squad was spinning its wheels.

Of course, in addition to the above mentioned suspects, the Major Case Squad did pursue numerous other leads of varying degrees of significance—officially 136 in all. They were, however, unable to develop the necessary probable cause to make an arrest. Two names did arise in the initial investigation that would later become important factors in the case, but for now, the time limit had expired. The case was effectively dead in the water.

Two detectives—one from the St. Clair County Sheriff's Department, under whose jurisdiction the case remained, and one from the Belleville Police Department, whose missing-person report had initiated the investigation—continued on the case for a short while following up on the unfinished leads, but the case file eventually found its way into a dingy gray metal cabinet in a drawer marked "Unsolved Murders," while other, more pressing business took the detectives' attention away. There the file laid untouched for several months. It had become an unfortunate fact of life: The probability had decreased dramatically that the death of Kristina Povolish would be legally avenged, and there were other matters to attend to. At least for the time being, Krissie's killer was given a free pass.

By Illinois statute, the county sheriff is responsible

for staffing and maintaining a jail, and in St. Clair County, the patrol and corrections divisions of the sheriff's department share a common facility. Therefore, it is not surprising that sheriff's department detectives are particularly adept at tapping an important source of information: the 300 or so detainees in residence at any given time.

Inmates in the jail are in a rather unique position to be of value to cops smart enough to use them. The boredom and frustration inherent in that environment breeds conversation, even among the most unlikely of bedfellows. And the talk inevitably turns to what matters most to those inside — what put them there, or perhaps more importantly, what they hope the cops don't find out about so they won't be coming back. The talk may also be an act of self-preservation. Mention a murder (or two) that you were involved in, and even the hardest of people give you a wide berth.

But mention it loud enough and it comes back to haunt you. The old stereotype of a stool pigeon who barters information for favors holds true. Those who possess certain types of knowledge have a tremendous bargaining tool, a tool that can be used to gain everything from reduced bail, to reduced charges, to a walk right out the door. Those who used to be called stoolies in more arcane times are now referred to as rats or snitches — or, within the legal machine, confidential informants (CI), a title befitting the business it has become. A good CI operates in a seller's market; where cops have little choice but to pay the going rate.

In October 1987, the word was passed upstairs from the jail to the detectives' offices. There was a prisoner below, it seemed, who had some information about the Povolish case. A detective was immediately sent down to talk to the source.

Detective Ted Beatty met the CI in a private interview room, still behind bars. The informant's story was simple:

He shared a cell with a man named David Hamilton. After a while, they discovered they had a mutual interest in the death of Krissie Povolish: the CI knew her personally; David Hamilton knew her killer.

Hamilton told the CI that he had been riding around with two brothers by the name of Stephens in Mike Stephens' white Trans Am when they picked up Krissie Povolish on Main Street in Belleville. It was about 12:30 a.m., and the four of them went to a party in Cahokia. On the way back to Belleville, Terry Stephens began removing Krissie's clothes while David Hamilton held her down. Krissie started to scream, so Terry Stephens grabbed her by the throat. Soon she was silent, and soon she was dead. They then threw her body out along the roadway.

The CI told Detective Beatty that he weighed Hamilton's admission against what he knew to be true. He was familiar with the Stephens brothers, and he was aware that Krissie Povolish had hung around with them in the past. That Mike Stephens drove a white Trans Am was a fact, as was the part about Krissie disappearing along Main Street.

But something else was odd about the informant's story. According to Hamilton, Terry Stephens had been so distraught about the murder that he took his own life the very next night. Hamilton gave some details about the suicide that also corresponded with known facts—a gunshot wound to the head and a witness who tried to hide the weapon.

When the informant put it all together, he said, he

believed he knew who the killers were, and he decided to come forward. He then made an offer: Any way he could help in the investigation, he would—even, if need be, wearing an audio surveillance wire.

To be sure, the CI told a good story. But for all that Detective Beatty knew, it was just that—a story. Still, some parts did ring true.

The suicide, for example. Ted Beatty remembered that well. As the investigator on call that night, he had drawn the assignment. Terry Stephens had shot himself in the head with a 9mm semiautomatic handgun in the immediate presence of his brother Mike, his girlfriend, and another person. And no one tried to stop him. Indeed, no one apparently knew it was coming.

Mike, Terry, and the other man had been bar hopping earlier in the evening, and Terry hadn't displayed the slightest hint of distress. But when they got back to Terry's apartment, he sat down on the bed, pulled out his favorite toy—the 9mm—put it to his temple, and pulled the trigger. It was clearly no accident. Terry Stephens knew the weapon well. When the shooting was done, the other man picked up the gun and ejected the magazine, ran out the door, threw the gun on the roof, and vanished into the night.

Terry Stephens was still alive when the first officers reached him, but it was too late. Too much damage had already been done. He made no dying declarations, no admissions of wrongdoing that the soon-to-be-departed often make to purge their souls, and he left no notes. His suicide would remain forever a mystery.

A few days after Stephens' suicide, Krissie Povolish's body was found. There was no reason at that time to make any connection between the two cases. Krissie was from Belleville, Terry Stephens from Cahokia. Although the two cities are not that far apart geographically—about three miles at their nearest point—their populations seldom mix. And in the first few weeks of the investigation, no one had mentioned Stephens' name in any sense, much less as a suspect.

But now, more than three months after the fact, this CI was suggesting that David Hamilton and the Stephens brothers were responsible for the crime. Detective Beatty then considered what he knew to be true. Although the informant did provide some tantalizing details, he said nothing that could not have been learned from other public sources—newspapers, radio, etc. Statements he attributed to Hamilton were not necessarily authentic, for just that reason.

The CI did not appear especially bright, but perhaps he was more clever than he let on. And one thing was certain: Terry Stephens did kill himself less than 24 hours after the disappearance of Krissie Povolish.

The polygraph was again employed and then reemployed when the first test yielded ambiguous results. On the second run, the CI passed. His story deserved thorough consideration.

Rumors and innuendos began to flood the case. On the night of the victim's disappearance, a white Trans Am was reportedly seen parked in a church parking lot a quarter-mile from where Krissie Povolish was found. The Stephens brothers had been seen in a tavern on triple Lakes Road less than half a mile from the same spot on the same night. Terry Stephens had also shot a cop once and was therefore

418

capable of murder.

To interview Hamilton in the county jail would have created an unnecessary risk. If a detective were to question him about a homicide that he had only recently implicated himself in, presumably in confidence, the CI would be exposed as a rat, and he would have quite literally outlived his usefulness, both to the cops as a snitch and to Hamilton as a human being.

No, another strategy was needed. Hamilton was due to be released from jail shortly, and after consulting with the state's attorney's office, Belleville police detectives and sheriff's investigators decided to pursue an eavesdrop, a covert electronic surveillance in which the CI would wear a hidden body mike, while a team of detectives stationed nearby would listen in on the conversation. To that end, an eavesdrop order was issued through the courts and signed by a judge. Miraculously, the CI was released from jail.

When Hamilton obtained his own somewhat less miraculous release, detectives secured the services of the CI, who remained extremely cooperative. Three times he was wired and sent to David Hamilton's home. Despite prolonged interaction between the two, the conversation never gravitated toward murder. Hamilton simply would not implicate himself again; perhaps he smelled a rat. The eavesdrop had failed.

The surviving Stephens brother, Mike, was then brought in for questioning. His repeated denials earned him a trip to the polygraph machine, and, like all his forerunners, he passed. So the Stephens lead faded into oblivion.

During the fall of 1990, another scenario presented itself via the jail grapevine to sheriff's detectives, one that harked back to the earliest days of the Major Case Squad investigation. The murder, it was alleged, was the handiwork of two friends, Eddie Michaels and Tommy Flynn, who had picked up Krissie Povolish along Main Street, attempted to rape her, and then killed her.

This information was gleaned from a source (who would steadfastly refuse to act as a police operative) who had overheard someone saying that Tommy Flynn admitted he had not actually meant to kill Krissie—he just hit her and she died. Legally speaking, the information would be considered hearsay twice—or three times—removed. It was useless as evidence, inadmissible in court, but just maybe a launching point for the ultimate resolution of the case.

Eddie Michaels and Tommy Flynn were no strangers to the detectives. Their names had been mentioned in the first days of the investigation as possible suspects. Then, friends of theirs were overheard speculating about Michaels' and Flynn's involvement in the killing, but when the friends were interviewed, they backed off the speculation completely. No, they said, they would never suspect them of murder, and they certainly had no real knowledge of the case.

Eddie Michaels was initially interviewed in a detox center in southern Illinois, where he had checked himself in mere days after Krissie Povolish had disappeared. His alibi was weak, but verifiable—he was home that night with two friends, neither of whom was Tommy Flynn. A few days later, when his rehabilitation was complete (so the story goes), he passed a polygraph and was eliminated as a suspect.

Tommy Flynn, however, was never located by the task force. Apparently, he too had left town immediately after the victim's disappearance. Was he running from something? The Major Case Squad never had the opportunity to ask him.

It was not until the summer of 1991 before this newly revived lead could be pursued. Understandably, more current matters would take precedence over a four-year-old case, however important it might seem. Several close friends of both Flynn and Michaels were interviewed, and while all denied any knowledge of the Povolish killing, two of them stated unequivocally that if any in their immediate circle of friends did know who committed the murder—if indeed Michaels and Flynn were guilty—no one would ever tell. They were that tight with one another, and the detectives believed them. What the detectives did not believe, however, was that no one knew the truth.

Eddie Michaels was again picked up for an interview. Over the course of several hours, three teams of detectives took turns interrogating him, each using a different approach.

But in the end, even though Michaels had adopted the body language indicative of compliance and submission—head bowed, slumped in his seat, with an occasional tear welling up in his eye—he simply refused to confess, he said he just didn't do it.

There was, however, just prior to the end of the interview, a humorous, perhaps even revealing moment. Issuing yet another broad-brush denial, Michaels blurted out, "I can't confess to something I *did*." Catching himself a moment later, he continued, "No, wait, you guys are getting me confused." But if detectives had managed to break through the barriers, Michaels quickly recovered, and the denials continued. There would be no admissions.

Because Michaels had already passed one polygraph test, and because no new information had been gained in the four years since then—no trump card, as it were, for the polygraphist to play—no new test was given.

The other player in this scenario, Tommy Flynn, was by all reports now living in Florida. Again he had managed to dodge the investigative bullet. But even in his absence, detectives found witnesses who would alibi him for the night of the murder. Apparently, Flynn didn't do it either.

After four frustrating years, case #87-01-006, the murder of Kristina Marie Povolish, remains unsolved. The file folder, now thicker and more burdensome than ever, sits atop a greenish filing cabinet, taunting every investigator who has pursued the case since its inception.

Occasionally, as personnel are rotated within the St. Clair County Sheriff's Department, a newly appointed detective will pick up the reports and attempt to ferret out that one vital clue that has perhaps been overlooked by all his peers. And every one of them will fail, perhaps because the answer just isn't there.

And so the mystery remains: Who killed Krissie Povolish?

"WHO STRANGLED THE POPULAR COED?"

by Howard and Mary Stevens

Friday, September 17, 1972 was the beginning of what was expected to be an exciting week for dark-haired Pamela Milam, 19, a sophomore at Indiana State University (ISU) who was looking forward to the fall rush season on campus and activity in her sorority, Sigma Kappa. An honor graduate of Honey Creek High School at Terre Haute, Indiana, Pam worked as a full-time employee of the Southland Branch of the Vigo County Library.

Pamela was busy getting ready for the traditional campus sorority rush and last-minute details filled her head. Her good looks radiated through her personality; she was a warm, caring person with a broad, infectious smile. She met fellow students easily. Deeply religious, she took an active role in her campus ministry.

Pam's father was her most loyal supporter, so when she didn't show up on Saturday at the family home as she had promised, he became worried. He headed for the downtown university campus and the Lincoln Quad residence hall to which Pam had been assigned during the fall rush season.

The Milams had always been protective parents.

423

They were the first to admit it and would tell friends "one can't be too careful, especially with a daughter." Pam was the baby of the family, and they delighted in her achievements in high school and now in her second year at the university.

Pam's father beamed when word came to him that his daughter had reached out to others in the campus ministry and at school. No, he didn't mind checking on her when she worked at the branch library; after all, it was just a few blocks from their home. But nothing would prepare him for that moment when he took an extra set of car keys and opened his daughter's car trunk after he found it parked near her campus dorm.

Inside the trunk was the crumpled body of his daughter. Thick tape was wrapped around her mouth and head. A rope was tied around her neck and wrists. She had been strangled. Her father bowed his head and wept. The tears wouldn't stop running down his face.

The father's grief quickly drew a crowd of students. Campus police were notified and they, in turn, summoned Terre Haute officers. Chief of Detectives Frank Hoffman was one of the first officers at the scene and he took charge of the investigation. The victim's car and the immediate area were cordoned off. Officers assigned to the police laboratory were directed to the scene to collect whatever evidence might be available.

Hoffman, six-foot-two and weighing nearly 200 pounds, tried to comfort the grieving father, who kept asking, "Who could have done this to my baby? Oh, God. I hurt all over." Hoffman directed a uniformed patrolman to take the father aside and get him away from the grisly scene.

"What can you tell a man who has such a deep hurt burning his insides?" Hoffman asked a fellow officer.

One of the brightest, most knowledgeable detectives with years of police work behind him, Ray Tryon, rushed to the scene to head the probe. He started questioning anyone who might have any information regarding the victim or the automobile in which her body was found. Tryon, Detective Hoffman knew, was the man for the job since he had special training in the FBI school at Quantico, Virginia and frequently taught classes on murder investigations to Terre Haute officers.

Detective Tryon was surprised that the victim's car was discovered on campus and parked in such a prominent spot near the coed's dormitory. He was even more surprised that the keys were not left with the vehicle. What did the fact mean? Were there inferences he could draw? Tryon asked himself.

First off, the automobile. Was it deliberately left where it could easily be spotted? Did the murderer want it to be found? Was he therefore guilt-ridden about the crime? "We work with what we have. What are these things telling us?" the veteran detective told another officer assigned to the baffling case.

Second, the car keys. Certainly the criminal should have tossed them away and perhaps he did, making it more difficult for the police. The natural thing for the killer to do, Tryon reasoned, was to leave the keys in the ignition or in the floor well. The killer had been around and was not a novice in crime or violence, Tryon was sure.

What about the method of murder? Tryon's extensive schooling had taught him that this phase of the probe was perhaps the most important. Murder cases are, for the most part, solved or unsolved according to this particular aspect of the investigation.

"Let's face it," Tryon told a colleague. "Sexual attacks are usually the work of younger men . . . Sex murders are associated with stabbings, strangulations or beatings. This case has the earmarkings of a random killing—a spur-of-the-moment murder. The victim was in the wrong place at the wrong time."

Down the road, the veteran detective knew that there would be bits of information authorities could not share with anyone. "I would much rather have the suspect guessing at what we know and what we're doing to solve this case. Besides, I never was in favor of telling the press too much. I've mellowed somewhat but I still believe in the principle—it's us against them," Tryon confided to his colleague Hoffman.

Uniformed officers quietly asked the curious to move on. Other lawmen moved through the nearby dorms to talk to anyone who might have seen the victim's car, a 1964 dark red Pontiac Tempest, driven around campus or through the downtown area. The vehicle also had a distinctive feature, a brightly colored, license-plate-sized tag on the front bumper with the name Jesus boldly spelled out. The right rear hubcap was missing from the vehicle.

Ambulance attendants gently removed the body, in near-fetal position, from the car's trunk. The victim's blue pantsuit was rumpled and streaked with grime. Her face was swollen and appeared battered, her hair tangled and matted. A large red welt circled her neck where the raw rope was tied. In some places, the rope had cut into her neck and specks of blood oozed from the wound. It was a gruesome sight.

Homicide detectives fanned out in all directions looking for anything that might provide a clue to the killer. A cigarette butt might be important or even a button from a coat or a piece of cloth.

A white sheet covered the victim. Onlookers gasped as the body was placed in the white ambulance. The flashing red light on top continued to churn in the fall air.

Ducking under the bright yellow crime scene ribbon, Detective Tryon moved toward his detective car, where he stopped long enough to study notes he had scribbled in his spiral-bound notebook. "Maybe the autopsy will tell us something. Perhaps a psychological profile will help. We work with what we have," he tried to convince himself.

Back at headquarters in the City Hall building, Tryon and other officers assigned to the case compared notes. The questions mounted, the answers did not. They all agreed on one thing: a solution to this case was not going to be easy.

Twenty-four hours after the body of the young coed was found in the trunk of her car, fear of further violence permeated the ISU campus. Male students volunteered to escort coeds to and from night classes. Most coeds accepted the offer with no argument.

In a number of residence halls there was talk of leaving school and going home until the murderer was apprehended. Dorm counselors promised additional protection as a means of combating the growing fear of violence on campus. An incident in which a coed was slashed with a knife three days after the body of Pam Milam was found did not improve campus unrest.

"The girls in the residence halls are in a state of near panic. If something else happens, I don't know what I will tell them," a dorm instructor admitted.

The brother of Ray Tryon, an officer in charge of the university's security department, coordinated efforts of campus and municipal police to solve the baffling slaying. The horror of the brutal murder shocked Terre Haute residents, as well as university staff and students. Everyone wanted this case solved — and quickly.

After a series of tests were conducted on the body, Pam Milam was buried in a cemetery near her country home. There were no known breaks in the case and no suspects. Detectives were at a dead end after putting more than 100 hours of overtime into the frustrating case. Hundreds of reports, photographs, telephone calls and crime lab results were reviewed. A quick break in the case eluded investigators.

Police Chief Jim Swift took an active role in the probe when he released to the press a photograph of the victim's car. He asked west central Indiana residents to notify police if they saw the distinctive car over the weekend, from the time the coed was last seen on Friday until her body was found on Saturday.

As the investigation continued, members of the ISU Foundation offered a $1,000 reward for information leading to the arrest and conviction of Pam Milam's killer. At the same time, the university president expressed shock and sadness over the murder.

"Pam was a lovely young woman and her tragic death will never be understood by her many friends at the university and in the community," he noted.

One of the most startling developments in the preliminary probe caught investigators by surprise. Dr. Robert Burkle, county coroner, reported there was no evidence that the victim had been assaulted. He attributed wounds about the face and head to sharp taillight fixtures located inside the car trunk. Burkle said Milam was probably dead before being placed in the trunk of her car. He listed strangulation as the cause of death.

Chief of Detectives Hoffman announced that the interior of the victim's car revealed some fingerprints. He said they would be examined at the Indiana State Police Laboratory in Indianapolis. He refused to comment on the coroner's preliminary results until he had time to examine the report with other officers assigned to the case.

While sleuths pressed their probe into the Milam murder, a rape involving another coed was reported on campus. The incident touched off another round of panic among coeds on campus and prompted townspeople to demand some progress in the investigation.

One suspect, Pam Milam's boyfriend, was questioned at length, but he was released when detectives checked out his alibi and found it to be legitimate.

But bad news continued to plague the probe into the death of the pretty university student. A suspect taken into custody in neighboring Putnam County a week before the Milam murder was released because of lack of evidence. He was returned to Miami, Florida, for questioning in a homicide involving the strangulation of a young woman. In that incident, a rope was used and the victim had been bound with thick tape.

Ten days after Pam Milam's body was found in the trunk of her car, a strange twist developed in the case. Police revealed that evidence suggested the victim's clothing had been removed sometime during the time she was missing and carefully replaced before her death. Tryon and others believed the young coed had been attacked and that the condition of her body was disguised by the long ride in the car trunk.

Interviews of students, male and female, consumed

most of the investigators' time. Hoffman and Swift estimated that more than 200 persons were questioned during their investigation, many of them on more than one occasion. At least two suspects flunked polygraph examinations, and they drew special attention.

One detective assigned to the case, Tommy Tanoos, was convinced that someone, somewhere, must have witnessed the scuffle between the victim and her assailant. Why didn't someone see it? Was Pam abducted in broad daylight? Or had Pam known her slayer and gone willingly with him? "It is a haunting case. It never goes away," Tanoos said at the time of the probe.

Detective Tryon said he was consumed by questions without answers. Was the strangler a person who committed the act on the spur of the moment? Or was he an old hand at homicide who coolly blinked at chances he would get caught? "I really believe the latter theory," Tryon said.

The veteran detective was bombarded with questions from reporters. He still is. Most go like this: "Don't you think you can wrap this case up in a hurry?"

"There are no quick fixes on this case," Tryon has said recently. "I think, someday, that we will know who murdered Pamela Milam. Whether we will be able to convict him on this charge, I really don't know. I know he is out there and sooner or later we will turn him up. Right now, he's probably laughing at us. But somewhere down the road, we'll get him and we will know that he is the one." Detective Tryon is convinced of this.

Tryon and his brother never let the case get out of their minds. The Milam case represents a challenge they do not take lightly.

What kind of a person was Pamela Milam, the victim of the grisly slaying?

"She was the kind of person you would have enjoyed having as a daughter. In all the hours I have devoted to this case, I never heard her described in a negative manner," says one central figure in the probe. The father of two daughters himself, he was thrust into the investigation as head of the university's security force. He is a retired Terre Haute policeman and detective.

Milam was active in groups associated with campus ministries. Her devotion to those causes might have contributed to her death, he believes.

"I saw her as a champion of the underdog," he added. "She may very well have attempted to reform the wrong person. She was a believer that there was good in most people. Pam probably subscribed to the theory that there just weren't any bad people out there. That is the way I saw her and I am sure she was determined to find the best in everyone she met."

Had she lived, she would have made an excellent elementary school teacher, was his opinion.

Terre Haute's Police Chief Gerald Loudermilk — world renowned for his statement: "Fight crime, shoot back!" — is convinced his slogan has something to do with his town's low crime rate. Under his policy of getting tough on felons, Terre Haute's crime figures have gone down in most categories.

Loudermilk, 55, is the father of four children. One son is a police officer, another a city fireman. He is convinced that the nation's courts are too lenient on repeat felons.

"Drugs are our biggest problem. Forty percent of all crimes are drug related," Loudermilk says.

Although he has advised his police officers to shoot back if they are fired upon, he notes that none has been called upon to defend himself in a situation involving a fleeing felon. "It is unbelievable how many cards, telephone calls and letters I have received praising me on my stand," he reports.

Loudermilk is hopeful that the Milam homicide will be solved before he hangs up his badge. "We welcome any information on the case and we will continue to hunt for her killer," he insists. He praised the many officers who have devoted hours of work to the case and he promised that a solution was inevitable — sooner or later.

Terre Haute police didn't have far to look back to find a similar slaying near the ISU campus that has also gone unsolved.

Five years earlier, and within five blocks of the parking lot where Pam Milam's body was found, officers investigated the suffocation death of Joan Fox, 30, who lived in an apartment on the university campus. Fox was criminally assaulted and suffocated with a pillow. More than 100 persons were questioned in the case, but no one was officially charged or convicted of the crime.

Information on the Fox slaying is still sought by Chief Loudermilk. Although a person who is now dead was believed to have murdered Joan Fox, the strange case remains unsolved.

Two months after the Fox murder, the apartment house in which the body was found was the site of a suspicious fire in the early hours of a summer morning. Only the rear portion of the apartment where the victim died was destroyed. Later, the building was demolished to make room for university expansion.

An autopsy revealed that Joan Fox's death was due,

in part, to a blow at the temple that had knocked her unconscious, investigators theorize. A bloodstained soft drink bottle was recovered from beneath the bed. The young woman's body lies in an unmarked grave at Highland Lawn Cemetery. Few people, caretakers report, ask to see the Fox burial site.

Authorities have not given up on either of the unsolved cases, and they continue to ask for help in solving them. They promise absolute anonymity to any and all informers.

"There is nothing to fear from cooperating with lawmen," Chief Loudermilk stresses. "There is everything to fear if these killers are allowed to remain free and perhaps strike again. It has happened in the past and it may happen again."

APPENDIX

"Who is 'Baby Hope' and Who Smothered Her?"
True Detective, May, 1992
"The Unknown Horror Behind Pretty Pixie's Slaying!"
True Detective, August, 1990
"Who Killed Krissie Povolish?"
Inside Detective, May, 1992
"Tennessee Mystery of the Vanished Nurse!"
Master Detective, July, 1989
"Two Infernos — Three Corpses — No Suspects!"
True Detective, June, 1990
"Family Massacre . . . But Who Did It?"
Official Detective, June, 1991
"Cleveland's Gruesome Mystery of the Mad Butcher's Dozen!"
Master Detective, October, 1990
"Golden Girls' Horrible Mutilations"
Official Detective, December, 1988
"Does a Sex Monster Prowl for Little Girls?"
Official Detective, November, 1988
"Who Blasted the Beloved Teacher in the Gold Car?"
Official Detective, April, 1991

"Who Laced the Brunette's Tylenol with Cyanide?"
Official Detective, August, 1991
"Florida's Easter Sunday Murder Mystery"
Inside Detective, May, 1992
"Lisa Gibbens Murder—Half Her Head Was Blown Off!"
Official Detective, October, 1992
"Strangest Hollywood Murder Mystery Ever!"
Official Detective, October, 1990
"Strangled Bible Lady Clutched a Bizarre Clue!"
Inside Detective, February, 1986
"Who Strangled the All-American Boy?"
Master Detective, March, 1984
"Who Murdered Cathy Dawes?"
Master Detective, July, 1985
"Slain Socialite in the Townhouse"
Official Detective, February, 1991
"Oregon's No. 1 Murder Mystery"
True Detective, February, 1976
"Reign of Terror of the Green River Killer!"
Master Detective, February, 1985
"The Skulking Sex Monster Who Preys on Young Lovers!"
Official Detective, February, 1988
"Who Murdered Evelyn Marie Smith?"
Master Detective, March, 1986
"I've Been Shot. Send Help!"
True Detective, November, 1991
"Catch the Cruising Cabbie Killer"
Official Detective, July, 1991
"Who Strangled the Popular Coed?"
True Detective, October, 1990